Intelligence
Requirements
for the 1990s

Intelligence Requirements for the 1990s

Collection, Analysis, Counterintelligence, and Covert Action

Edited by
Roy Godson

Lexington Books
D.C. Heath and Company/Lexington, Massachusetts/Toronto

Library of Congress Cataloging-in-Publication Data

Intelligence requirements for the 1990s : collection, analysis,
counterintelligence, and covert action / edited by Roy Godson.
p. cm.
Highlights the major aspects of the discussion at the Colloquium
on Intelligence Requirements for the 1990s, organized by the
Consortium for the Study of Intelligence, held Dec. 1987, Washington,
DC
Includes index.
ISBN 0–669–19555–3 (alk. paper).   ISBN 0–669–19556–1 (pbk. : alk.
paper)
1. Intelligence service—United States—Congresses.   2. United
States—National security—Congresses.   I. Godson, Roy, 1942–   .
II. Colloquium on Intelligence Requirements for the 1990s (1987 :
Washington, DC).   III. Consortium for the Study of
Intelligence.
JK468.I6I58   1989
327.1′2′0973—dc19   88–23030
                                                                 CIP

Copyright © 1989 by National Strategy Information Center, Inc.

Published simultaneously in Canada
Printed in the United States of America
Casebound International Standard Book Number: 0–669–19555–3
Paperbound International Standard Book Number: 0–669–19556–1
Library of Congress Catalog Card Number: 88–23030

The paper used in this publication meets the minimum requirements of
American National Standard for Information Sciences—Permanence
of Paper for Printed Library Materials, ANSI Z39.48–1984.

ISBN 0–669–19555–3

89 90 91 92 8 7 6 5 4

Contents

Acknowledgments

This book, more than most edited works, is a product of the endeavors of many. For almost a decade, the Consortium for the Study of Intelligence (CSI) and the National Strategy Information Center (NSIC) have provided forums to bring current and former practitioners from the United States and abroad together with students of intelligence in academia, Congress, the media, and other organizations. Members of CSI, who come from universities and public policy centers throughout the United States, and the participants in the nine colloquiums have contributed invaluable intellectual skills, time, encouragement, and wise counsel. In the process, they have made a unique contribution to the national debate about intelligence.

NSIC has housed the Consortium and given material assistance from the beginning. It has also provided an environment where scholars and practitioners, not necessarily sharing a common political agenda, have been able to consider how best to identify overall U.S. intelligence requirements as a means to enhance national security.

I would like to express my appreciation to the current and former U.S. government officials who have been willing to participate in this endeavor. Their collective experience spans the entire history of modern U.S. intelligence. It should be noted, however, that the views expressed in the publications of the Consortium as well as in the chapters and the discussant comments in this book are not necessarily those of any individual agency or department.

Finally, I am especially grateful to a few individuals who have had the patience and skill to turn this particular complex manuscript into a finished product very quickly and who, in intelligence lingo, "handled" me—particularly Jeff Berman and Jill Fall of NSIC, Bette Janson, who prepared the manuscript for publication, and Jaime Welch-Donahue of Lexington Books for her help and encouragement.

Abbreviations

ASW	antisubmarine warfare
BND	Bundesnachrichtendienst—Federal Republic of Germany's foreign intelligence service
C³	command, control, and communications
CA	covert action
CC&D	cover, concealment, and deception
CCP	Cuban Communist Party
CI	counterintelligence
CIA	Central Intelligence Agency
CPSU	Communist Party of the Soviet Union
CSI	Consortium for the Study of Intelligence
DCI	director of central intelligence
DDCI	deputy director of central intelligence
DDCI/CI	deputy director of central intelligence for counterintelligence (proposed)
DDI	deputy director of intelligence (CIA); also used to refer to the CIA's Directorate of Intelligence
DDO	deputy director of operations (CIA); also used to refer to the CIA's Directorate of Operations
DGI	Direccion Generale de Intelligencia—Cuba's intelligence service
DIA	Defense Intelligence Agency
DoD	Department of Defense
DRV	Democratic Republic of Vietnam

FBI	Federal Bureau of Investigation
FEC	Far East Command
GRU	Soviet Military Intelligence
HUMINT	human intelligence
INF	intermediate range nuclear forces
INR	Bureau of Intelligence and Research (Department of State)
KGB	Committee for State Security (Soviet Union)
LIC	low-intensity conflict
NATO	North Atlantic Treaty Organization
NIE	National Intelligence Estimate
NKPA	North Korean People's Army
NSIC	National Strategy Information Center
NSC	National Security Council
PFIAB	President's Foreign Intelligence Advisory Board
PLA	People's Liberation Army (China)
PLO	Palestine Liberation Organization
R&D	research and development
RAF	Royal Air Force (U.K.)
RFE/RL	Radio Free Europe/Radio Liberty
ROK	Republic of Korea
SBDP	Soviet Battlefield Development Plan
SDI	strategic defense initiative
SIGINT	signals intelligence
SLBM	submarine launched ballistic missile
SOSUS	sound surveillance systems
SSBN	ballistic missile nuclear submarine
S&T	scientific and technical
START	Strategic Arms Reduction Talks
VPK	Military-Industrial Commission (Soviet Union)

1
Intelligence for the 1990s

Roy Godson

hat kind of foreign intelligence does the United States need to meet the national security challenges of the 1990s? What should be the objectives or missions of U.S. intelligence? What kinds of procedures and organizational arrangements will achieve these objectives? How can the attention of the president and other senior officials be brought to focus on these matters?

These questions are not new. They have been posed throughout the 1980s and no doubt will be on the agenda into the twenty-first century. What is new is the emerging recognition that U.S. intelligence, as it has been constituted, does not fully match the challenges that almost certainly lie ahead. In the 1970s, this was the focus of neither the academic study of intelligence nor the policy debate about it. Instead, the president, Congress, the media, academia, and the intelligence community leadership came to focus almost exclusively on abuses—real and alleged. What many then considered to be an overactive and overzealous intelligence apparatus was constrained, and the intelligence budget was cut dramatically.

By the late 1970s and early 1980s, attention began to shift away from abuses to the weaknesses and inadequacies that had become apparent in U.S. intelligence effectiveness. However, during that period most leaders of the intelligence community were reluctant to admit that there were serious problems. They belittled and even ridiculed White House, congressional, academic, and internal critics of U.S. performance, although, at the same time, they began to request and to receive additional funding.

By the mid-1980s, the tide had turned, helped, in no small measure, by a series of costly hostile intelligence successes and counterintelligence failures sometimes characterized as "the year (or even the decade) of the spy." A growing consensus—though by no means unanimity—began to emerge among congressional, academic, and media specialists as well as among senior leaders of the intelligence community, that the missions of U.S. intelligence needed refinement and reorientation; that the methods and procedures used to achieve these missions required considerable improvement; and that the organizational arrangements of the past did not match the needs of the future. This diagnosis has led to some experimentation and reform inside the intelligence community.

The consensus was apparent during the December 1987 Colloquium on Intelligence Requirements for the 1990s, organized by the Consortium for the Study of Intelligence (CSI). The more than sixty participants included current and former senior intelligence and Department of Defense (DoD) officials, members and staff of the President's Foreign Intelligence Advisory Board (PFIAB), members of the National Security Council (NSC) staff in the 1970s and 1980s, current and former members and staff of the congressional intelligence committees, academics, journalists, and other specialists in the subject.

The inquiry of the colloquium was based loosely on four sets of assumptions. First, that the outlines of the global context of the 1990s are already coming into view. Here, the participants relied for the most part on the findings of an April 1987 CSI colloquium on the likely global environment in the 1990s. Seven geostrategic regions and two functional areas—the international economy and terrorism—were analyzed at that meeting. Among the conclusions that emerged were the following:

1. The Soviet Union, despite its chronic economic and social ills, will become in some respects a stronger strategic power in the 1990s. It may be able to project more military power than ever before at most levels of conflict. It will have greater diplomatic and political power, assisted by the rejuvenation of its diplomatic and active measures apparatus. At the same time, it will be constrained by serious internal and economic difficulties.

2. The cohesion of both blocs will be weakened. The Soviet bloc and the Western alliance will become more strained and unstable. Eastern Europe will be especially difficult for Moscow. Western Europe and Japan increasingly will pursue their own independent policies, with less emphasis on U.S. partnership.

3. A new international economic pattern is already emerging. The economic patterns of the postwar era are breaking down. Relative

economic dominance is shifting away from the United States and toward Western Europe and the Asian rim of the Pacific. This will impose great strains on the United States, and the domestic political ramifications in the 1990s are likely to be significant.

4. Varying degrees of instability are to be expected in the Third World—particularly in areas of geostrategic interest to the United States—above all Mexico, Central America, and the Caribbean, but also the Middle East, southern and central Africa, and strategic regions in Asia.

5. Terrorism will continue to be a serious threat to U.S. interests. The most critical threats are likely to emerge from and take place in the Middle East and in adjacent regions rather than in the United States itself.

Not everyone at the April 1987 colloquium agreed with each of these assessments. However, it was agreed that prudent planners will want to take into account issues and problems that cannot now be anticipated. Nevertheless, intelligence planners consciously or unconsciously must begin with assumptions about the likely nature of the global environment. These basic assessments were used to lay the foundation for consideration of U.S. intelligence in the 1990s.

A second set of assumptions was made about the nature of U.S. national security policy in the 1990s. It was taken for granted that intelligence ought to be designed to help formulate (collection, analysis, and counterintelligence) and implement policy (covert action and counterintelligence). Hence, it is difficult to examine intelligence requirements without knowing the policy preferences of the U.S. governments of the 1990s. Nevertheless, planners today must assume that there is an enduring core of national security concerns to ensure that the capabilities are in place to address these concerns when and if they are needed. Again prudent planners also must take into account uncertainties, but it was assumed at the December colloquium that there would not be changes in the fundamental precepts of U.S. policy and strategy in the 1990s.

Third, it was recognized that we are not starting from a tabula rasa. In recent decades, U.S. intelligence has developed a particular set of missions, doctrines, personnel, and resources. Important technological and human intelligence means, procedures, and organization are already in place. They cannot be modified radically, at least not in the immediate future. Many of the strengths and weaknesses of U.S. intelligence identified in the 1980s will continue in the 1990s, regardless of what we do now.

Fourth, it was assumed that intelligence consists of four major interrelated elements—collection, analysis, counterintelligence, and covert action—that are linked to overall national security policy. Affecting any one element is likely to affect the others and have consequences for national security policy formulation and implementation.

The December colloquium looked at the capabilities required of each element to meet the challenge of the 1990s. Each element was the focus of two papers, which were critiqued by two panelists before the floor was open to general discussion. The participants were asked to address the following questions:

1. What missions (purposes, objectives, and type of intended products) should be undertaken by each intelligence element? How adequate are the missions of the past and the methods of determining those missions for future needs?

2. How should we go about pursuing these missions and producing the required products? What personnel, training, technology, methods of production and operation, and processing and dissemination of data do we need?

3. What organizational arrangements within and between bureaucracies concerned with these elements would help achieve these missions?

The following summary highlights major aspects of the discussion, and places recent proposals for intelligence reform in the context of the postwar evolution of U.S. intelligence.

Analysis

The mission and the resultant analytical products of the intelligence community, along with many of its intellectual and bureaucratic procedures, were subject to incisive criticism at the colloquium. Identified weaknesses in U.S. analysis are likely to be compounded by the peculiarities of analytical requirements in the 1990s. Hence, a new doctrine of analysis intended to produce new types of products as well as major changes in analytical procedures was proposed.

In general, political and military intelligence estimates were seen as being prone to be too academic and too divorced from the needs of policymakers. They often reflect the doctrine or school of thought institutionalized in the Central Intelligence Agency (CIA) by the first generation of senior analysts, illustrated most notably in the work and writing of Sherman Kent.[1] According to Kent, analysts were to describe empirical trends in foreign societies based on evidence from history and overt and clandestine sources. They were not to allow their values and policy preferences or those of the policy "consumer" to affect their work. This prescription became a key tenet of the analysts' ethos.

To ensure the above, analysts were not to become directly involved in helping policymakers. A barrier was to be maintained between analyst and policymaker to prevent the policymaker from perverting the analyst's product. Analysts should be close enough to policymakers to be aware of their concerns and should tailor analysis to meet policymakers' needs, but they should not become involved with policymaking lest they lose their objectivity. Moreover, the proponents of this view, which became dominant within the intelligence community, do not believe that intelligence, as a matter of course, should be involved in identifying options or opportunities for policymakers or in conducting audits to help determine whether policy is achieving its intended objectives. The role of intelligence, this school believes, is to lay out the facts, identify trends, and thereafter leave policymaking to the policymakers.

This doctrine also had the additional, if unintended, effect of helping to screen analysts from criticism by outsiders privy to their necessarily classified products. Policymakers, the NSC and its staff, the PFIAB, the presidentially-appointed director of central intelligence (DCI), and others who challenged the analysis were seen as almost ipso facto interfering with the scholarly, objective work of the analysts. If they brought other values, paradigms, and policies to bear on the problem, they were politicizing intelligence to suit their policy preferences. To a large extent, this resulted in shielding analysts from substantive debate over the quality of their products.

A second school of analysis also developed in the early days of the CIA. From the late 1940s, when the first school became predominant, until the late 1970s, there was little explicit dialogue between the two, although the arguments within the intelligence community about the scope and format of analytical products often reflected, albeit implicitly, the controversy between them. In the 1980s, a number of factors (among them congressional and academic criticism of national estimates from the 1960s and the 1970s; requests for specific types of analysis from various components in the White House; and the interest of DCI William Casey and Deputy Director of Intelligence [DDI] Robert Gates) combined to fuel interest in the type of analysis envisioned by the second school. And indeed innovations in some analytical products in the 1980s have blurred the distinction between them.

The characteristics of the second school and its differentiation have not been fully explicated in the literature on intelligence. Indeed, most practitioners, policymakers, and scholars usually talk and write about intelligence analysis as if there were only one major type of analytical estimative product—that past practice is the model for the present and the future. Components of the second perspective can be found in the writing of, among others, Willmoore Kendall[2], and in the essays and commentary of Adda Bozeman, Angelo Codevilla, and Kenneth deGraffenreid in *Intelligence Requirements for the 1980s* Vols. I-VII.[3] They are also addressed in more detail in the chapter on analysis in this volume.

Among the major characteristics of the second school are the following:

Opportunity-Oriented Analysis. According to proponents of the new analysis, estimates should not focus exclusively on descriptive trends in other societies. Instead they should use descriptive trends explicitly to demonstrate to the policymaker where and when opportunities to advance policy lie. They should illuminate opportunities to advance U.S. interests through diplomatic, military, and economic means, public diplomacy, and covert action. Opportunity-oriented analysis is designed to complement descriptive analysis. However, it would focus on the strategic and tactical vulnerabilities of foreign leaders, parties, and/or movements. It would identify those factors subject to external influence and those that are relatively immutable.

The analyst would not be asked to become a party to decision making. He or she would be asked to identify opportunities and the likely results of given courses of action on foreign societies based on U.S. interests in the region as defined by policymakers. The desirability of this type of contingent prediction was noted by Willmoore Kendall in 1949, but it has been undertaken by the intelligence community only rarely, and usually reluctantly. Noteworthy exceptions would include the Bureau of Intelligence and Research (INR) in the Department of State, which sometimes prepares this type of analysis for senior State Department officials, and some military analytical products that attempt to anticipate the defensive countermeasures an enemy might use.

Awareness of the Otherness of Foreign Societies. Proponents of the second school are particularly concerned about the tendency of Americans to believe that foreign societies are, if not identical, much like ours. This is called mirror imaging. Americans have a tendency to universalize theories that may explain U.S. society and statecraft but do not explain the behavior of others. Policymakers need to be informed by analysts about the exact and peculiar ways in which foreign societies and their elites are different from ours. They need to know the methods that others use to pursue their ends and how they differ from ours.

This is no easy analytical task. Fully understanding one's own society is difficult enough. Penetrating foreign cultures so that one understands them without succumbing to exaggerated fears or contemptuous denigration, such as labeling them irrational, crazy, or barbaric, requires even more effort. Analysts are required to understand the values, doctrines, decision-making procedures, and perceptions of foreigners, as well as their capabilities. They must not assume that foreigners will behave much like Americans (or any "rational person") if they have the same capabilities. Analysts must point out that the values, doctrines, and behavior of foreigners are often very different from those of Americans.

Interaction with Foreign Societies. Intelligence analysts are not scientists investigating the natural phenomena of the physical world. Understanding nature is difficult enough, but intelligence analysts are trying to understand foreigners who not only are changing as the analysts study them, but also are attempting to shape the analysts' perceptions of them and hence the decisions the analysts make concerning them. This is the Heisenberg principle applied to social phenomena, and therefore the problem is multiplied.

Dissimulation is normal in many cultures. In some cultures, it has been institutionalized in government bureaucracy so that one or more senior leaders and whole departments under their direction specialize in denying information and in selectively allowing their targets to see what they expect or want to see. While traditional analysts do not rule out this type of inquiry, proponents of the second school believe that this interactive process deserves much more careful attention than it receives from traditional analysts.

Self-Conscious Epistemology. Proponents of the second school believe that analysts must be self-conscious about their analytical methods and their strengths and weaknesses. They propose making much more explicit what the analysts know, what they do not know, and how they came to know what they think they know. These proponents tend to be skeptical of the notion that intelligence can just gather facts and infer trends. Rather they believe that analysts (and collectors) use models or theories to decide what facts are relevant, whether they are conscious of it or not. They propose making the theories or paradigms that guide the analysts much more explicit and ensuring that policymakers are aware of what basic premises underlie major analytical products.

The propositions of the new school of analysis are not incompatible with those of the traditionalists. Proponents of the new school maintain, however, that the traditionalists usually pay only nominal attention to these concerns. Hence, the new analysis emphasizes the significance of these concerns, not their originality or their incompatibility with the traditional approach.

Advocates believe that this new approach not only would have improved the product of previous decades, but its relevance will be even greater in the emerging world environment of the 1990s and beyond. The roles played by Europe, Japan, and China in world affairs will increase. Many smaller powers also might find it possible to play a more independent role in world politics. Thus, the need to be attuned to many different cultures and political and military systems will be pressing. Also, the United States will have to maneuver with greater dexterity with respect to both its allies and to a more complex Soviet bloc. U.S. policymakers will need to know a great deal about the opportunities to influence both friends and adversaries and, at the same time, will need to protect themselves from being maneuvered or manipulated by foreign governments.

The United States has had a difficult time understanding Soviet political and military developments with precision. Even after more than four decades, the United States still finds it difficult to get its bearings, particularly when confronted with new developments. This problem is likely to be compounded as traditional cultures come to the fore in the more fragmented international system of the 1990s. Unless there are major changes in analytical products, policymakers will be ill-equipped to cope with the choices before them.

How can the United States obtain these new products? Certainly, there is no quick fix or short-term solution. A number of measures, some very difficult to implement, might help, however.

First, both policymakers and senior managers of the intelligence community must decide that they need the types of products that would result from the new analysis. In the 1980s, they began to move in this direction. But according to participants in both the policy process and the intelligence community, in the Reagan era (as well as in previous Administrations) it was difficult to focus the attention of senior policy officials on matters of analytical intelligence policy. At the same time, as was noted, there have been changes in some analytical products. There also has been determined bureaucratic resistance. Another factor inhibiting innovation may have resulted from the Iran-Contra affair, where some senior officials, politicians, and people in the media charged—with relatively little evidence—that the DCI and senior intelligence officials had politicized intelligence and "cooked" analysis to suit their policy initiatives.

After four decades of the traditional school's dominance, however, there is a growing view that change is needed. Proponents of the second school have not yet systematically developed a comprehensive doctrine. Participants believed that policymakers and the DCI should charge them with doing so.

Second, even if there is an agreement among policymakers and intelligence managers about the necessity for a new type of analysis, there is concern about finding the required personnel. Very few Americans have experience doing opportunity-oriented political-military analysis. Few are trained for this in the formal education system. And until recently, even professional analysts have not been encouraged to develop these skills. Moreover, most of them have had little practical experience in political, military, or economic affairs before becoming analysts.

When it comes to analyzing the peculiar strategic and tactical opportunities afforded by a foreign state, U.S. analysts also are often ill-equipped. Even if they have language and cultural training, in general they have not had to live or operate in these cultures. To the contrary, they have been raised and trained in a society that disparages lying and deception. They live in a society that often teaches cultural relativism in its universities but is given to fits of seeking to universalize American social science theories as well as political and economic values. How, in this society and in this intelligence community, can the personnel be found to accomplish the new mission?

Fortunately, the personnel problem is not as acute as it may appear. Some analysts have demonstrated great skill in adapting to these analytic needs. In recent years, training programs have begun to focus on aspects of the new analysis in both the CIA and the Defense Intelligence Agency (DIA), but bureaucratic patterns in place for many years cannot be changed overnight. The normal process of turnover at the top is beginning to have its effect. While now recognized as a priority, training can still be substantially changed to address the new needs.

Another source of new analysis is new personnel. While the intelligence agencies believe that they are attracting better quality analysts, the more important question is the mission the new analysts are to perform. Higher grades, good SAT and GRE scores, and academic experience indicate something about qualifications. Although they might be necessary conditions for employment (and even this is debatable), they certainly are not sufficient for the new analysis. There is a need for analysts who can understand the peculiarities of foreign cultures and their statecraft. Many will have to be fluent in foreign languages, and they will have to understand what is required to operate in these cultures, that is, to actually influence events.

If the United States were a small, insular, homogeneous society, this would be an almost insoluble problem. But, of course, it is not. Within the polyglot American society a remarkable diversity and range of such individuals are to be found. Indeed, compared to most, the U.S. possesses a natural advantage. It is true that members of diverse ethnic groups and those who have the requisite political skills may not be volunteering for employment in U.S. intelligence. In addition, there are sometimes other complications in employing such individuals, such as security considerations. But why should U.S. intelligence not actively recruit the needed talent that is available in American society, just as universities actively recruit athletes? In reality, the subject has rarely been a high priority for busy senior officials and managers caught up in pressing daily analytical tasks. New recruitment practices are likely to receive the requisite attention only when policymakers and the leadership of the intelligence community realize that this is an important component of the new analysis.

Collection

Determining the collection missions of the 1990s and ensuring that the United States will have the required capabilities remain high priorities. First, there is a necessity to change the method the United States uses to determine its collection priorities. Second, unless there are changes in the collection process, the United States is unlikely to achieve its collection objectives, whatever their ultimate substance.

Determining collection priorities has never been easy, and the problem is becoming ever more difficult. Requirements are outstripping capabilities. Policymakers, analysts, and other intelligence consumers (for example, covert action practitioners) need more and more information. Although the Soviet Union is likely to remain the major target, the new global context of the 1990s will increase the demand for more intelligence information on non-Soviet targets.

Additionally, collection requirements, particularly military collection requirements, against the Soviet target must be reassessed. Collection against the Soviet military is the largest part of the U.S. effort. The paradigm and methods that guided the selection of U.S. collection priorities with respect to this target from the 1950s through the 1980s appears to be in need of modification.

Until now, the focus has been on scooping up facts about Soviet military capabilities. The nature of military technology in the postwar period and technical collection breakthroughs by the United States in the 1950s and 1960s produced a collection paradigm that served the country reasonably well. That analysts misassessed the meaning of data (important National Intelligence Estimates [NIEs] of the period were flawed in major respects) was not primarily the fault of the collectors. Take, for example, the PFIAB-inspired competitive intelligence exercise conducted by the CIA in the mid-1970s. Two teams, A and B, used the same data. Team B, which did not comprise intelligence analysts, came to a much more accurate assessment of Soviet capabilities than Team A, which was composed of these analysts.

Collection priorities from the 1960s to the 1980s grew out of the nature of military technology during this period. Missiles, for example, were for the most part land based, large, immobile, and difficult to hide. Moreover, the United States had taken the lead in developing much of the military technology during this period. The American collectors knew the basic characteristics of these weapon systems—what to look for and how to interpret ambiguous data. In the conventional arena, during the same period, it was relatively easy to count divisions, tanks, and airplanes. The technology was already well known, and much of it had been used in World War II and Korea.

The second factor that shaped the collection paradigm from the late 1950s to the 1980s was U.S. reconnaissance breakthroughs. The United States developed the technical capabilities to see, hear, and sense facts about Soviet capabilities. This drove the requirements in a particular direction, concentrating on objects that could be seen, heard, and sensed. At the same time, the collectors were placing less emphasis on "soft" subjects, notably doctrine and intentions, which were less amenable to collection by technical means. Another factor affecting collection priorities was the tremendous growth of the place and importance of monitoring arms control agreements by the intelligence community. This new task, particularly keeping track of Soviet weapons, has not only consumed large resources within the intelligence community but has also tended to affect collection processes, often to the exclusion of other approaches.

Now, however, much of the collection equation has changed. First, innovation in military technology, for example, has enabled Moscow to develop smaller, mobile missiles designed to be hidden from collectors. Moreover, the Soviets have built weapons for which there is no U.S. equivalent. They already have a limited strategic defense capability, and they are likely to have a much bigger program on-line in the 1990s. In addition, Moscow is investing heavily in various forms of exotic technologies. Much less is known about these defensive weapons and new technologies than when the United States first developed nuclear weapons and missiles, although their strategic impact might turn out to be equally decisive. For the most part, they are not nearly as observable, and since the U.S. database is so limited, the nation will have great difficulty fully understanding the information it does acquire.

The technology of conventional weapons also has changed and will continue to evolve. It has been more than fifteen years, however, since some of this technology has been battle tested, and qualitative changes are much more difficult to assess than quantitative ones.

It should also be noted that U.S. collection was developed primarily for a peacetime environment or an environment in which the United States needed to know only if it was being attacked so that it could retaliate against fixed targets. This too has changed. Now Moscow has developed the command and control facilities and offensive and defensive mix of forces designed to destroy or neutralize much of U.S. collection in wartime. These forces are also designed to be able to fight protracted nuclear or nonnuclear war.

Second, the Soviet Union and other countries possess a vast amount of information about U.S. collection capabilities and their vulnerabilities. This has come about as a result of global progress in intelligence collection technologies and also from U.S. and British counterintelligence and security failures, such as the Kampiles, Helmich, Boyce-Lee, Prime, Walker, Whitworth, and Pelton cases, to name only a few of the more serious failures. By learning about specific U.S. capabilities and methods, Moscow (most importantly) learned where it was vulnerable to U.S. collection. This enabled the Soviet Union (and other countries) not only to take countermeasures limiting the effectiveness of U.S. collection but also to "steer" U.S. collectors in directions they wish us to pursue—and away from others.

True, because of the substantial investment of the early 1980s, U.S. technical capabilities are likely to improve in the 1990s. For example, new technologies will be used to expand coverage to parts of the electromagnetic spectrum not currently accessible. This will make possible some forms of coverage despite, for example, darkness and clouds in some areas. In addition, it may be possible to use computer-based artificial intelligence systems to help analyze the mountains of data these systems will produce. However, these improvements will not be revolutionary. Major breakthroughs in the 1990s comparable to those of the 1950s cannot now be expected. There will remain important limitations on what the United States can collect.

As a result of these changes in military technology and capabilities, as well as U.S. reliance on improved systems about which Moscow already possesses much information, collection that focuses on the mission of the 1960s is less likely to fare well in the 1990s and beyond. The United States is less likely to know where, how, and for what to look. As a result, the United States will see less than it did, and it will be harder to make sense of the even more ambiguous data it collects.

How then should the mission of U.S. collection on the Soviet military be determined? The beginning of the answer is to be found in the intellectual context. It will be difficult, if not impossible, to understand Soviet capabilities without knowing the context or intellectual underpinnings of Soviet military power. The United States must more fully understand what Moscow intends to do with its military forces and how it plans to employ these forces, both in peacetime and in wartime. The Soviets believe military science really is a science. They plan with great precision for both eventualities.

The United States also must understand Soviet doctrine and political-military planning. Furthermore, U.S. collectors must identify the problems or constraints Moscow envisions and how Soviet leaders plan to circumvent them. The United States literally cannot afford to collect facts about Soviet military capabilities. Thus, the collection mission must be devised from one or more intellectual frameworks. These frameworks will suggest questions or hypotheses to guide the collectors.

But short of sources in the Soviet Defense Council, how are the collectors to obtain the paradigm to be used to guide their activities? A major implication of this analysis is that the methods used to determine the collection of previous decades cannot be continued in the future. Senior policymakers cannot simply authorize the continuation of past practice with enhanced capabilities, that is, collection of facts with more and better images and communication channels. Instead, they will need to consider intellectual scenarios or theories to explain Soviet military planning. Then they must select those scenarios, theories, or models that should receive collection resources. The argument here is that the United States should not continue to seek only to collect all available facts. It must also determine which facts are more significant and what they might mean.

The danger in this approach is that policymakers might select the wrong scenarios or theories. Collection and resources might be wasted and U.S. vulnerabilities increased. It should be realized, however, that even were policymakers not to be aware of alternative scenarios or models, there would still be scenarios or models guiding collection. Popular mythology notwithstanding, the United States now is not photographing, listening, and processing data pertaining to everything. Some areas, subjects, and channels are receiving much more attention than others. The model and the intelligence collection budget are now being set by collection managers, more or less on their own, according to implicit rather than explicit choices. These are based on the often unconscious intellectual habits of the collectors, the inevitable bureaucratic battles over resources, and what collection managers believe their capabilities might allow them to learn.

The new approach would require the model to be made explicit and policymakers to make explicit choices. It would necessitate alternative models being presented to senior policymakers. They, in turn, would become involved in choosing the model or models and in setting the resulting collection priorities. The intelligence community budget, most of which is devoted to collection, would come to be driven by the much more explicit choices of policymakers—which is not the way it has been determined in recent decades.

These collection models or choices also could be developed in a new way by teams of analysts, collection specialists, and even counterintelligence (CI) analysts. The various types of analysts (analogous to theoretical scientists) would develop hypotheses (and methods of testing them) that might explain Soviet behavior. The collection specialists (analogous to experimental scientists) would determine how such hypotheses and methods could be tested through available future collection methods. The counterintelligence analysts would help screen both the hypotheses and collection methods for deception. In addition, they would determine what kinds of positive intelligence could be gleaned from CI operations. Counterintelligence could tell us, for example, about the Soviet Union's Committee for State Security's

(KGB's) external and internal collection and active measures priorities, which in turn tells us about Soviet intentions, capabilities, and vulnerabilities.

There have already been limited precedents in the intelligence community for this approach, although collection planners usually work relatively independently. The U.S. Navy has developed innovative methods for teaming intelligence collectors and analysts, and in the early 1980s the U.S. Army developed a model of Soviet ground force doctrine (the Soviet Battlefield Development Plan), which served as a hypothesis in tracking new Soviet developments. In sum, collection priorities in the 1990s should entail a tighter integration of the elements of intelligence—analysis, collection, and counterintelligence—and greater involvement of senior policymakers.

In addition to devising new ways of ascertaining collection priorities—the bulk of which concern technical sources—other major innovations are needed in collection from human intelligence (HUMINT) sources. The Soviet target is likely to remain the highest priority, but other important targets are likely to include Iran, Libya, and terrorist groups.

Although there are a variety of techniques used in HUMINT collection, one dominant pattern prevails: collection managers talk to generalist case officers, often operating under thin cover, whose status as U.S. government officials restricts their contacts to a relatively narrow circle abroad.

Therefore, their task of recruiting foreign agents who can provide them with secret information is made quite difficult. (This is the dominant, although not exclusive, mode of HUMINT collection.) As a result, case officers are given general guidelines, and only rarely are they themselves specialists in the subject matter they are required to obtain. Hence, the officers are often not in a position to task the agent or evaluate his or her information properly. Because most case officers serve under official cover, they approach the target as U.S. officials. Moreover, after one or two assignments abroad, for the most part they are known to sophisticated foreign intelligence and counterintelligence services, even if they are competent in clandestine tradecraft.

There are, however, alternative patterns, which are only rarely used. The essence of the alternatives is to find different ways of gaining access to the individuals and repositories of knowledge the United

States seeks without using official cover. There are at least two ways to do this. One is to use nonofficial case officers who, in the course of normal business or social relationships, gain access to the relevant sources. This is a riskier and more expensive approach than the dominant current pattern, but its proponents believe that it provides better access to targets. The second approach is to enlist the services of Americans and foreigners who are not professional intelligence officers but are specialists in the subjects assigned by the collection taskers. They would be able to interact with sources and glean from them both generalities and details to help form a mosaic. They would not recruit or run agents, but, because of their special knowledge of a particular subject and continuous contact with the source, they would be in a position to acquire significant information and at the same time screen for fabrication or deception. It is hard for one specialist to deceive another for very long. As is discussed in chapter 2, this type of collection has already led to fruitful results. One area in which much has been accomplished is science and technology. The pattern has worked in perhaps the most difficult environment, the Soviet Union, even prior to the onset of *glasnost*. In Mikhail Gorbachev's Soviet Union, this approach should reap even higher dividends, especially if it is properly tasked and coordinated.

To strengthen this approach, detailed planning would be essential. Case officers would have to be retrained, and the motivations and subcultures of both U.S. and foreign collectors/specialists in this program would have to be assessed. There will be reluctance to do this work in some professions or in some sectors of some professions, but not in others. Although this alternative requires an adjustment in the HUMINT collection pattern, it could in time lead to major breakthroughs.

Counterintelligence

Proposals for reform of counterintelligence, initially the focus of controversy, have led to a much greater consensus. In the early 1980s, the intelligence agencies, Congress, the media, and academic specialists were generally satisfied with U.S. counterintelligence capabilities. Efforts to reform counterintelligence both by the White House and by outside specialists were stifled. But then the country was shaken by a series of revelations of major hostile intelligence successes and CI failures. Apart from the overall damage to U.S. national security, it was clear that the major intelligence agencies themselves had been penetrated at some point—and not only by the Soviet bloc but also by the People's Republic of China, Israel, and Ghana, among others. One result was that many people began to pay serious attention to long-standing proposals for improving counterintelligence.

One of the more significant proposals concerns changing the method used to determine the national CI mission. Traditionally, the mission has emerged from ad hoc departmentalism—that is, each department or agency makes its own decision on what it should be doing to identify and neutralize the activities of foreign intelligence services in its area of jurisdiction. There has been little central coordination. There have been efforts to determine the nature of the total foreign intelligence threat to the country, but there has been neither an overall assessment of the values, secrets, and institutions we need to protect nor overall consideration of how CI can perform this function as well as any ancillary intelligence and policy functions. Responsibility has been split among the major components of the intelligence community, particularly the CIA, the Federal Bureau of Investigation (FBI), and components of the DoD. There have been periods of cooperation and sometimes coordination among them, but there has been no standard method to set national goals or priorities. Each agency sets its own. Sometimes this has served the national interest; sometimes not. (There is little reason to believe that this method has been a bulwark or a bane of civil liberties. Contrary to popular mythology, there does not appear to be a necessary relationship between the method of determining the national CI mission and the level of intrusion into civil liberties.)

An alternative method of determining the mission would be to institutionalize the following procedures. First, make regular, systematic, and comprehensive assessments of the threat that the hundreds of foreign intelligence services arrayed against the United States pose to overall U.S. security interests. This would include identifying the broad range of targets and the means used by foreign intelligence and security services operating in the United States and abroad. Some are more hostile toward the United States than others. Even many foreign intelligence services with whom the United States maintains cooperative relationships pose a threat (by targeting U.S. technological secrets or seeking political influence in the United States, for example). The U.S. government must understand the intelligence objectives of these services, their priorities, and their modus operandi. Presumably U.S. diplomatic, intelligence, and military installations and personnel both abroad and at home are major targets, both in peacetime and in wartime. American businessmen, scientists, students, and journalists at home and abroad also may be targets. The techniques and capabilities of foreign intelligence services also must be assessed, both in terms of their human and technical characteristics. How effective are these techniques? What are they likely to accomplish in the near and longer term? This information must be collected, assessed, and collated if the U.S. government is to understand the magnitude of the threat.

Second, there is a need to determine which secrets, institutions, and values are to be protected. Obviously, protection cannot be extended equally to all. The government as a whole must determine what the most important secrets are so it can mount greater defensive security measures to protect them. To do this, paradoxically, it may be necessary to disseminate and centralize information about secret programs more widely than before in an effort to provide security and CI officials with a better sense of what is important. In the absence of such understanding, it is difficult to deploy CI resources rationally.

Moreover, the threat must be matched up against those secrets, values, and institutions the United States seeks to protect. It may turn out that the priorities of foreign intelligence services are not the same as those of the United States. Many of their targets and methods might not be as important or as effective as U.S. officials imagine. Hence, the United States might not need to dispense its resources to cover every conceivable target. Instead, it can concentrate resources on key priorities. (In recent years there has been some experimentation along this line in the intelligence community, for example, pertaining to technology transfer, which indicates that this is a promising approach.)

The same is true for protecting U.S. institutions and values. Foreign intelligence services—particularly the Soviet KGB and Cuban Direccion Generale de Intelligencia (DGI)—have targeted U.S. institutions and values. They seek to gain influence in the media, churches, trade unions, and other nongovernmental organizations. Do we care?

If so, which values and institutions are most important to the United States? The proposed alternative brings together knowledge of the threat and knowledge of what is threatened.

Third, what ancillary benefits can be obtained from CI programs? Can U.S. knowledge of what foreign intelligence services are trying to do contribute to satisfying positive collection requirements? For example, most of the world is ruled by authoritarian and totalitarian governments in which intelligence and security services play a very important role. Knowledge obtained from penetrating and understanding these organizations (the job of counterintelligence) can tell U.S. officials much about the vulnerabilities and priorities of the ruling elites in those countries. If the United States recruits high-ranking security service officials close to the ruling party leaders, they are likely to know how the leadership perceives its domestic and foreign enemies. Knowledge of KGB and Soviet military intelligence (GRU) tasking is a potentially important indicator of Soviet political priorities abroad, as well as their priorities for developing particular offensive and defensive weapon systems.

In addition, as Washington learns how a foreign government, through its intelligence capabilities, sees and hears the United States, the United States gains the capability to use an important channel to influence that government. This might help reinforce messages that the United States is already sending to that government, perhaps through diplomatic channels. It also might mean being able to send altered or partially false information to deceive foreign governments into behaving in ways the United States considers desirable. Using intelligence channels allows this to be done without disinforming the public. To exploit CI capabilities fully, however, the government as a whole must be aware of the state of U.S. knowledge and capabilities, as well as what the various parts of the government are doing to enhance national security. This is not now the case.

Only when senior U.S. policymakers know what is most important to protect, what the priorities and capabilities of foreign services are, and when they can weigh the value of the potential ancillary services of counterintelligence, is the U.S. government in a position to determine the precise missions of CI. The current method of determining the U.S. counterintelligence mission does not adequately utilize these procedures.

At the colloquium, a series of proposals were put forward pertaining to (1) centralizing the formulation and implementation of CI;

(2) developing unilateral CI policy capabilities abroad; and (3) training and professionalizing intelligence and particularly CI personnel.

While there is a consensus that the coordination and implementation of CI policy needs improvement, there are different views about the type of reorganization required. Proposals range from the creation of a government-wide analytical and coordination group, to the creation of a deputy director of central intelligence (DDCI) to coordinate the CI work of the foreign intelligence agencies, to incremental changes only.

Two former CIA officials who held senior CI positions and also have broad experience in other intelligence disciplines, suggest that, although the performance of the various entities concerned with counterintelligence has improved in recent years, the system as a whole is inferior to its fragmented parts. They argue in chapter 4 of this book that

> [r]esponsibility for the establishment of national CI policy, allocation of tasks to the various CI organizations, monitoring of progress, resolution of interagency conflicts, and so on, must be lodged in some entity or person. Continuation of the piecemeal and parochial approach to counterintelligence can be expected only to perpetuate the great national security damage that the United States has suffered to date.

They propose that a new DDCI would be the best place to lodge this function, although they concede that such a move might not give the office government-wide authority. Other senior CI professionals are not convinced, however, that this type of major organizational reform is required.

A second proposal is for a dramatic increase in U.S. capabilities to conduct counterintelligence abroad independently of local intelligence services. The United States faces a major multidisciplinary intelligence threat first to its personnel and installations abroad and second from hostile intelligence services that work against U.S. personnel and installations inside the United States from overseas facilities. The decade of the spy demonstrated, for example, that Americans recruited in the United States are run from abroad and that Americans recruited abroad are contacted when they return to the United States. The United States' ability to identify and neutralize foreign intelligence activities directed at Americans abroad must be improved. This requires a shift in priorities. It has been demonstrated that the United States cannot rely on friendly local security services to monitor hostile intelligence threats directed at Americans. Instead, the United States must increase its capability to perform this mission itself, something the United States has been reluctant to do in recent decades.

A third set of proposals discussed in chapter 4 is the recruitment, training, and professionalization of CI personnel, as well as CI training for all operational intelligence personnel. The United States needs to recruit, train, and retain CI specialists. It cannot afford to have counterintelligence depend completely on personnel with relatively little training and assigned for relatively short tours (two to three years), as they are in most agencies. While CI specialists need operational experience, they also need extensive training and would benefit from remaining in CI career tracks. Most CI personnel have little specialized training, and few remain lifelong CI specialists. There is little incentive to remain a CI specialist and little institutional memory.

An ancillary training program and distribution of CI information also should be established for non-CI intelligence personnel. Operational officers, whether collectors or covert action specialists, should have much more training and receive more CI information than they do now to help protect the security of their operations. This combination of operations security—at almost all levels of intelligence and even for nonintelligence operations personnel (such as some military personnel)—together with improved and coordinated CI specialization, will enable the United States to meet its CI needs in the 1990s.

Covert Action

A major focus of concern is the mission or role of covert action (CA) in U.S. national security policy. When or under what circumstances should the United States be prepared to use this instrument? In the late 1940s, the consensus was that covert action in all its manifestations—propaganda, political support, intelligence support, and paramilitary activity—was a normal instrument of U.S. statecraft.

With the breakup of the foreign policy consensus in the 1960s, doubts about the wisdom of this proposition began to affect the Washington foreign policy establishment. Even before the congressional investigations of the 1970s, the utility of covert action was being questioned.

In the mid-1970s, to all intents and purposes, covert action came to a halt. The Church committee concluded that covert action dominated the CIA and the CIA dominated the rest of the intelligence community. With the rise to positions of influence of Church committee staffers in both the Carter administration and the newly established permanent congressional intelligence committees, as well as the selection of Theodore Sorenson and then Stansfield Turner as DCI, there were few movers and shakers in the Washington intelligence establishment who believed in the need for a major CA capability. CIA specialists in the discipline retired or were fired. The new senior managers in the CIA were not champions of the CA instrument, and the infrastructure—the personnel, agents, and communications—atrophied. In those years efforts also were made to use Congress to outlaw covert action or to impose so many legal restrictions on its use that it could never again become a significant policy instrument.

World events acted as a counterweight to these developments. The Iranian revolution and seizure of U.S. hostages, the Nicaraguan revolution and the rise of Marxist-Leninist elements inside the Sandinista government, and the Soviet takeover of Afghanistan and the uprising of the *mujhadin* altered the political kaleidoscope in the late 1970s. They demonstrated that there were threats and opportunities where covert means were necessary either by themselves (for example, to rescue the hostages or the U.S. diplomats who had taken refuge in the Canadian embassy) or as part of a larger overt effort to contain Soviet expansionism (Afghanistan) or the expansion of violently anti-American elements in Central America (Cuban-supported Marxist-Leninists). These events also demonstrated that covert action could not be started from zero. There was a need to maintain a CA infrastructure—trained personnel and equipment—in place that could be used when needed.

In the late 1970s, plans to use covert action on a selective basis were proposed both in the White House and in Congress. Legislative efforts to outlaw and restrict covert action foundered. The 1974 Hughes-Ryan reporting requirements for covert activities were somewhat relaxed by the Intelligence Oversight Act of 1980.

Despite the reduced suspicion surrounding covert action, the predominant view in the Carter administration and in Congress was that such activities were to be used only under extreme circumstances, or, as Cyrus Vance, Secretary of State during most of the Carter administration, told the Church committee in 1975, when "absolutely essential to the national security."[4] Similarly, Stansfield Turner, Carter's DCI, believed that covert action accomplishes very little and should be used extremely sparingly.

Nevertheless, as a result of the imperatives of world politics and despite misgivings, CA programs, from political support and propaganda to paramilitary activities, increased—even before the Reagan administration came to power. This trend has continued in recent years. Indeed, some paramilitary programs have become so large and so widely known that Congress debates them in public. But the increase in CA programs did not resolve the question of the doctrine or mission of covert action. Should it be regarded, as it was in the 1950s and 1960s, as another instrument to be coordinated with other tools of statecraft, albeit with the special oversight mechanisms established in the 1970s? Or should it still be regarded as an exceptional tool to be used only when other instruments have failed or will not work?

These questions were raised but not resolved by the Reagan administration. They remain the focus of debate both in the Executive Branch and in Congress, and occasionally they spill out into public view. As a result of the Iran-Contra affair, where the Reagan administration was caught circumventing its own covert action and congressional oversight procedures, the debates of the 1970s and proposals for restrictions on covert action surfaced anew.

Most of the participants in the December 1987 colloquium favored regularizing covert action in U.S. statecraft. They generally agreed that there will be major opportunities for the United States to advance its interests in the 1990s through a broad array of CA techniques. These techniques will succeed only if there is support throughout the government and the general public to use this instrument as part of the panoply of foreign policy tools used to advance U.S. interests. In the absence of such a consensus, it will be difficult if not impossible to use the instrument effectively.

To do this it was suggested that the executive branch and Congress should establish and maintain oversight procedures and that the administration should not seek to use the covert instrument as a substitute for overt policy. If U.S. national security policy is well understood and accepted, chances are good that the major means necessary and proper to its success will not be opposed. In the context of carefully formulated policy, a variety of actions, both overt and covert, will seem natural.

In addition to institutionalizing the CA mission in U.S. statecraft, a number of other measures are necessary. First, CA planning must be integrated into government-wide national security programs. To some extent this is already happening, although covert action is often regarded by many in the Washington foreign policy establishment as potentially dangerous and controversial. Few outside the CIA help develop CA plans, and only rarely are CA specialists included in national security planning and implementation groups. The CA dimension should be considered as a matter of course when policy is made regarding a given region or issue, even if a decision not to use the instrumentality is made.

There is also a need to integrate covert action more fully into the CIA. Since the 1970s, covert action has been regarded as problematic within the agency. CA specialists need to benefit more from analysis and counterintelligence. Both these disciplines have much to offer CA specialists, yet only rarely are they well integrated with CA planning. Although there may be more scrutiny of CA proposals by analysts than in earlier years, there is a need for more CI analysis and scrutiny of CA planning and operations to ensure that such action is not compromised or otherwise turned against the United States.

To gain acceptance as a regular part of U.S. statecraft, recruiting and training CA specialists is vital. Some believe that, for the most part, general case officers, who also do collection and counterintelligence under official cover, can fulfill this mission. This is the dominant U.S. pattern. Another view is that covert action is a specialty unto itself requiring training and experience in political operations and policymaking. CA planners, especially operators, should have the linguistic, cultural, and political skills needed to operate covertly. More case officers will be needed who possess these skills.

Another approach to enhancing U.S. capabilities concerns broadening the resource base for political action programs to influence events abroad. One method is to do overtly what used to be done covertly. Several Western countries now overtly support political groups in other countries. This is not considered controversial in the donor country. An example of a relatively successful overt political action was the West German quasi-governmental foundation support of democratic parties in Portugal in the mid-1970s. The essence of this support is giving governmental funds to nongovernmental organizations that can dispense the money overtly without the political liability of being identified with donor governments. This kind of assistance has begun in the United States with the creation of the National Endowment for Democracy, but supporting political parties or subgroups in the midst of turmoil in other countries is still regarded as controversial in the United States. In addition, there are other major inhibitions about supporting political groups abroad, particularly in Congress, which must appropriate the funds. Overt support of pro-Western political forces abroad might, however, pay high dividends in the complex world of the 1990s.

Another method of increasing U.S. capabilities to influence events is to seek help from foreign intelligence services. There has often been a reluctance in the United States to utilize foreign intelligence services for CA objectives. Sometimes, for very good reasons, the United States prefers to go it alone or not to become involved at all. These reasons might include the fear that a foreign service has been penetrated or that it will request an unacceptable quid pro quo. At other times, the reasoning is far from adequate, as when the United States believes it can go it alone, that its operatives are superior, or that there is no tradition of cooperation with a particular country's services.

The second line of reasoning might have been adequate in the past, but in the more politically demanding world of the 1990s, it will not be. Of course, securing foreign cooperation will be more difficult than in the past, given the relative decline of U.S. influence and the reputation the United States has acquired for leaks and exposures (including the Iran-Contra investigation) and for abandoning friends. Still, the United States has many allies abroad. Where it is possible and the price is not too high, the United States should attempt to use the capabilities of others to achieve what would be difficult if not impossible by itself.

Finally, the need for public understanding of and support for covert action was stressed. Public support would translate into all types of benefits. There would be less tendency to leak, both in the executive branch and in Congress, and both Congress and executive branch agencies would be more supportive of covert action. A number of steps can be taken to achieve a higher degree of public support, even without tragedies abroad, which would demonstrate the need for covert action.

First and above all, the administration must be clear about its policy. The goals and the overall means reasonably calculated to achieve these objectives must be laid out for the American people. The administration should not, as a rule, embark on foreign initiatives unless it is willing to fight a sustained public campaign for them and there is reasonable support for its policy. In those circumstances, there is likely to be little opposition to most forms of covert action in support of policy. It is not necessary for the administration to spell out its CA programs. These programs must, however, fit in with policy, and they must not seek to circumvent the oversight process. In this case, even if they are leaked, they will not lead to public displeasure and disarray. In the context of carefully formulated and supported foreign policy, overt and covert action are less likely to be opposed.

Second, the U.S. government can go a long way toward building support for covert action not only by following its own oversight procedures, but also by explaining to the American people, in a sustained fashion, the necessity for covert action. The United States cannot return to an earlier era when intelligence activities were the preserve of a few Washington insiders and an elite inside the CIA. Intelligence activities of almost all forms are now accepted by the American people. The subject is taught in universities, and specific CA means are debated on television. In this context, both the president and Congress must be prepared to discuss and defend the general use of covert action—which has been done too rarely—if the government is to have public support for these instruments in the 1990s. This is easier said than done, but it is important.

Conclusion

The colloquium did not address all aspects of the product, process, and organization of each element of intelligence or the elements' relationships to each other and to policy. It focused on political and military analysis, not on economic analysis. There was no discussion of the need for presenting policymakers with competing analytical products. The colloquium did not discuss all forms of collection. There was little discussion of counterterrorism, narcotics, and technology transfer. The discussion of requirements was based primarily on the perspective of the intelligence professional and not on that of the policymaker or Congress.

Nevertheless, the proposals set forth major requirements for U.S. intelligence. To meet the threats, opportunities, and challenges of the 1990s, the following general requirements would seem to follow from the summary conclusions reached in regard to each of the four intelligence elements.

First, despite the progress of the 1980s, the missions of U.S. intelligence need to be adjusted, refined, or altered. This requires assisting and encouraging those in the executive branch and Congress who have begun to change the methods we have been using to determine the mission of each element and the substantive missions themselves. There is growing recognition that the traditional methods and doctrines of determining products should be complemented by new or revised doctrines of analysis, collection, counterintelligence, and covert action.

Second, the procedures used to achieve U.S. objectives in previous decades are unlikely to be adequate for the next decade. The most common concern is the recruitment and training of personnel. Unless past patterns are altered, U.S. personnel will not be able to accomplish their likely missions.

Fortunately, the types of individuals needed are available in the United States' multiethnic, heterogeneous, creative, and dynamic society. A new recruitment process can find analysts who are familiar with foreign languages, cultures, and political action; collectors able to operate clandestinely in foreign and particularly exotic cultures; counterintelligence specialists who not only know foreign languages and cultures but are also street smart and familiar with the operations of foreign intelligence services; and covert action specialists who have similar skills but are also skilled political operators themselves.

The required skills that new recruits do not possess can be provided in training programs. The United States should not expect even good students trained in American universities to be skilled analysts. It should not expect street smart investigators to be familiar with the modus operandi of foreign intelligence services. It is unreasonable to expect bright young Americans with advanced degrees to be able to understand and influence events in other societies solely on the basis of their academic training. A great deal of sophisticated training is required. Ensuring that the trainers and the curricula are adequate to the missions should be a high priority for senior management.

Finally, throughout the discussion there was a call for greater integration of the elements themselves and greater integration of the elements with policy. Analysis would benefit from more interaction with counterintelligence and collection. Collection requires much more support from analysis, counterintelligence, and policy; counterintelligence needs more involvement with policy; covert action requires greater support from all the elements. Policymakers themselves must become intimately involved in ensuring that intelligence policy serves overall national security policy.

The need to implement many of these changes was recognized in the 1980s, and action was taken in some areas. In the latter part of the decade there is a growing consensus that past practices should not be the only guide to the future and that traditional missions and procedures need to be modernized. Translating this consensus into effective intelligence policy is the challenge of the 1990s.

Notes

1. Sherman Kent, *Strategic Intelligence for American World Policy,* (Princeton, N.J.: Princeton University Press, 1949).

2. Willmoore Kendall, "The Functions of Intelligence," *World Politics* 1 (July 1949): 540–552.

3. Roy Godson, ed., *Intelligence Requirements for the 1980s,* vols. 1–5 (Washington, D.C.: National Strategy Information Center, 1979–1982), vols. 6 and 7 (Lexington, Mass.: Lexington Books, 1986).

4. U.S. Congress, Senate Select Committee to Study Government Operations with Respect to Intelligence Activities, *Hearings* vol. 7, "Covert Action," 94th Cong., 1st sess., December 4 and 5, 1975 (Washington, D.C.: Government Printing Office, 1975), 54.

2
Collection

Essays:

I.   Robert Butterworth
II. R. Keeler and E. Miriam Steiner

Discussion:

I.   Fred Ikle
II. Donald Nielsen

I. ROBERT BUTTERWORTH

A generation ago, the Soviet Union could not hide its missiles in Cuba from U.S. overflights, intercepts, and agent reports. Since then, the Soviets have lost many other secrets to U.S. intelligence. Some observers expect even more losses in the future, thanks particularly to satellite reconnaissance.[1] Others, however, note that during this same period, the Soviets relentlessly pursued the secrets of U.S. collection and built programs to frustrate them, eventually finding successes of their own. Indeed, judging by the headlines of the mid-1980s, a replay of the Cuban missile crisis today could turn out very differently: Nothing useful would come from eavesdropping or overhead reconnaissance, and the agents would turn out to be doubles working for Fidel Castro.[2]

Which characterization will the future resemble? Regrettably, I fear that the gloomy one seems much more likely. To be sure, there will be triumphs in the 1990s. More intelligence will be available against some problems everywhere and against all problems in some locations. U.S. collection will profit from clever applications of technical wizardry, the Soviet anomie spawned by the regime's inner rot, the magnetism of the United States' promise abroad, and the skill and courage of the people in its service. Analysis will benefit from new techniques for mathematical inference, more flexible computerized aids for exploring hypotheses and patterns, more interpretive guidance from visitors and émigrés, and new analysts trained by those who produced the critical insights of the past. Nonetheless, I fear that all of this will not meet the future challenge and that current plans will result in a mismatch pitting emerging future Soviet strengths against developing U.S. weaknesses.

Key elements of the future security balance are already clear. The balance of forces in Europe, the primary strategic theater, is unlikely to shift markedly in favor of the West, and problems of command and control are sure to continue bedeviling the North Atlantic Treaty Organization's (NATO's) approach to coalition warfare. It is also unlikely that the central strategic balance will become substantially more favorable, either through U.S. investments, Soviet weakness, or arms limitation treaties.

Other developments also will complicate U.S. planning. Soviet capabilities for protracted global war are growing. British, French, and Chinese nuclear forces are likely to be improved in some respects, although their future roles, survivability, and operational effectiveness are problematic. In addition, the balance of general purpose forces might move increasingly to favor the Soviet side, at least according to several static measures. The global power projection balance might also do the same.

Unfortunately, the collection balance is also changing unfavorably. The different strategic situations, resources, and objectives of the two sides have generated asymmetric competitions, and the Soviet approach is increasingly opaque to U.S. intelligence.

"More of the Same" Collection

Physical signatures of interest to U.S. efforts to assess Soviet strategic programs are now much more difficult to collect from overhead. This is because the subjects of interest have changed, the Soviets have pursued deliberate programs to deny collection, they have learned a great deal about U.S. collection operations, and the number and type of U.S. collection systems are limited. Some crucial arenas, moreover, are still not adequately represented in U.S. collection planning. Space objects (or the absence of them), for example, are increasingly important to Soviet programs and postures, yet U.S. planning has emphasized looking down rather than up. Furthermore, the prospects of finding human intelligence (HUMINT) to supplement the collection by technical systems, although impossible to rule out, seem fainter in light of the breathtaking amount of information that the KGB has acquired about the U.S. approach to espionage during the past decade.

Some important phenomena will be hidden completely from U.S. collection. Leaders in bunkers buried under meters of earth and concrete, missiles inside canisters inside garages, subterranean production facilities, and laser testing inside closed buildings and tunnels are illustrations of things that are likely to be sensed in very sketchy fashion, if at all. There will probably be little to be gleaned from staring long and hard at their suspected locations, while HUMINT accounts are likely to be fragmentary and contradictory.

Although detectable in principle, some items will remain quite obscured for all practical purposes. This occurs when a collection system is not in the right place; it was not built, delivered, launched, or completed in time; its location and geometry led to processing algorithms that confused certain signals with noise; its location was known (through compromise or because it was otherwise obvious); or it was poorly designed or located. Bad luck also plays a role in some situations. In some cases, items of interest remain unseen because their signatures match a different pattern (camouflage). In other instances, phenomena have remained hidden because there is no pattern (synoptic collection is inadequate to allow accurate interpretation of the collected pieces, and contextual elements for pattern recognition are absent). Sometimes these problems occur because of the difficulty of fusing information collected in different ways and times, and sometimes it happens because the information is being collected in such detail that it cannot be processed sensibly.

Amrom Katz describes the problem this way: "Suppose one day . . . the Soviets proposed the acceptance of recce aircraft overflight of the Soviet Union by the US, but on two new conditions: 1) The aircraft can fly no higher than 100 feet altitude over the terrain; 2) All the Soviet Union must be overflown and photographed. This is a recipe for unmitigated disaster. *We would drown in the film.*"³

More generally, the importance of pattern development and recognition to understanding is now widely understood. Noam Chomsky's linguistic analysis and Jean Piaget's studies of learning by children are two salient examples. Even more prosaic illustrations emphasize the point that pattern matching is an essential element in inquiry. Donald Campbell, for example, suggests trying to

> imagine the task of identifying the same dot of ink in two newspaper prints of the same photograph. The task is next to impossible if the photographs are examined by exposing only one dot at a time. It becomes more possible the larger the area of each print exposed. Insofar as any certainty in the identification of a single particle is achieved, it is because a prior identification of the whole has been achieved.⁴

Roughly, then, if the whole cannot be identified, the meaning of the part is unclear. (This is the problem, mutatis mutandis, with verifying compliance with negotiated ceilings rather than prohibitions on numbers of mobile missiles.)

Finally, some signatures of interest are collected and eventually identified and interpreted accurately, but the process requires so much time that it does not provide useful intelligence; inscrutability is a time-dependent function. For example, an accurate assessment of the Polyarnyy "rubber ducky" as described by Andrew Cockburn could not be denied to U.S. peacetime collection, but were the time for assessment more compressed, Soviet denial efforts might have been successful.⁵ Disruptive painting on runways, optical and thermal obscurants, communications that become accessible only on occasions that oddly coincide with the need for them, and defectors bringing critical information at convenient times illustrate the problem of the time required for collection to provide enough data to support an accurate assessment. Some things, in other words, remain hidden not because they cannot be detected but because they cannot be detected soon enough. These considerations should temper the confidence of some observers that "new technologies . . . will help the United States overcome Soviet efforts to deceive Western spy satellites."⁶ Quite often, the question of *when* something might be knowable is as important as *whether* it is knowable. The time required for unraveling several intelligence puzzles in the past seems virtually geological in scale; in many circumstances, a late answer is useless.

The envisioned battery of new technologies, moreover, is not likely to come along very quickly. As Amrom Katz pointed out a few years ago, requirements are set in response to capabilities, beloved Washington mythology to the contrary notwithstanding.[7] Evolutionary improvements to existing collection tools have been, understandably and predictably, the persistent hope of the community. If a $2 billion package has been found lacking, there is sure to be a $3 billion design in the works that will do better. The new design is touted as sure to do the job—provided critical secrets can be kept, funding profiles protected, and the target fundamentally unchanged during the decade or more required for the tens of thousands of people involved to move the program from "Authorization to Proceed" through "Full Operating Capability."

New Technologies Won't Solve the Problem

What are the prospects for new generations of collection technology once again coming to the rescue? Today they seem quite dim, partly because truly revolutionary technologies are unlikely to be fielded in any large way. Reliable data are lacking, but it often seems hard to avoid wondering whether the U.S. government is still sufficiently agile to leapfrog Soviet *maskirovka* efforts with revolutionary collection technologies. In some cases, officers that began as innovators have mutated bureaucratically into managers of routine line operating systems. In other cases, real competition in ideas and technological approaches has been squelched by political competition among program headquarters staffs inside the Beltway. In most cases, statements of need and requirements are removed from any ultimate consumer by layers of bureaucracy, each of which serves as a consumer to the next, and all of which contribute little detectable in value added to the product. Finally, the overall planning and programming process embodies powerful incentives to protect ongoing activities at the expense of advanced research and development.

Prospects also seem dim because of the difficult analytic requirements that must be satisfied to make even evolutionary improvements work productively. One major source of these requirements is the production function, which itself creates powerful demands on analysis. Target signatures have to be forecast further in the future, in more detail, and with more at stake than in earlier years. At the same time, there is less tolerance for uncertainty and inaccuracy. Greater accuracy is needed partly because the signatures themselves tend to be narrower and more specific and partly because limits on resources have made it more difficult to build new systems that are over-designed in terms of currently validated requirements. Money is not the only constraint here. Equally important is the availability of certain critical skills and facilities, which could not be increased for practical purposes in the near term even with major increases in program funding. In addition, in earlier years the probability of significant unanticipated collection could be used to help justify overdesign. Today there seems to be less likelihood of such bonus kills except against targets that are much less sophisticated than the Soviets and their allies, again owing to both intrinsic design developments and Soviet planning for *maskirovka* and operational security.

Similar considerations will force more demands on analysis for help in developing the concept of operations for the proposed new tools. These systems are expensive to operate even in a benign peace-time environment, and many are intended to be useful across the conflict spectrum, which adds substantially to the price tag. Moreover, there will probably be more need to look at items of interest in different ways, which then entails the expense of command and control over several different tools and correlating the processing of their collection. And again, there will be less to see. (True, there may be more collection, particularly if new sensors are fielded to collect signatures in novel frequency ranges. It can be expected, however, that the learning curve—the processes of accumulating data, becoming familiar with sensor effects and peculiarities, correlating signatures with various other phenomena, and testing hypotheses and interpretations sufficiently to gain confidence in the new tool—will require considerable time.) In sum, both the operation and the design of future collection systems will be looking to analysis for guidance that is more timely, precise, and extensively justified than heretofore.

Altogether, these changes mean that even with sharp revisions in past collection practices, it will be a struggle to find data adequate to meet future competitive needs. It will be hard to see with the desired detail and confidence enough of the more important strategic elements. Some will be impenetrable to collection, some will be missed, some will be misinterpreted, and many will be assessed correctly only after a very long time. When it comes to intelligence, it seems, U.S. standards have slipped from full frontal nudity to glimpses of stocking.

Other Problems

It also has become apparent, albeit more slowly, that projections of U.S. concerns and habits will not serve to explain Soviet programs. John Hines and George Kraus have analyzed major differences between the Soviet and U.S. approaches to developing force postures and show how U.S. intelligence has often been surprised when Soviet planning turned out not to follow U.S. rationales. One illustration involves the "narrow, weapons-oriented, and mirror-imaged" U.S. appreciation of the Soviet development of the SS-N-8 submarine-launched ballistic missile (SLBM): "[T]he Soviets had a long-range, sea-based missile and they would probably use the capability to hide in the world's oceans (as would the US Navy)." In fact, as the authors demonstrate, "this perception inhibited understanding of the overall effect of the Soviet achievement and retarded development of effective countermeasures against SSBNs [ballistic missile nuclear submarines] hidden under arctic ice."[8]

> [T]he Soviets used the extended range (4,900 nautical miles) of the Delta SSBN/SS-N-8 missile system (nuclear missiles launched from submarines), in effect, to defend better their seaborne strategic nuclear forces against superior US antisubmarine warfare (ASW) capability—all in behalf of the larger objectives of enhancing the security of their strategic nuclear reserve. They achieved this not by deploying the longer-range subs in large expanses of ocean where superior US ASW could be brought to bear more easily. They used the capability, instead, to hide the SSBNs under or near arctic ice near the Soviet Union and thereby greatly complicate their detection and destruction by three of the four major components of the US ASW system—air- and surface-based ASW platforms and the SOSUS (sound surveillance systems) fixed surveillance sensors. Protection against the fourth threat, US SSNs (nuclear attack submarines),

was provided by integration of the Delta SSBN into a system of defenses comprised of Soviet SSNs, ASW surface ships, land-based ASW aircraft, and land- and sea-based air defenses. The Soviets advanced toward the objective of improved security of their strategic nuclear reserve in a systemic way by integrating enhanced offensive capabilities (the SS-N-8/Delta) into a defensive capability that was largely already in existence. It is almost certain that this was the intended Soviet deployment scheme all along. It should be noted that the extended range of the SS-N-8 was made possible by Soviet superiority in an "inferior" liquid missile fuel technology which the United States had abandoned earlier in favor of solid fuel. (The United States did not deploy sea-launched ballistic missiles [SLBMs] of comparable range for another decade.)[9]

The intelligence challenge of the next decade is also made more difficult by the recent confluence of developments in Soviet military technology and *maskirovka* programs with U.S. security losses. Soviet plans and programs for strategic conflict include enormous and sustained investments in programs intended eventually to provide enduring survivability for key elements of their leadership, society, and economy, as well as strategic nuclear and general purpose military forces.[10] These programs, separate and apart from considerations of operational security and surprise, effectively hide or obscure many of the signatures that U.S. sensors previously would have detected. In addition to these developments, there is the Soviet overlay of *maskirovka*, enjoying a salience and priority sanctified by doctrine, organization, leadership, and resources and instructed by a hemorrhage of U.S. secrets. Altogether, it seems, U.S. collection systems have obtained directly observable hard data on central items of interest less and less frequently. Estimates and assessments have correspondingly come to depend on ever more mediated chains of inference at increasingly greater analytic distance from direct empirical truth.

As this process continues, the possibility of being fooled increases dangerously. It would seem attractive to the Soviets to control the relatively few directly observables in order to influence U.S. views and assessments, even if this required substantial investments. Moreover, just as the rewards for undertaking a major deception program are beginning to look commensurate with the costs, the Soviets must also be finding that the risk that such investments would prove ineffective has been greatly reduced by U.S. security losses. The United

States, after all, just suffered through the decade, not the year, of the spy,[11] during which a series of major generic collection capabilities were compromised. As a result, beyond gaining insight into a particular U.S. collection system, the Soviets might also be able to gain a better understanding of the U.S. approach to future investments, and in so doing stay inside the U.S. decision–action cycle.

These developments threaten U.S. intelligence with a quadruple whammy. As collection becomes increasingly more difficult, the opposition is becoming increasingly more knowledgeable about how the collection occurred, which means U.S. analysts will probably have less hard data with which to work and must be less trustful of the apparent facts and what they might indicate. The environment will become more difficult to read, while the usual U.S. tools for reading it will become less relevant and less probative. These circumstances will increase the chance of the United States' reaching critically wrong intelligence assessments, either because the collection process was manipulated by adversaries or because analysts, locked into omphaloskepsis, took a wrong intellectual turn that could not be diagnosed or corrected in time by further collection.

Looking to the Future

If collection will prove less useful, U.S. intelligence must depend more on understanding Soviet assessments and plans. The process of developing explanations can be helped to some extent by organizational design. Today's organizations and their plans for tomorrow embody the more disjointed and piecemeal approaches to inquiry that better suited an earlier day. The problems of the 1990s, I think, will be better met with tighter integration among the various strategic planners, collectors, and analysts to define more clearly the central puzzles to be attacked, the strategies and timing for addressing them, and the effective allocation of very limited resources.

To implement this outlook, the community, or at least those sectors of it dealing with critical problems of the future strategic competition, might be restructured into research teams of analysts, collection specialists, and planners to attack the major Soviet intelligence subjects of the next decade: How, where, and why the Soviets intend to conduct the strategic competition. The business of the teams should produce theories of increasing scientific merit, which might well entail ploys designed to force the Soviets into revealing signatures that can be collected and interpreted usefully. This process could make it easier to shape the balance within collection strategies among resources, needs, and programs. In any event, there would be a tighter focus on intelligence needs and less likelihood of mistaking that goal for the preservation of particular collection businesses.

Some intelligence elements may be moving in these directions already. The reorganization of the CIA's Directorate of Intelligence (DDI) along geographic lines was a useful beginning. Some collection program offices, particularly those building expensive systems, have been reaching out to find broader customer support in recent years, if only to help protect their budget requests. Others, particularly in the U.S. Navy, have pioneered creative and highly successful approaches to teaming intelligence collectors and analysts with force operators and designers. Above all, there is the definitive model, the Soviet Battlefield Development Plan (SBDP), established within the U.S. Army by Lieutenant General William E. Odom when he was assistant chief of staff for intelligence. Though restricted by organizational charter to addressing only part of the Soviet military system, the SBDP exemplifies the merits of approaching intelligence problems as processes of scientific inquiry.

In addition, it seems likely that only this type of approach can begin to confront the challenges of Soviet cover, concealment, and deception (CC&D). Recent exhortations to analysts notwithstanding, the repeated careful testing of each piece of evidence simply does not begin to do the job. Evidence does not come along like cars on an assembly line, and analysts are not like robot welders. Sensor activity alone cannot distinguish fact from fake, determining whether the opponent intended to be observed or whether he or she appeared to lose something valuable in order to protect a greater treasure. As many have noted, "by and large, acquisition of additional data does not serve to change people's minds. . . . The problem is not [that] we are limited to an inadequate view, but that we have a (particular) view of the whole . . . the context which makes something the problem that it is pervades every aspect of the matter in question."[12] It is developing and testing patterns and theories, not the rote iterative checking of each would-be datum, that seems most likely to guard against fraud and misdirection.

Notes

1. Phillip Elmer-Dewitt, "When In Doubt, Check It Out," *Time*, 11 January 1988, 64–65.

2. "U.S. Said to Be Unable to Verify Missile Ban," *Washington Times*, 18 November 1986, A6; Robert C. Toth, "Soviet Arms Total Is Surprise to U.S.," *Philadelphia Inquirer*, 15 November 1987, 27A; Walter Pincus, "U.S. May Have Miscounted Some Soviet Missiles," *Washington Post*, 16 December 1987, A6; John Walcott, "War of the Spies," *Wall Street Journal*, 27 November 1987, 1.

3. Amrom Katz, "Technical Collection," in Roy Godson, ed., *Intelligence Requirements for the 1980's: Clandestine Collection* (Washington, D.C.: National Strategy Information Center, 1982), 105.

4. Donald T. Campbell, "Pattern Matching as an Essential in Distal Knowing," in K.R. Hammon, ed., *The Psychology of Egon Brunswick* (New York: Holt, Rinehart, and Winston, 1966), 83. John Raser suggested that "we think of the difficulty of identifying a particular star on a clear summer night without the pattern of stars around it to give it its identifying context. The frame of other stars, though each of them is also unidentifiable by itself, provides the information necessary to give meaning to what would otherwise be uninterpretable." See his discussion in John Raser, *Simulation and Society* (Boston: Allyn and Bacon, 1969), 32–37. Relationships among data morphology, inference validity, and distal knowledge are explored more fully in Robert L. Butterworth, "Soft Data and Theorizing about International Relations: Some Aspects of Validity," *International Studies Notes* (Summer 1977): 4–7. Similarly, radar can collect data so quickly that humans are unable to interpret it quickly enough. This is the conclusion of studies conducted by the Applied Physics Laboratory at Johns Hopkins University in the 1960s and 1970s that showed that "radar operators often missed targets even when they were detectable." John A. Adam, "Radar: Shooting for Tomorrow," *Washington Post*, 22 November 1987, C3.

5. Andrew Cockburn, *The Threat* (New York: Random House, 1983), 277. This account, incidentally, seems inaccurate, although not in a way that vitiates the points made in the text. Cockburn's account has it that photo interpreters working with satellite pictures "noted that a new ballistic missile submarine had joined the Soviet Northern Fleet at Polyarnyy, near Murmansk. Its appearance was duly recorded for insertion in the updated assessments of enemy forces. Not long afterward, there was a severe storm in the Barents Sea, which raised heavy seas and effectively blocked out all satellite surveillance for a number of days. When the next batch of [satellite] photographs finally arrived, the analysts saw that something very curious had happened to the new submarine: it had bent in half, which is something

that real submarines made of metal do not do." From this account, of course, the analysts could see no such thing; they had two data points separated by "a number of days," but nothing in Cockburn's account suggests why they should have thought that the submarine they first identified and the bent object subsequently noted were in fact one and the same item.

6. William J. Broad, "U.S. Is Designing Spy Satellites to Be Far More Secret Than Ever," *New York Times*, 3 November 1987, C1.

7. Katz, "Technical Collection," 103.

8. John G. Hines and George F. Kraus, "Soviet Strategies for Military Competition," *Parameters* 16 (Autumn 1986): 29. See also Jan S. Breemer, "The Soviet Navy's SSBN Bastions: Evidence, Inference, and Alternative Scenarios," *Journal of the Royal United Services Institute for Defense Studies* 130 (March 1985): 18–26.

The importance of analyzing, replicating, and working against Soviet assessments has been pressed for years, particularly by Andrew W. Marshall, director of net assessments, Office of the Under Secretary of Defense (Policy). Many elements of the case and methodology have been presented by Eliot Cohen in chapter 3 of this volume; by Cohen and Steve Rosen in their manuscript *Thinking Strategically* (New York: The Free Press, forthcoming); and by Robert L. Butterworth, "On Estimating Enemy Capabilities," in Edward Kolodziej and Patrick Morgan, eds., *National Security and Arms Control: A Reference Guide to Theory and Practice* (Westport, Conn.: Greenwood Press, forthcoming, 1988).

9. Hines, 29.

10. *Soviet Military Power: An Assessment of the Threat, 1988* (Washington, D.C.: GPO, 1988), 59–62.

11. I am indebted to Gary J. Schmitt for this observation.

12. Tracy B. Strong, "The Activity of Political Science as Science" (Paper delivered at the American Political Science Association Convention, New Orleans, LA., 6 September 1973, mimeograph) 32–33.

II. R. KEELER AND E. MIRIAM STEINER

Intelligence on scientific and technical topics (S&T) often can be better obtained by nontraditional means—that is, by persons other than professional intelligence officers, because these people normally are generalists, not scientists. Indeed, such intelligence officers (known in the community jargon as case officers) and their sources often lack easy and frequent access to the very people from whom S&T information is most likely to be collected. They also lack the knowledge of the subject necessary to recognize what is valuable and how to elicit it. In addition, the case officer who is lucky to get close to a source is frequently handicapped by having been given requirements that are naive and one-dimensional. As physicist Edward Teller once said on rejecting such a set of requirements, "All of them were stupid; except two, which were obvious."[1]

Fortunately, S&T information also can be obtained by carefully trained and briefed technical and scientific personnel during the course of personal contacts and other interactions that occur at international S&T conferences. These conferences can provide a better means than traditional clandestine channels for collecting intelligence about scientific and technical developments in closed societies. Generally, they include scientific paper presentations and roundtables or panel discussions, in-depth one-on-one discussions of scientific topics, and social occasions such as mixers and banquets. Frequently, visits to nearby scientific centers are offered as part of the overall program or are arranged on an individual basis. The well-briefed scientist knows what information he or she is looking for and how to pursue targets of opportunity.

Over the past fifteen years, professional contacts such as these have yielded S&T information that is difficult to obtain in closed societies. Although the information may not be considered secret in the classification sense, it is nonetheless very difficult to obtain by more traditional means. Examples range from items that may become available through personal contacts—such as the home telephone number and address of a member of a given country's academy of science and the professional or personal links between specific scientists and programs—to the formal release of scientific material in papers or discussions that reveal hitherto unknown research programs or capabilities. In addition, so-called military or state secrets have occasionally surfaced or been released by the authorities or other designated officials for some specific purpose. The S&T human intelligence (HUMINT) obtained by all these means may be unique and original in nature, or it may corroborate and expand on signals intelligence, electronic intelligence, communications intelligence, photographic intelligence, and HUMINT obtained by clandestine means.

In addition, scientists and engineers of high professional stature who are widely known to their professional counterparts in closed societies are more likely to have frequent and easy access to the technical personnel from whom S&T information can be obtained. Leadership positions in national or international scientific bodies may further enhance access. When a respected and widely-known scientist has political contacts with prominent national figures or holds a high government position, foreign hosts may be particularly open in hopes of future reciprocity. The Soviets, for example, have been known to reveal high-level plans through these types of contacts.

The reputations and expertise of comparable foreign scientists, along with their natural desire to display their own status and accomplishments, strongly militate against a frequent use of deception. In dialogue with U.S. colleagues of equal stature, it is difficult for a foreign scientist of international reputation from a closed (or open) society to misrepresent scientific facts. The scientist knows that his colleagues will evaluate the validity or reasonableness of his statements. This reluctance to engage in deception is further enhanced by the fact that deceptive practices would hamper future dialogue with foreign colleagues and might even result in public embarrassment. This is why techniques such as the use of *dezinformatsia* and *maskirovka* are of little utility in the international scientific environment and, although occasionally attempted years ago, are virtually unknown today.

The purpose of this chapter is to document significant S&T intelligence that has been gathered over the past twenty years through professional S&T channels such as those described above, to cite some of the problems that have inhibited a more aggressive and effective nonclandestine collection program, and to assess the opportunities for this type of HUMINT in the future. The ideas put forth in this chapter are not intended to downplay the importance of more traditional forms of intelligence collection (that is, case officers recruiting foreign agents and national technical assets). Rather, the purpose is to emphasize the complementary role that can be played by nonclandestine collection through professional S&T channels. The analysis begins with a historical review of improvements in the opportunities for S&T HUMINT collection.

Continuing Improvements in Opportunities for Noncovert S&T HUMINT Collection

The opportunities for obtaining S&T HUMINT in the Soviet Union through nonclandestine means have steadily improved over the past fifty years. Although there was considerable opportunity for scientific exchange in the immediate postrevolutionary years from 1922 to 1928, in 1929 the Soviet government began to increase restrictions. By 1935 scientists and engineers were forbidden to correspond or exchange manuscripts and reprints with their foreign colleagues. Foreign travel to meetings was forbidden, as was any personal contact with outsiders, and international scientific meetings were no longer held in the Soviet Union.

This situation began to change in 1955, when the Soviet Union sponsored major participation of its scientists and engineers in the First United Nations Conference on the Peaceful Uses of Atomic Energy held in Geneva. Some sixty or seventy scientific papers were declassified, with final approval coming from Nikita Khrushchev himself. The First Pugwash Conference was held in 1957, with Soviets and Eastern Europeans in attendance. The Second United Nations Conference on the Peaceful Uses of Atomic Energy was held in 1959, again with exceptionally strong Soviet attendance. Finally, in August 1961, the first international scientific conference since 1931 was held in the Soviet Union—the Fifth International Biochemical Conference—and the normal process of international scientific cooperation began to return to the Soviet Union.

In 1961 the Soviet Union reached a steady state in its procedures for handling international scientific matters. Scientific attachés were appointed, exchanges were initiated, and Soviet scientists began to show increased interest in participating in international scientific organizations. (Along with this activity came an increase in spying in the West and in the transfer of Western technology to the East, while at the same time Western scientists were seriously restricted in the Soviet Union.)

The Soviets presented the West with a rather tarnished mirror image in their response to the customary Western behavior in these matters. For example, the nomination of Soviet scientists and engineers for elective positions on the governing bodies of most international organizations had to be done with the concurrence of official representatives of the Communist party or the Soviet government. Nevertheless, the presence of Soviet scientists in these organizations often provided leverage to encourage the Soviets to host meetings and to participate in subsequent international scientific exchanges. Although surveillance and other defensive measures have become more sophisticated, general travel restrictions in the Eastern countries, particularly the Soviet Union and the People's Republic of China, have been progressively loosened. They are now at a point where individuals conducting military research in the Soviet Union are allowed to travel to the West, and various institutes previously closed have been opened to both Eastern European and Western visitors. Now there are even a number of instances in which individual scientists have become long-time collaborators and associates across international East–West boundaries.

Examples of Significant Noncovert S&T HUMINT

A noted Western scientist working in the field of pulsed power and accelerators attended a 1973 international plasma physics meeting in Novosibirsk. At the get-acquainted reception, one of the Soviet scientists working in the same field engaged him in a long discussion, during which some major Soviet advances were mentioned that revealed technology completely unknown in the West. These advances, although later cited in the open Soviet literature, indicated that the Soviets were developing the technology base for a strategic defense initiative (SDI) program.

In 1974 the late Harry Sahlin of the Lawrence Radiation Laboratory attended a physics conference in Novosibirsk. Many of the Soviet attendees were aware of his frequent collaboration with Edward Teller and were intensely interested in some of his novel schemes for producing thermonuclear fusion. During this trip, Sahlin was able to see Nobel Laureate Peter Kapitsa and Academician E.P. Velikhov. He was also the first Westerner to visit Kharkov and Krasnaya Pakhra. During the visit, he learned the whereabouts and status of many of the Soviet scientists working in his field. Dr. Sahlin also was able to lay the groundwork for subsequent trips to these facilities by other U.S. personnel. It is interesting to note that another scientist who attended the conference but had neither the personal nor the professional stature of Sahlin was given a hostile reception and was unable to visit institutes outside the main area of the conference. This is an excellent example of how scientific stature can enhance access.

A solid-state physics meeting was held in Moscow in 1976. Almost five hundred Soviet scientists were in attendance, most completely unknown in the West. Among them were several individuals whose work was directly applicable to defense programs. Some people, previously known only by name, were identified and available for discussion. The U.S. scientists in attendance were allowed to visit a number of local institutes and take photographs of some of the facilities. A large number of preprints were obtained, among them proceedings of several "All Union" meetings, which are not normally open to foreigners. Through this meeting, the U.S. scientists were able to gain a much deeper understanding of Soviet research in a number of fields, which is particularly important since many published Soviet articles are rather cryptic and frequently omit important details. Unfortunately, only three U.S. scientists participated in this meeting. A larger attendance by trained and briefed U.S. scientists would have resulted in the acquisition of much more information, particularly had they been given an understanding of what trends and progress could be considered significant.

In 1981, at a plasma physics conference in Kiev, a whole area of research was disclosed in which the Soviet Union was far ahead of the United States. This research dealt with low-density fluid equilibrium and transport properties. Some of the top Soviet experimentalists and theoreticians are now known to be pursuing work in this area. The performance of many newer weapon systems is tied to this scientific and technical base. A number of Soviet scientists thought to be involved in military work described their results to the audience (including the two or three U.S. scientists in attendance). As a result, this work has been followed carefully by U.S. scientists over the past four years, and it is clear that Soviet expertise in the field gives them a unique capability that the United States still does not possess. Again, a larger attendance by well-informed scientists would have resulted in a better understanding of these new developments.

At a 1986 physics meeting in Leningrad, scientists from a closed institute appeared before an international audience for the first time. It was revealed at this meeting that the institute had been in existence for twenty years, had been established by direction from the highest level, and was manned by top-notch scientists who had been intensively recruited. Their presentations were first-rate and contained material that would have been considered classified had it been presented in the United States. (This is reminiscent of an occurrence at the Livermore Laboratory in 1976 when a Soviet scientist made a blackboard presentation and local security officers later erased the board because it contained information regarded in the United States as sensitive.) Because of careful planning by U.S. attendees prior to the meeting, it was possible to obtain copies of this work, discuss it with the authors, and make copies available to scientists working in the same fields in the United States.

Problems in Nonclandestine Collection of S&T HUMINT

Nonclandestine S&T HUMINT collection by scientists and engineers continues to represent only a tiny part of the U.S. intelligence community's S&T efforts. Various intelligence agencies have failed to take advantage of these new opportunities, especially the availability of prominent scientific figures and their latest scientific work, which have increased markedly in recent years as the political climate in the Eastern bloc countries and mainland China has changed. Few attempts have been made to systematically anticipate new scientific and technical developments, and there is no plan to prepare scientific personnel to take advantage of these opportunities. In general, little effort is made to see that international conferences are covered by the personnel most qualified to attend.

The reasons for this problem are applicable to other professional fields besides science and technology. The following is a description of the current situation:

The intelligence community devotes little, if any, advance planning to a particular project.

The quality of the intelligence personnel supervising and executing HUMINT collection programs is spotty. Many such personnel are only marginally qualified, and others are not strongly motivated.

Briefing and debriefing of sources is frequently done by scientifically unqualified personnel.

Requirements are rarely given to attendees at international conferences.

Personal motives of scientists visiting the Soviet Union are often not well understood.

Screening of conclusions evaluating Soviet S&T is not done.

In establishing reciprocity, no care is taken to ensure that no more information than is necessary is supplied to the scientists of the country visited.

Above all, the intelligence officer is not prepared to take more risks, given the relatively low level of risk inherent in gathering noncovert S&T HUMINT.

Although the debriefing of returnees from various international events is usually relatively thorough, it is often done by personnel with no technical background. The scientist is not normally given requirements or items to consider in advance and has no way to participate in establishing requirements.

Although there are many panels that consider questions of requirements, they often suffer from a surfeit of senior scientists and technologists who are far from current. Even if more qualified personnel were added to the panels and substantial improvements in the quality of requirements were made, there is no assurance that the requirements would be given to the most active and capable scientists attending conferences in the Eastern countries. Such scientists are often quite young, and at present there is a natural reluctance to allow the younger scientists access to sensitive information, again demonstrating the United States' inability to take reasonable risks.

In one recent instance, the director's office of a national laboratory asked intelligence officials to give one of its prominent scientists some background information before his upcoming overseas trip. The response was "We wouldn't touch him with a ten-foot pole!" In another instance, a staff member was denied high-level clearances because he had made trips, and planned a future visit, to the Soviet Union. In a third instance, a young scientist was denied sensitive briefings just before his departure to Vienna to meet his opposite number from the Soviet Union in a lengthy and exceptionally sensitive negotiating session. The government response to the request was "We don't want to use those clearances for that purpose." One might ask what those clearances are to be used for if not to prepare individuals to handle matters of utmost national security. This attitude again reflects the unwillingness to take risks that are, by almost any perspective, negligible. The individuals involved had held high-level DoD clearances and had occupied positions of high responsibility. It must be recognized that any operation of this kind entails some risks. In view of the importance of the information needed, intelligence administrators should be prepared to increase the risks they are willing to take.

The quality of intelligence personnel in these areas is uneven. In the military services, the intelligence field must compete with lines that are considered more career enhancing. The U.S. Navy has avoided this problem by creating a special intelligence designator, which improves the situation slightly. In the other services, the situation is not so clear. Selection boards try to balance personnel among the various lines whenever possible. In the U.S. Air Force and U.S. Army, changes in lines often take place at relatively junior levels, particularly with the Air Force's nonrated (nonflying) personnel. When personnel are more or less arbitrarily ordered to a duty such as intelligence, the results can be less than satisfactory.

As an example of the damage one unqualified person can do, consider the case of a small U.S. Air Force group operated for years by a few highly motivated and dedicated officers. Several civilians providing technical background and long-term continuity were attached to the group. The activities of the group were highly successful, providing much information of the highest value to national security. Many of the officers went on to distinguished careers both inside and outside the defense community.

In 1984 this situation changed. Because of an imbalance in the relative number of officers of a given category in that service, a certain officer was ordered to the group to take charge of the program. This officer immediately terminated a number of significant programs, eliminated several valuable consultants to the program, refused to pay legitimate program expenses, revealed the names of program participants to unauthorized personnel, and generally antagonized the staff. In a short period of time, the officer was removed and transferred to an innocuous public relations position on a large joint staff in Europe. The program never really recovered, and its performance has been marginal ever since.

This incident reveals what can happen when the proper care and discretion are not exercised in choosing junior military personnel for sensitive intelligence billets. It also indicates the impotence and lack of initiative in civil service personnel who stood by and watched all this take place. Unfortunately, this trend reflects the high-level policy downgrading of the relative status of intelligence work in the services.

Assuming competence on the part of the intelligence community, some practical difficulties must be overcome in order to do well in nonclandestine S&T HUMINT. The first of these is that although individual scientists or engineers may be willing to participate, their employers might not be willing to do so. For example, the national laboratories, with their tremendous personnel and material assets, are natural bases for technical exchanges with the Soviet Union, China, and other Eastern bloc countries. Their opposite numbers in these closed societies are the many institutes of their academies of sciences. These facilities host meetings, symposia, and conferences and are appropriate sites for reciprocal visits. But the view of the various U.S. laboratory directors toward the gathering of HUMINT is mixed.

Two large national laboratories with the same sponsor illustrate this point. In one laboratory, a previous director steadfastly asserted that he didn't want his scientists to become spies. In only one case during his tenure did he permit outside funding for foreign travel. Intelligence personnel were not welcome on-site. His attitude probably reflected a fear of controversy and a lack of trust in his own personnel. At the other laboratory, the director provided his scientists and engineers pretravel briefings through an internal organization. The appropriate intelligence organizations were welcomed on-site. The long-term result was an increase in significant S&T HUMINT obtained and a far greater understanding of the scientific work being carried out overseas in institutes in the Soviet Union and elsewhere.

A second problem lies in the very nature of professional contacts, which requires reciprocity. He who wishes to get something must be willing to give something in return. Between technical colleagues, a reluctance to share research quickly becomes obvious and leads to a slowdown in communications. Alternatively, when information is exchanged in scientific meetings, considerable discretion must be exercised in what information is brought forth.

In one case, a prominent hydrodynamic code developer for a Department of Energy laboratory made frequent trips to the Soviet Union to a facility near Semipalatinsk providing support for Soviet nuclear explosive testing activities. Some of his activity came to light when a group of his coworkers from the United States were visiting an office at the Institute of Hydrodynamics and were shown a stack of print-outs and a number of reports from their own laboratory. These had been brought into the Soviet Union by the code developer, who did not make the same reports available to his own coworkers in the United States. This particular individual was cautioned by his associates, and some of this activity stopped. Although none of the code developer's activity was illegal (all the material in question was unclassified), he was carrying the idea of exchange a step too far. Clearly, defensive briefings by the proper agencies should make potential overseas travelers cautious about the material they take with them.

In this case, a natural question arose as to why this individual was transferring this software and other reports to Soviet scientists. It was the general impression that he was willing to provide the Soviets with this type of information in exchange for VIP treatment in the Soviet Union.

Other scientists who have traveled to the Soviet Union have returned with somewhat unrealistic perceptions of Soviet society. U.S. scientists will often meet more senior personnel on trips to the Soviet Union than their Soviet counterparts will meet on trips to this country. Because of this, Westerners are likely to encounter individuals in the Soviet Union who are politically sophisticated, and it is important to view their experiences with senior Soviet officials in this light.

A related problem involves the reliability of U.S. scientists for this type of intelligence work. For example, a scientist employed by a large laboratory had worked for some time as a consultant on a project evaluating Soviet advances in a particular field. He had represented himself to his sponsors as "the expert" in this field. In the summer of 1984 on a trip to the Soviet Union, he called attention to himself by attempting to enter several institutes in Kiev without previous authorization. As a result, he was placed aboard an Aeroflot flight by the local authorities and returned to Moscow where his trip had originated. Two years later, the existence of some of his reports was alluded to in the popular media; at that time he was identified, also in the open literature, as one of the sources of information for the study. At the same time, he began negotiations with the Soviets for an extensive tour of the Soviet Union scheduled for the summer of 1987. Some time before his departure, his security officer, aware that the scientist had been revealed in the open literature as a source for intelligence, ordered that his trip be canceled. In cases such as these, where a certain individual appears to be unreliable, it is important that the briefing officer understand the personal motives for overseas visits and act to prevent possible incidents or harm to the visitor.

The problem of potential conflicts of interest should not be seen as an insurmountable barrier. It exists and must be dealt with. For example, émigré sources may be unreliable for two reasons. First, there has been a subtle effort in the Soviet Union to remove Jewish scientists from sensitive areas of research and development, so Jewish émigrés would have little or no knowledge of the large body of the more recent classified work being carried out. Second, émigrés have little or no reason to praise the technology base of a country that they feel, in effect, has rejected them.

Biases can appear in other ways. In one summary report dated 1983, the claim was made that in the Soviet Union a great deal of effort was being put into various exotic types of chemistry. A specific description was given, with the claim that useful products could be prepared through applying these techniques. The author of this section of the report, himself engaged in exactly this type of chemistry, used this material to justify a request for large amounts of funding to support his own work—to keep up with the Soviets. What he did not report, however, was that this work is not supported strongly in the Soviet Union and, in fact, several groups in this field have been dispersed and put to work in other institutes.

At present, there is a running dispute in the field of physical oceanography. One school of thought contends that the Kolmogoroff turbulence hypothesis, one of the great classical concepts of modern physics, holds for ocean turbulence. This view is accepted by almost everyone who works in the field of turbulence. An alternate view is held by a group of oceanographers in the United States who make experimental measurements of various quantities in the ocean. In a comprehensive survey of Soviet oceanography, this group viewed the Soviet failure to embrace the group's views as a sign of backwardness on the part of the Soviets. It is well known, however, that the Soviets are the world's experts in this field. The misleading claims made in the summary report gave U.S. analysts an erroneous picture of the Soviet ability to understand oceanographic phenomena as related to antisubmarine warfare.

Another problem pertains to the security clearances held by scientists and engineers attempting to collect S&T HUMINT who might attend international meetings. From time to time, technical personnel involved in defense work in the United States are asked to participate in sensitive projects. This requires upgrading clearances. If the individual in question is planning to travel to Eastern countries, his or her clearances can be withheld until the trip is completed. There is an additional tendency to delay granting of upgraded clearances even when no trip is planned if the individual periodically travels abroad to Eastern European countries. Unfortunately, the information that could be gained through the upgraded clearances might be useful in providing perspective on the HUMINT collected during the trips. Security officers are often put in the position of asking themselves, "If I authorize the additional clearances or a trip, what will happen if the individual gets in trouble abroad? How will this affect U.S. security and me?"

Giving requirements generally depends on the discretion of the laboratory director (as mentioned previously), the commanding officer, the cognizant corporate officer, or another appropriate supervisor. Some of these people will be supportive, but others will not. It is important for the individual briefing officer to understand the views of all concerned and respect them, while at the same time advocating the maximum in cooperation in the interest of national security.

In the preceding sections, we have stressed the value of nontraditional HUMINT and the desirability of increased emphasis on this area. Potential sources must always ask themselves whether the various intelligence agencies are reliable enough for them to assume nontrivial risks to their careers and personal safety. Suppose a source consistently uncovered HUMINT that was construed to be contrary to the prevailing beliefs held in the intelligence community. Would this source's participation in HUMINT gathering continue to be welcome? Could the source rely on security from his or her sponsors while in potentially risky situations? Could the source be sure that his or her activities would not be leaked to potentially hostile colleagues? Could the source really trust the sponsoring agencies? This last question is the basic question that every individual participating in these programs must answer for himself or herself.

These examples of what can happen in activities associated with obtaining nonclandestine HUMINT point out the need for professional intelligence officers to be astute and aware of the nature of the individuals and the various environments around them in their work, the nature of the challenges they may face in their travels, and the value of the HUMINT they may obtain and how it relates to the existing body of knowledge in their given field. The wide spectrum of personalities and views within the scientific community makes it particularly important that intelligence briefers and debriefers be astute and sensitive to the risks and pitfalls that might be incurred in dealing with this community.

Outlook

Travel restrictions in the Soviet Union are loosening. For example, the late academician Ya. B. Zel'dovich was granted permission to travel to New York in 1987 to receive the Maxwell Award of the American Physical Society. Zel'dovich is thought to have worked with Andrei Sakharov on defense problems for a significant period after World War II. He was Jewish and not a Communist party member. The decision to permit him to travel to the West was reputed to have been made at the Politburo level, perhaps by Gorbachev himself. The result has been a pronounced effort by many Soviets in sensitive positions to pursue overseas travel opportunities, particularly to the West.

Increased access to previously closed Soviet facilities is expected to continue. In the summer of 1986, a number of highly placed Soviets attending the Megagauss IIII meeting in Santa Fe, New Mexico, were taken through the dynamic test area at the Los Alamos Laboratory— the first time ever for Soviet visitors. It was made clear to them that reciprocity was expected on future visits to the Soviet Union. They agreed, and because one of them (Gennady A. Mesyats) is a potential president of the USSR Academy of Sciences, there is some justification for expecting more opportunities for visits to sites hitherto closed. In 1988 a junior nuclear weapons designer from the Soviet Union appeared at the Geneva verification negotiations. The appearance of such a young, high-level individual involved in defense work was unusual and was a further indication of a relaxation of control over Soviet nationals involved in sensitive projects. This relaxation might make these individuals and their work far more accessible to the scientific community.

Western visitors have been encouraged to extend their visits to Eastern countries when on business or official trips; sightseeing excursions are offered in addition to trips to various institutes. In 1984 a Swiss delegation was invited to the Institute of Chemical Physics—the first time Westerners were allowed to tour this facility. They were briefed by the late Academician N. N. Semenov, the institute director, and several new programs were revealed. In the past few years, there has been a conscious effort to expand these types of exchanges.

Part of this is due to some of the changes taking place in the Soviet hierarchy. As one of the young Soviet scientists expressed it, "Fifteen years ago, I would pick up the telephone, and on the other end of the line would be a seventy-year-old man. What can I say to a seventy-year-old man, and what can he say to me? But now when I make such calls, it is my friends who answer the telephone, and between us, we get things done." Obviously, many of the younger Soviets, encouraged by the recent changes in their government's policies, proud of their own work, and eager to learn about what is going on in the West, are chafing at the old restriction.

Recently, scientists from Eastern countries have sought participation on editorial boards and collaboration with Western colleagues in joint review papers. A Soviet academician was recently made the guest editor of a major international journal so that the proceedings of a conference he hosted could be published in that journal. Westerners have been encouraged to coauthor review articles with their Soviet counterparts in major Soviet journals such as *Uspekikh*. Perhaps this kind of interaction will continue to increase.

Recommendations

The present policy in U.S. intelligence circles is to downgrade the value of HUMINT relative to other means of obtaining technical and scientific intelligence. This attitude must change for two reasons. First, the aggregate of other means of obtaining information is decreasing. That does not mean that other means are not more important than HUMINT at this time, but there is a trend away from those means, and we cannot foresee the end of it. Second, opportunities for obtaining HUMINT are increasing with the opening (if only slightly) of Eastern bloc societies. The imbalance between the open and closed societies is a powerful lever. Westerners are always free to disclose more than their Eastern counterparts, with the result that the Easterners, in an effort to cling to some shred of reciprocity, must reveal more than they otherwise might have.

To make the best of this situation, the intelligence community must have as clear a vision as possible of the United States' opponents' potentially deployable military systems. This vision requires special skills to conceptualize a future system from basic scientific accomplishments. S&T intelligence officers must not be afraid to attempt this conceptualization, and they must gather around them a support system that can assist in this effort. Officers must be able to look far into the future for opportunities that are often quite dependent on time, situation, and personnel. To do this they must have a keen understanding of the scientific personnel available and a determination to employ these assets to the limit of their capability.

Examples of success in obtaining noncovert S&T HUMINT are instructive. The problem now is to generalize from these specifics. Once generalizations are made, they should be institutionalized within the intelligence community with high-level, broad-based coordinated support as a matter of established policy.

Notes

1. From a discussion about intelligence at a conference sponsored by the Lawrence Livermore Laboratory, Livermore, Calif., June 1974.

Discussion

Fred Ikle

Is the United States facing a darkening dusk, as Robert Butterworth suggests? Is it losing capabilities—relative to changes taking place in targets of interest—rather than gaining them in an era when it may need more? The way I see it is that although the United States is not losing capabilities in absolute terms, it has greater and more difficult needs that are outpacing its anticipated capabilities.

Perhaps the most important difficulty is gauging the research and development (R&D) that the Soviet Union, the United States' principal adversary, is conducting. Why is that more important in the 1990s and beyond than it has been heretofore? Simply because the Soviets have caught up with the United States in many areas of technology. Because the United States' technical edge is narrower on all fronts, it is important for the United States to see where the Soviets may be pulling ahead, pulling even, or perhaps coming up with something entirely new. Research is very hard to observe by most of the means currently available. The HUMINT approaches that Norris Keeler and Miriam Steiner mention may be some of the more relevant in addressing this problem, but they are not being emphasized in the intelligence community.

The authors address a second broad question: U.S. openness versus Soviet concealment (*maskirovka*). A curious paradox is at work here: An excess of data in itself provides a certain type of concealment. It may be the best defense the United States has against Soviet intelligence collection. Soviet representatives at official functions often complain, "You guys publish so much we don't know what to read, and we don't know what to follow." The Soviets probably see the plethora of data as U.S. deception because much of it is contradictory. So even when the Soviets have the truth, they tend to treat it as the "Minsk to Pinsk" story—the Americans published this in an open hearing because they were really doing the opposite.

This phenomenon also might begin to have an impact on the United States. What if the Soviets were to agree to more on-site verification requirements? Imagine that you were given a million dollars and charged with counting the population in a given place in the United States with a margin of error of less than fifty thousand people. Think of how many tricks could be played on you in this open society! Now imagine an attempt at deception under conditions of excess data in a period of crisis and pressure. Having too much data helps cover up the deception. If you go through the histories of the major intelligence failures, there was usually too much data piling up on people's desks, and the junk obscured the significance of the correct information.

Thus, the question of openness versus concealment is richer than how much or how little information Soviet intelligence gets. The authors stress the need for innovation in the instruments of collection in order to take advantage of the richness and diversity of existing opportunities. But I am afraid that perhaps the official intelligence community—the Pentagon and other agencies—are not adept and quick enough to explore new ways of gaining access, either with new people or new instruments. There is a need to make it possible for inventors, who more likely than not are in industry rather than government service, to introduce new ways of gaining information.

A key dimension is missing in the essays. The authors addressed peacetime intelligence and collection, but it behooves the United States, particularly those people in the Pentagon and in the intelligence community, to look at wartime collection.

In considering wartime collection, the United States should not emphasize apocalyptic contingencies, such as the so-called nuclear exchange, but rather the question of a large-scale or small-scale conventional war, a war in which (1) conventional instruments may be hurt, damaged, destroyed, or eliminated; and (2) the ground rules for collection instruments totally change. Let me cite some historic examples.

Think of the things people did with collection in World War II, with HUMINT and sending in instruments. The United States is not doing those things now. Imagine the results the United States could get from industry today under wartime ground rules, and you get a different picture. Some people have thought about this, but the subject has not received enough attention. By and large this is symptomatic of the way those in the intelligence community program and discuss things.

Also note that in wartime collection, you need things much more quickly. There is not enough time to do a two-year national intelligence estimate to determine where the enemy will hit you next. The problem of how to shift gears and mobilize collection resources is an important gap in U.S. intelligence work.

What are the main missions of U.S. collection and analysis? Presumably, the purpose of intelligence is primarily to enlighten government actions and decisions. What the United States wants from collection and analysis is a basis for making predictions. There could also be a secondary purpose for collecting intelligence—to adjudicate a case in the past. Examples of this are the Iran-Contra investigation and the continuing collection of data on World War II war crimes. But the bulk of the intelligence is really for future government action—to anticipate the chemical weapons capability of a Third World country, future Iranian-sponsored acts of terrorism, or the Soviet military potential, for instance.

I will illustrate this in just one domain—arms control—where the United States tried to collect what is called information on Soviet cheating. The United States did not want to adjudicate the past crimes of the Soviet Union, even though it is useful to do that sometimes. The General Advisory Committee of the Arms Control and Disarmament Agency did a good job of recording all Soviet violations back to the peace treaties with the Baltic republics. The Reagan administration wanted this information on Soviet compliance primarily to guide future Pentagon and other government actions. Note that although actionable information must not have much ambiguity, ambiguity is unavoidable in intelligence. Outside of mathematics, there is considerable ambiguity even, as all historians know, in interpretations of history.

The salient fact is that the level of ambiguity tolerable in the intelligence needed to make a certain decision depends on the amount of pain the decision will create. Curiously, or maybe frighteningly, in the 1980s the United States found that the pain level regarding violations of arms control treaties was really very low. All the Reagan administration was trying to do in this regard was answer a congressionally mandated question about whether or not there had been violations. The pain level was low because the administration did not rush up to Congress with a $100 million supplemental request for defense appropriations or with proposals to cancel all arms control agreements or radically change relations with the Soviet Union. The administration found it relatively easy to deal with what little ambiguity there was in the evidence because it was only writing the scorecard for arms control without giving any thought to acting on the basis of that scorecard.

Although this was only an intellectual exercise with a very low level of pain and practically zero dollar cost, there was a hell of a battle among the agencies in the administration over whether or not this or that kind of ambiguous or semiambiguous thing constituted a violation. There were, what you would call in the juridical process, the lawyers for the defense (the accused), who made the case that this or that was not a violation, and the lawyers for the prosecution, who made the case that it was. This made for an exhausting judicial proceeding inside the very innards of the executive branch.

Against this backdrop, as one looks ahead to the possibility of much more far-reaching agreements than the Intermediate Range Nuclear Forces (INF) Treaty, such as the Strategic Arms Reduction Talks (START), one must imagine this quasi-judicial process within the innards of the United States government operating when the pain level is higher, when action is likely to be the result of adjudication, and when, therefore, the toleration for ambiguities would probably be lower. One must also consider that Congress has to play a key role in any decision to respond to arms control violations.

How can the United States ensure serious decision making? Senator Malcolm Wallop has made an interesting proposal in this regard. Congress would mandate itself to raise the defense budget when a future administration certified that the START (or INF) treaty had been violated. Thus, when members of Congress judge the verification provisions of proposed arms control treaties, they will have to look at how their successors will be able to cope with the problems the treaty will generate. In so doing, they might find that the agreements contain ambiguities that create insoluble intellectual problems.

For example, consider the range and carrying capacity of cruise missiles. What happens if a treaty calls for a limit of 600 kilometers for nuclear armed cruise missiles, as in SALT II, and a limit of 590 kilometers on conventionally armed cruise missiles? First, you cannot distinguish whether a cruise missile is nuclear or conventionally armed. Second, suppose the conventional missile actually flies only 590 miles, but if you equip it with a nuclear warhead, which is much lighter, it will go three times as far, which is well into the prohibited range for nuclear armed cruise missiles. Clearly, you cannot fix the cruise missile problem by simply establishing a prohibited range for both conventional- and nuclear-armed cruise missiles as long as any kind of cruise missile is allowed.

My point is that ambiguities can have very serious consequences if there are changes in the policies of foreign governments. And changes in policy are not infrequent. One example is the naval arms agreement of the 1920s. There was some cheating at the margins because of Japanese foreign policy in the 1920s, but when the leadership change in Germany occurred in 1933, the question of the limits on naval armaments became very dangerous. Germany and Japan decided to take advantage of the ambiguities in the treaty in a big way. Fortunately, the Roosevelt administration started to react before it was too late. Now consider a START agreement with the Soviet Union. Is the United States prepared to deter the Soviet Union from taking massive advantage of START if in the 1990s the Soviet government decides to carry out a policy different from the treaty commitments of today's Soviet government?

The time factor is crucial. When you have collected ambiguous information, sorted it out, gone through the contortions in the executive branch with the advocates for the defense and the advocates for the prosecution, and then gone through the contortions before the two congressional intelligence committees, how can you prove without a doubt that the evidence shows a significant change rather than simply the actions of an overzealous Soviet colonel here or there? Let us assume that the United States is unusually capable of collecting unambiguous evidence and that the government is able to reach a definitive finding that there have been serious violations. And let us assume that Congress agrees to allocate large amounts of money to redress the violations. Has the country then pulled itself out of danger? Probably not. Consider the time factor. In 1981, for example, the United States discovered that it would take ten years to deploy the Trident D-5 missile to redress anticipated deficiencies in its strategic posture.

Donald Nielsen

Robert Butterworth's assessment is somber. He takes a realistic and pessimistic view of the collection environment, which is getting tougher and more impenetrable due to factors such as *maskirovka* and the complexity of technical requirements. In discussing the perception that a technological breakthrough will make a difference in the future, he quite properly points to the fact that better human intelligence (HUMINT) alone is not going to solve the United States' problems.

The first part of Butterworth's essay discusses the fact that requirements are growing and capabilities are lessening. That's correct. Visualize two lines—the one representing requirements is ascending at a dramatic rate, and the other, representing capabilities, is level or perhaps declining. At some point in the distant past, those two lines may have converged—that is, there may have been a point at which the United States had parity of requirements and capabilities. Butterworth suggests that this might have been the case during the Cuban missile crisis, but I think the Garden of Eden is probably more likely. The United States has never had enough collection capabilities. The problem has always been to satisfy that gap between the upper line—requirements—and the lower line—capabilities. What can the United States do to diminish or make more practical that gap in what it wants to know?

The first thing it can do is reduce requirements. Today everybody talks about how requirements are growing and how we want to know more about everything. Yet I think it should be possible to reduce requirements. The intelligence community must take a very harsh attitude about accepting every requirement levied on it. In some cases, the only honest response is to admit that they cannot all be filled and that decision makers will have to do without some information.

Second, requirements should be formulated from the top down. Today requirements tend to be built from the bottom up. The military services manage the collection resources; naturally, their interests are in satisfying their requirements first and then acting on other requirements with what is left. This may lead the United States to an environment in which it knows everything about a T-72 tank except where it is going to be used. It is important to start looking at requirements from the top down and design a system that reduces the slope of the top line.

Another way to redress this situation is to add more to U.S. collection resources. This certainly does not look promising in today's environment. In fact, it seems as if that line might recede even more.

Some things can be done, however, with the resources the United States has today. First, the technical systems that are currently being fielded are and should be limited to technical requirements, the "now" sorts of things, such as order of battle, technical capabilities, and force dispositions. The HUMINT system must be improved and targeted strictly at "soft" information such as intentions. HUMINT should be used to collect data that can be gathered by access to the human mind. In other words, the United States should use each system primarily for what it is best designed to do.

Second, as Dr. Ikle has noted, the United States must address the problem of the principally peacetime nature of its collection systems and the importance of transferring those capabilities to a wartime environment. If the United States went to war today, the technical systems available would not change. The question is how well the United States could adapt them to optimal usefulness in the tougher wartime environment. Unfortunately, the current U.S. HUMINT system is only a peacetime system. Much more attention must be devoted to developing a system that can be used in wartime. Today HUMINT is essentially reduced to the role of verifying what can be learned from other means. "Low risk, low gain" is a fairly accurate assessment of current HUMINT operations. The United States also needs to develop a better means of assessing the effectiveness of existing HUMINT systems. One way might be to judge HUMINT collection systems by the access they give and not by the number of self-evaluated reports they generate.

Third, particularly in the HUMINT area, the United States must pay more attention to Soviet requirements. The international scientific conferences Dr. Keeler mentions are a case in point. Although the United States sometimes obtains invaluable information at these meetings, I believe it is far more important to know what information Soviet scientists are there to get. There is a direct connection between their questions and their capabilities. Thus, a great deal more time should be spent collecting and analyzing information on what the Soviets are trying to find out: The Americans must listen to Soviet questions and not trust their answers.

The United States also should concentrate on analyzing Soviet special activities. Again, there is a direct link between Soviet active measures and their intentions. If the United States can discern what Soviet active measure goals are, it will have a glimpse into a hidden world. The following serves as an example: Suppose the United States discovered a Soviet forgery campaign intended to show that Corazon Aquino was throwing the Philippines open to unlimited U.S. basing. Such a discovery would leave no question about Soviet intentions toward the Aquino regime.

Although these examples illustrate counterintelligence targets, they are also targets that yield valuable positive intelligence. I hope this serves to illustrate the fact that the United States needs far more cooperation between the counterintelligence and positive intelligence communities.

The United States builds many of its collection capabilities on well-documented requirements, but I think a basic collection capability should be independent of requirements. A case in point is the need to develop networks of agents in the Third World. Even though the United States might lack specific requirements today, it needs to develop networks to warn of problems before they arise. U.S. networks must be flexible, survivable, and capable of retargeting in times of crisis. This is more important in the HUMINT world than in the technical world, although some aspects are applicable to both.

Even though the outlook is gloomy, the United States can improve its lot. One important factor is to scrub down the number of requirements and collect less junk. A great deal of the HUMINT information that is collected simply clogs the system. It is important that the United States optimize its technical and human systems, seek greater cooperation with the counterintelligence community, and build new networks. It must strengthen and restructure its intelligence forces, particularly those engaged in HUMINT.

General Discussion

At the colloquium, people generally agreed that there is a growing gap between what U.S. human and technical intelligence systems are capable of gathering and what the United States will need in the

1990s. The discussion focused on the nature of the gaps and the difficulties in closing them.

There was some discussion about collecting information on objects in space, where Dr. Butterworth stated much of the challenge from the Soviet Union is likely to come. An academic argued that it is very difficult, if not impossible, to learn much about these objects by observing them. Suppose the United States was able to take pictures of the *Mars Probe,* which the Soviets say contains a high-energy laser, or could even record the laser beam scattered off the Soviet craft's test target. The United States still would not know the key parameters of the device—for instance, its power, jitter, or retarget time. Thus, he concluded, although the United States must surely shift the focus of its technical collection, the results will not be very great.

U.S. decision makers will have to learn to work with much less hard information about Soviet weapons than they have been accustomed to having. Dr. Ikle concurred, adding that intelligence by observation is particularly difficult with regard to advanced research and technology. A government official pointed to an even more difficult problem—simply identifying objects in space.

There was some disagreement about the future role to be played by human collectors with substantive expertise. An intelligence officer wondered about the usefulness of the HUMINT described by Dr. Keeler, particularly in obtaining the types of specific information that everyone seemed to agree technical systems are unable to obtain. Dr. Keeler acknowledged that there is a problem examining information collected by scientists and engineers concerning operating military systems. He agreed that the information scientists are likely to collect will seldom be as cut-and-dry as, for example, the measurement of a missile silo. But it would be a mistake not to notice that from these nontraditional sources of collection the United States can find out things more important than the measurement of silos, such as the yield-to-weight ratio of Soviet nuclear weapons.

Another U.S. official cautioned that the opportunities for Soviet deception increase with greater access to Soviet scientists. He argued that whenever one is gathering information on subjects the Soviets know to be of interest to U.S. collectors, one must expect the Soviets to employ deception. He cited as an example the time Mikhail Gorbachev warned Soviet officials at the 27th Party Congress not to continue to refer to "peaceful coexistence" as a form of class struggle.

Gorbachev did not say that peaceful coexistence is not class struggle; he simply forbade people from saying it to Western audiences. Dr. Keeler accepted the general validity of this point but added that the most difficult target imaginable for *maskirovka* is an intelligence collector who happens to be an authority in that particular field.

If there is to be a greater reliance on substantive expertise in the 1990s, a participant mentioned, we surely will need language-qualified case officers. How, a journalist asked, will the United States produce experts in exotic languages? An academic noted that although there is a problem finding certain language skills in American society, the intelligence community has been unwilling at times to use those skills that do exist. He cited the example of the United States failing to fill posts dealing with a key country with officers who speak Spanish—a language millions of Americans speak well. He also added that this is not a new problem, as the need for language-qualified case officers was prominently noted in the 1970s and 1980s.

A number of participants addressed the problem of setting collection requirements. A former White House official noted that there is more information to be collected and more potential collection targets than are possible to use usefully. A former high-ranking intelligence official explained that "everybody tasks" but that no one does the "quality job" of authoritatively prioritizing. A military intelligence officer argued that unnecessary requirements are seldom edited out because no one wants to be responsible for saying "let's not look at this." So these requirements are passed on, and the resulting tasking and collection clogs the system, wasting limited resources.

There was a general consensus that in order to make the best use of available U.S. collection resources in the 1990s, a better job must be done in setting priorities. To avoid obtaining less useful material, several participants suggested a greater measure of top-down control of tasking and increased dialogue among collectors, analysts, and policymakers. But an academic noted that it has been next to impossible to get political leaders to pay attention to these issues—that is, to exercise their responsibility for tasking or for ordering the community to change the kinds of case officers or satellites it uses.

The government's inability to change its collection procedures also was discussed. As an explanation for this problem, a former White House official pointed to bureaucratic resistance and the lack of follow-up on the part of political leaders who do not question why an order is not carried out. An academic argued that it is not enough for political leaders to order that more resources be devoted to human or technical collection. A clear rationale must be developed as to why this is important and what purposes it is designed to serve. The specific collection requirements should be based on how the elected leaders of the United States view the world of the future.

Finally, a former intelligence officer argued that because good intelligence can help avoid war, it should be seen as a "peace event." An academic disagreed, noting that there is little justification for spending billions of dollars for satellites and agents if war does not loom as a clear and present danger.

3
Analysis

Essays:

I. *Eliot Cohen*
II. *Paul Seabury*

Discussion:

I. *Robert Gates*
II. *Andrew Marshall*

I. ELIOT COHEN

The "No Fault" View of Intelligence

Over the past two decades, students of intelligence failure have focused their attention on the question "Why do statesmen fail to heed intelligence?" Implicitly, they have assumed that intelligence agencies and analysts have, generally speaking, performed their analytic missions well. In an article on "Why Policy Resents Intelligence," a former national intelligence officer explains that because intelligence "seeks to reflect complex reality, its product often makes for hardship in the lives of harassed decisionmakers."[1] Another senior intelligence

The author is grateful to Stephen Rosen, George Kraus, Gary Schmitt, Abram Shulsky, George Pickett, and others for their help, which has taken many forms. A very special debt is owed to Andrew Marshall. Parts of this essay are derived from a chapter in a book he is writing with Stephen P. Rosen on net assessment and strategic planning. The Free Press has graciously given permission for publication of excerpts and paraphrases of parts of that chapter.

officer writes that statesmen are "ideologically motivated, driven to action, and because of pressures to succeed, impatient with those whom they perceive to be impeding their progress."[2] Such a view implies that the fault for failure, however we define it, rests not with the intelligence organizations, but with those dyspeptic, dogmatic, and uninformed politicians who resent the sting of dispassionate analysis.

Other, more generous students of intelligence (most of them from academia rather than the CIA or kindred organizations) claim that failures of warning or estimation stem not from the poor judgment or the bad character of policymakers but from the intractability of the intelligence problem itself.[3] A variety of causes—"noise" produced by fragmentary data and organized routines that lead statesmen and analysts alike to expect incremental rather than quantum changes in international politics—lead some to conclude that failure is simply a "burdensome concept."[4]

In many cases, these theories reflect reality. Nonetheless, I believe that profound flaws at the working level contribute mightily to defective strategic intelligence. By this I mean estimative intelligence in political-military affairs rather than other varieties of intelligence such as indications and warnings and the like. The training of analysts and management of their work, and not simply the foibles of politicians (or the human predicament more broadly), account for serious weaknesses in U.S. intelligence. These problems stem from a flawed doctrine of analysis and from the broader problem of mirror imaging. Although one may conceive of remedies, they will not prove easy or simple. After examining these two fundamental problems, I will suggest an approach to understanding the nature of strategic intelligence based on "the otherness of the enemy." From there, I conclude with a brief discussion of specific intelligence problems the United States is likely to face in the 1990s and offer some suggestions about how analysts might be better prepared to cope with these problems.

Pathologies of Analysis

The Working Assumptions of Analysis

A recently declassified article titled "Managing/Teaching New Analysts" published in a government journal in 1986 provides a peek into the world of analysis. Its author—for the sake of convenience let us call him Mr. Z—provides his colleagues with guidance for handling new analysts, a task in which he clearly has some experience. One cannot, of course, treat a single source such as this as an infallible guide to the analytical world. However, by looking carefully at Mr. Z's assumptions and passing remarks, as well as at the substance of his argument, the careful reader will glean some interesting insights.

Mr. Z notices that many analysts do not, apparently, have a great deal of experience in their work. "With the proportion of analysts in their probation period running over fifty percent in many offices, managers are facing a daunting training burden in addition to reviewing an increased volume of production, providing vital hand-holding services during the adjustment period, and passing on tribal lore."[5] The 50 percent figure is striking, as it reflects either recent rapid growth in the size of the analytic community, personnel turbulence of large proportions, or both. Moreover, these new analysts do not appear to have much, if any, formal training for their work: "[I]nterviews of new analysts at the end of their first year [reveal] a desire for a manual describing how to do analysis."[6]

It would appear, then, that supervisors must train new apprentices from scratch. Where do they begin? Mr. Z believes that "the manager's first task is akin to deprogramming—undoing habits formed in four to ten years of college-level work."[7] The remark about deprogramming reveals a disdain for (or perhaps, as we shall see, a deep ambivalence toward) universities that pervades the paper. The reasons Mr. Z offers for his contempt suggest that U.S. institutions of higher education do not do a competent job of providing a liberal education even to the talented few. Thus, Mr. Z finds that college students have been trained to "gather facts" and "pile up detail" to "demonstrate their expertise" in college, without ever having to think about broader implications; in the academic world, "what passes for 'conclusions' is more often than not a summary of the preceding pages."[8]

To help break in the new analyst, Mr. Z recommends that the manager hammer home a three-part understanding of the intelligence analyst's mission. The first of these is that "[t]he job is to make judgments about the future." Indeed, "we are less concerned about what actually happened than the significance of the event for US interests. . . ."[9] The "real job of analysis [is] thinking about the future."[10] This view has a lineage of at least three decades. In the mid-

1950s, Roger Hilsman, who once served as director of the State Department's Bureau of Intelligence and Research (INR), concluded from interviews with many intelligence analysts that they regarded the future as "predetermined, inevitable." The task of intelligence, in this view, was "merely to find the key to these locked books of future history and read the pages."[11]

Curiously enough, one common complaint by consumers of intelligence concerns the proclivity of analysts to make predictions in the most tentative fashion—or, less politely, to weasel. Thus, Henry Kissinger recalls that in the days immediately before the outbreak of the Yom Kippur War, an INR assessment cautiously raised the possibility of a limited Syrian attack on Israel. The head of INR defended the assessment later, declaring that it was "far from saying that it [an Arab attack] was not at all likely." Kissinger sourly remarks that "the reader will have to judge whether a harassed policymaker could possibly draw the inference suggested by Mr. Cline from the conclusion of the INR report."[12] Analysts, no doubt, have the sense to know that mushy predictions rarely expose their authors to humiliation. More honorably and more importantly, they must also know that the future is inevitably so contingent that virtually no worthwhile forecast can have the ring of certainty.

The following is Mr. Z's second message for new trainees: "*We are the interpreters of foreign cultures and alien problems.* As such, our job is to expose the logic behind the actions of a Middle East madman and to render intelligible to the general reader the physics underlying a Soviet barrage attack on a US missile system."[13] This obviously makes sense. Mr. Z's phrasing, however, has certain unsettling implications.

Note that Mr. Z lumps in the same category the interpretation of foreign cultures and what is, in effect, popular science. There is no suggestion here that the two constitute completely different kinds of problems. By way of contrast, Abram Shulsky has argued that the problem of penetrating another government's workings does *not* resemble the challenge of unraveling "a hidden, but ultimately knowable process of nature." Rather, it is "a struggle between two human intelligences each of which is trying to outpsych the other, i.e., a chess game the prediction of which is inseparable from the playing."[14] Alternatively, Mr. Z seems to suggest that the two problems pose similar challenges in terms not only of the intellectual process that wrestles with them but also of the amount of experience needed to pursue those processes: "After a few months on the job [new analysts] are among the most knowledgeable people in the government on a particular issue. . . ."[15]

Now, a technically competent analyst who can write clear English can, in all likelihood, handle the description of the physics of a nuclear barrage within a few months. But can one acquire expertise about another government and, more broadly, another culture in such a short time? Is "the logic behind the actions of a Middle East madman" really so amenable to understanding by someone with no prior background?[16] Again, the idiosyncrasies of Mr. Z do not alone account for this view. Hilsman found that his generation's analysts shared a similar belief in the ability of versatile analysts to figure out what any country was up to. According to Hilsman, they believed that

> the basic motivations of Americans were almost universal. Although everyone seems to agree that some foreigners had peculiarities, for example, that Latins are excitable, there was a feeling that the soundest approach in trying to explain events that are puzzling is one of searching for motives that would actuate an American in similar circumstances rather than for a different set of motives particular to that people alone. One official, for example, said that when one came down to it, intelligence was just pick and shovel stuff, digging out the facts plus common sense. All one did was to put oneself in the other fellow's boots—what would you do if you were Stalin with his capabilities?[17]

Not surprisingly, such analysts place little "value on the idea that peoples of other cultures have different habits of thought, different values, and different motivations. They apparently reject the idea that someone who presumably has an intimate knowledge of cultural differences has any particular usefulness."[18] Furthermore, admittedly old evidence suggests that personnel practices, including frequent reassignments, often prevent desk officers in the intelligence community from developing the kind of familiarity with an area that would mitigate such parochialism.

Mr. Z's third concept is, again, unexceptionable on the surface: "Our job is to support decision makers."[19] But here, too, his elaboration of the point proves troubling. He says that new analysts must learn that "for the first time in their lives, they are writing for an audience that knows less than they do."[20] A professor would probably say that this misstates the relationship between a university professor and an advanced student. Far more importantly, it suggests a lack of awareness concerning the intellectual range of policymakers. Although analysts may quickly acquire expertise in very narrow areas, they may very well have less overall knowledge than an assistant secretary or National Security Council (NSC) staffer who has lived in the country in question and perhaps knows the language or has studied the region for years. A policymaker may have direct access to information unavailable to the analyst (confidential conversations with foreign officials, for example) and, in any case, knows U.S. policy—often a key piece of the puzzle—far better than the analyst.

The remainder of Mr. Z's article deals with the guidance new analysts should get in writing intelligence papers. He does not appear to cover the issue of how to evaluate evidence or address the problem of deception or concealment by the intelligence target. The problem of understanding decision making in a very different polity and society also receives no mention. Instead, Mr. Z concentrates on the challenge of forcing analysts to "begin with conclusions, and then explore their implications."[21] He seems to prize smooth speculation above a securely anchored argument.

Mr. Z's article—assuming it reflects substantial elements of intelligence community thought and practice, helps us understand why policymakers disregard much intelligence analysis. Predictions that "begin with conclusions," no matter how ingenious, will carry little weight with statesmen, particularly in areas where they rate their own expertise highly. Unless analysts lay out their chain of reasoning and the nature of the evidence supporting their conclusions, policymakers have little reason to prefer intelligence assessments to reliable newspaper reports, cables from overseas representatives, or their own hunches. Yet the style of intelligence writing taught by the community will not, apparently, provide such validation. What is worse, there is nothing to suggest that analysts trained in such a doctrine will, in fact, enable policymakers to understand the workings of a foreign state better than they otherwise would.

Mirror Imaging

A far more serious problem exists than that of policymakers displaying little regard for estimative intelligence. This problem centers on the possibility that if policymakers read such intelligence, it will mislead them or reinforce inappropriate prejudices. The official school of intelligence writing seems to pay very little heed to problems of deception and concealment, a serious deficiency in view of the premium placed by many regimes (most notably, but not exclusively, that of the Soviet Union) on such activities. But more pervasive, and even more pernicious, is the phenomenon of mirror imaging by intelligence analysts. The problem may seem obvious and concern about it antique, but it merits some exploration, for mirror imaging infiltrates and corrupts analysis by circuitous and often scarcely visible paths. It is a varied and subtle phenomenon and can afflict those who pride themselves on their hardheaded realpolitik as much as it does those who take a sunnier view of international relations.

One of the most recent cases of the distortions caused by mirror imaging appears in the decision to sell arms to Iran in 1985.[22] The decision seems to have emerged in part from an analysis of Iranian politics based on a typically U.S. understanding of a division between "moderates" and "extremists" in the Iranian government. The very use of such words suggests a vision of politics and religion that probably diverges sharply from the reality of contemporary Iran. Such terms imply that factions form in most countries along lines demarcated by programmatic preferences rather than according to personal allegiances, clan relationships, theological disputes, or other criteria. The words *moderate* and *extremist* further imply that factional differences extend (as in the United States) across a range of issues. In the United States, for example, one would not use the word *moderate* to describe a Republican who on the one hand favored higher taxes, affirmative action, and a comprehensive arms control treaty with the Soviet Union, while on the other hand called for the imprisonment of abortionists and an invasion of Nicaragua. Yet in other polities, similar juxtapositions frequently occur. That bloody "extremist" Robespierre initially opposed a warlike foreign policy, as did the no less radical Lenin.

U.S. intelligence analysts have applied their presuppositions not only to the structure of politics in foreign countries but also to the ways in which foreign officials supposedly think. The presumption of "rational" calculation (based on the U.S. definition of rational) seems to have played a role in the belief that a limited air campaign against North Vietnam would lead Ho Chi Minh to defer or set aside Vietnamese Communist plans to overrun South Vietnam. This presumption is evident in the following quote: "It is reasonable to infer that the DRV [Democratic Republic of Vietnam] leaders have a psychological investment in the work of construction they have accomplished over the last decade."[23] Similarly, the intelligence community's own postmortem on the nature of the intelligence failure before the 1973 Mideast war held that "[c]ertain substantive preconceptions . . . turned the analyst's attention . . . toward political indications that the Arabs were bent on finding nonviolent means to achieve their objectives and away from indications (mainly military) to the contrary."[24] Henry Kissinger offered a blunter verdict: "Our definition of rationality did not take seriously the notion of starting an unwinnable war to restore self-respect."[25] On another front, in 1980 a senior intelligence official still defended the National Intelligence Estimate (NIE) of 1962 that indicated that the Soviets would not put missiles in Cuba: "In that case, as Sherman Kent often said, his estimate of what was reasonable for the Soviet Union to do was a lot better than Khrushchev's, and therefore he was correct in analyzing the situation *as it should have been seen by the Soviets.*"[26]

Mirror imaging can skew even seemingly straightforward military assessments. An intelligence organization might collect accurate technical information (for example, how many airplanes an enemy has and the airplanes' ranges, bomb loads, and so on) but completely misunderstand the data because of a failure to understand the workings of the target government and society. In the 1930s, for example, although British intelligence agencies had a fairly good grip on the current German order of battle, their projections consistently fell wide of the mark. Royal Air Force (RAF) intelligence expected that the German Luftwaffe would have the same teething problems that the RAF did and that, like the RAF, it would wish to develop an efficient organization before creating a large force structure.[27] When straightforward mirror imaging ceased, RAF intelligence officers replaced it with a stereotyped vision of how the Germans differed from themselves: "We do not believe that Germany with her ability and love of good organization would adopt the methods which X states she has adopted" ("X" being a German Air Ministry official who had just handed a highly sensitive plan to MI6).[28]

Such crude assumptions about national culture were matched by equally simplistic assumptions about ideology. These included the assumptions that totalitarianism translated into efficiency and that even the Nazis viewed the world as one in which "decisions were taken on the basis of careful calculation of risks and rewards."[29] In fact, the Nazi state was highly disorganized and riddled with feuds between the services, Party barons, and other social groups. Rearmament proceeded at a breakneck pace, disregarding efficient absorption of weapons, supply and production bottlenecks, and the suitability of the technologies for an upcoming war.[30] Hitler did, no doubt, calculate risks and rewards, but his calculating process was utterly different from that of reasonable Englishmen, a fact that some Englishmen, particularly Winston Churchill, intuitively understood.

At the most general, political level, British intelligence in the 1930s failed to grasp the basic facts about the nature of the Third Reich, in large part because it projected on Nazi Germany assumptions about society derived from Anglo-Saxon experience. British analysts did not fail to grasp the malevolent quality of German policy, but they did fail to see that German rearmament proceeded the way it did because of the peculiarities of the Nazi regime. Thus, mirror imaging is not only the improper attribution of benign motives to an opponent but also the failure to comprehend the dynamics of a society very different from one's own.

Mirror imaging occurs at the highest levels of strategic intelligence—the assessment of war aims and the fundamental strategy designed to achieve them. U.S. and Israeli analysts' failure to understand why President Sadat of Egypt would start a war (in 1973) he would inevitably lose provides one example of strategic level mirror imaging. Another is the persistent belief in the 1960s and 1970s that the Soviets aimed only at achieving nuclear parity with the United States, a mirror image of the United States' own belief in the meaninglessness of nuclear superiority.[31] This misconception of Soviet thinking led to persistent and prolonged underestimates of the rate of Soviet construction of nuclear forces.

At the operational level of war, mirror imaging leads to misunderstanding of the enemy's doctrines of war. In the 1970s, U.S. analysts assumed that Soviet submarines would, in the event of war, sally forth to attack U.S. lines of communication across the Atlantic, much as the United States had used its submarine forces against Japan in World War II. Only gradually did it become clear that the Soviets had a different operational concept, which envisioned the use of Soviet attack submarines to protect bastions in which the Soviet ballistic missile submarine fleet could ride out a prolonged war as a secure strategic reserve force. Similarly, in the interwar period, British and French intelligence paid only passing attention to the operational concepts that coalesced into the blitzkrieg. The British and French were not the only ones who misread the signs. One of the foremost experts on the Soviet military in World War II writes this about the Soviet defeats in the summer of 1941: *"The failure to comprehend the essentials of German military doctrine in a tactical, operational sense, and German 'war doctrine' in its widest context was the prime cause of disaster; the effect of this was and had to be devastating, for such a failure impeded and inhibited effective operational planning."*[32]

Mirror imaging occurs at the lower levels of analysis as well, where enemy tactics and technology are considered. Partly in reaction to discomfort with U.S. assertions concerning the superiority of U.S. armored forces, the director of Net Assessment in the Office of the Secretary of Defense commissioned in 1977 a study comparing U.S. and Soviet tank tactics and manning procedures.[33] Until that time, U.S. officers had generally believed that the additional experience provided by their three-year volunteers (versus two-year Soviet conscripts), superior U.S. training, and the initiative native to U.S. troops would provide a considerable edge over their Soviet counterparts. The study, only recently declassified, revealed that Soviet training and basic procedures not only differed from U.S. practices but also were in some respects superior, particularly in view of Soviet conditions and purposes. Soviet crews remained together for the duration of their tours, unlike their U.S. counterparts, who rotated every few months; Soviet crews trained on the same type of tank that they would later man, while the Americans did not; the Soviets made far more extensive use of simulators and other training technologies; and the Soviets understood the fundamental tactical problems of tank battles in ways far more suited to the central European battlefield than did the Americans.[34]

Tactical and technical mirror imaging can bring rude shocks in war. The surprising and crushing defeats suffered by U.S. cruisers and destroyers in nighttime battles with the Japanese off the Solomon Islands in 1942 had, as one of its causes, a failure to understand the differences between U.S. and Japanese tactics and technology. The U.S. Navy thought of cruisers as long-range scouts and screens for a battle fleet. These ships would rely on the superior range of their guns and weight of their salvos to defeat their counterparts and thus pave the way for a climactic clash of the main fleets. The Japanese had a concept of operations requiring prolonged attrition of a U.S. fleet crossing the Pacific before a decisive battle. This concept assigned greater weight to independent cruiser and destroyer engagements, particularly nighttime raids making heavy use of torpedoes and close-in gunfire. The Americans underestimated the range, speed, and warhead size of the Japanese torpedo (which it assumed to be equivalent to its U.S. counterpart), the number carried by Japanese surface ships, and thus the ability of the Japanese to fight the kinds of engagements that actually occurred in the South Pacific.[35]

This reflects the difficulty a technologically advanced power has in crediting its enemies with capabilities it does not itself have or does not think feasible—whether or not it would want those capabilities in the first place.[36] Mirror imaging in this case appears as the assumption that the opponent is uniformly only 90 percent as skilled as oneself. There is no notion that in some areas the enemy may be well behind and in others may have forged well ahead. This syndrome accounts for the widespread and comforting myth that Soviet military technology is invariably inferior to that of the United States. Many defense analysts adhere to this belief, although the Soviets produced far better tanks in World War II than did the Western powers. In the years since 1945, the Soviets have led in the deployment of infantry fighting vehicles, antiship cruise missiles, antisatellite weapons, and "weaponized" lasers.

The foregoing suggests that mirror imaging occurs not only when an analyst says, "The enemy is just like me." It also occurs when the analyst says, "The enemy is more or less like me"—slightly more irritable, aggressive, or unscrupulous, perhaps, or slightly less ingenious, intelligent, or determined, but basically the same. And it occurs when the analyst assumes that the enemy thinks pretty much the same way he or she does, even if the two sides have diametrically opposed ends. Mirror imaging is pervasive precisely because it so often takes this more insidious form, and it is only by mounting a frontal assault on it that sound intelligence gathering for strategic planning can begin.

The Otherness of the Enemy: Intelligence for Strategic Planning

Certain basic kinds of intelligence—order of battle information, geographic and demographic data, and the like—obviously constitute one part of the necessary information for strategic planning. So too do warning reports and predictive estimates, despite the caution with which both must be treated. But above all, strategic planners need intelligence on the otherness of the enemy—intelligence that will reveal the enemy's methods of operation, internal disputes, and ways of doing business, as well as the ways in which the enemy differs from the United States.

One of the best examples of this kind of intelligence, and how it feeds into net assessment and strategic planning, appears in Thucydides' *The Peloponnesian War*. The Spartan king Archidamus warned his compatriots in 432 B.C. against war with Athens in the following terms:

> In a struggle with Peloponnesians and neighbors our strength is of the same character, and it is possible to move swiftly on the different points. But a struggle with a people who live in a distant land, who have also an extraordinary familiarity with the sea, and who are in the highest state of preparation in every other department; with wealth private and public, with ships, and horses, and heavy infantry, and a population such as no one other Hellenic place can equal, and lastly a number of tributary allies—what can justify us in rashly beginning such a struggle? Where is our trust that we should rush on it unprepared? Is it in our ships? There we are inferior; while if we are to practice and become a match for them, time must intervene. Is it in our money? There we have a far greater deficiency. We neither have it in our treasury, nor are we ready to contribute it from our private funds. Confidence might possibly be felt in our superiority in heavy infantry and population, which will enable us to invade and devastate their lands. But the Athenians have plenty of other land in their empire, and can import what they want by sea. Again, if we are to attempt an insurrection of their allies, these will have to be supported with a fleet, most of them being islanders. *What then is to be our war?* For unless we can either beat them at sea, or deprive them of the revenues which feed their navy, we shall meet with little but disaster.[37]

Archidamus's picture of Athens contributed to his pessimistic answer to the central strategic question "What then is to be our war?" Similarly, Athens's great leader Pericles understood quite well the ways in which Spartan society created peculiar—and exploitable—weaknesses. He pointed out that the Spartans were a nation of farmers who were willing to serve in person. But they were citizens of a state poor in fungible resources and lacking experience in protracted wars fought far from home. In the end, he argued, the Spartans would be crippled by the nature of their coalition, which lacked a single council to debate and implement joint strategy. A strategy of protracted war conducted for limited aims would, Pericles argued, enable the Athenians to achieve the objective—the removal of Sparta as an obstacle to the growth of the Athenian empire.[38] The first half of the war proved both men right: The Spartans proved incapable of grappling with the Athenian strengths, and the Athenians, following a strategy dictated by Pericles, applied long-term pressure against Spartan weaknesses.

It is by no means an easy thing to penetrate an opponent's military culture or to understand it without succumbing to exaggerated fears or contemptuous denigration. As Aleksandr Solzhenitsyn once warned a disbelieving audience, "Any ancient deeply rooted autonomous culture, especially if it is spread on a wide part of the earth's surface, constitutes an autonomous world, full of riddles and surprises to Western thinking. . . ."[39] The reverse is equally true. Although the United States in the 1930s was nothing if not accessible to foreign agents, both legal and covert, it was in another sense impenetrable to the Axis powers because of their own failure to comprehend the workings of democratic states. Both the Germans and the Japanese repeatedly underestimated the American polity—its tenacity and ingenuity, as well as its ability to organize, improvise, and produce. And these colossal failures of intelligence helped doom both states to ruinous defeat. Today our tendency to judge Soviet organizational effectiveness by the standards of U.S. bureaucratic practice runs a similar risk of replacing careful analysis with contemptuous and misleading clichés.[40]

How does an understanding of the nature of the enemy's politics and culture contribute to success in warfare? The historical cases of military systems that have successfully sought and exploited such strategic intelligence are rather few. The Byzantine Empire, geographically indefensible, overextended, and surrounded by populous and warlike enemies, is one: "The generals of the new Rome made it their boast that they knew how to face and conquer Slav or Turk, Frank or Saracen, by employing in each case the tactical means best adapted to meet their opponents' method of warfare."[41]

In more recent times, British forces engaged in a bitter campaign against the Japanese in Burma in World War II soon discovered that tactical maxims applicable to war against European opponents made no sense in a war against an Oriental opponent. The British commander, General William Slim, described in his memoirs the importance of understanding the enemy, as well as the difficulty and time involved in figuring them out. After a while, for example, he discovered that the Japanese, "formidable as long as they are allowed to follow undisturbed their daring projects, are thrown into confusion by the unexpected."[42] On the basis of both his studies of the Russo-Japanese War and his own experience, he discovered that: "the Japanese were prepared to throw in every man, and more than once tipped the scales of victory with their very last reserves. . . . This was a source of great strength to them, but also properly taken advantage of might, in conjunction with their overweening confidence, be a fatal weakness."[43]

Throughout the campaign, Slim kept careful track of his opponents, at one point even intervening to prohibit an air raid on the headquarters of a general whom he regarded as so stupidly aggressive as to be a positive asset to the Allies.[44] Slim took the defeated Fourteenth Army and, after studying his opponents' tactics and way of war, trained his men to exploit Japanese weaknesses and counter their strengths. Rather than order encircled units to break out—a tactic that during the retreat from Burma had played into Japanese hands—he had them exhaust the enemy by battling them from defensive boxes. Realizing that his superiority lay in large part in superior logistics and knowing that he could count on almost unthinking aggressiveness on the part of his opponent, he deliberately enticed the enemy into a series of battles (Imphal and Kohima) at the end of a long supply line.[45]

Without otherness of the enemy intelligence, even the most accurate information on order of battle (the staple of most military intelligence) can prove worthless. Consider the advance of United Nations (UN) forces in Korea across the thirty-eighth parallel toward the Yalu River in October and November 1950. U.S. intelligence had a fairly good picture of the deployment of the Chinese People's Liberation Army (PLA) massing along the Yalu and moving into northern Korea. In early November, for example, several weeks before the Chinese onslaught, G-2 in Tokyo noted that two dozen Chinese divisions stood poised on the border, with more streaming in.[46] As the weeks wore on, U.S. and Republic of Korea (ROK) units captured nearly a hundred Chinese prisoners of war, who proved remarkably forthcoming about the size, mission, and location of their parent units. Even so, on several occasions when the opposing forces blundered into one another, the Chinese units inflicted heavy losses on UN (including U.S.) forces. When the Chinese onslaught began in earnest on November 26–27, the Americans and their allies suffered a bloody defeat. One U.S. and several ROK divisions dissolved in chaos, and shaken staffs in Tokyo and Washington began planning the evacuation of UN forces from the Korean peninsula.

The failure had many sources, some of which—undermanning, poor tactics, and faulty logistics—I cannot discuss here. But one of the chief causes may be found in the picture of the enemy. How did General MacArthur and other U.S. military chiefs, statesmen, and headquarters staff answer the question "What then is to be our war?" The Americans had, first and foremost, only a vague sense of what Chinese objectives might be. U.S. intelligence at that time offered descriptions that foreshadowed equally implausible assessments of another group of Asian Communists one and a half decades later. The Chinese would, the CIA believed, intervene only to defend vital power plants along the Yalu or if they thought that U.S. forces intended to base themselves along that river.[47] The notions that the Chinese would find a Korea unified by Western military power intolerable and that they would attempt to drive UN forces not only back to the thirty-eighth parallel but off the peninsula were not accepted. Far from conceiving of the Chinese Communists as demonic enemies of the West, the analysts conceived of the new People's Republic of China as having limited and "reasonable" concerns about such prosaic matters as hydroelectric dams.

The Americans did, however, take the prospects of Chinese intervention seriously and did have an answer to the question "What then is to be our war?" The answer was "victory through air power"—bombing and strafing to seal off Korea from China by cutting the Yalu bridges and, failing that, to destroy the PLA as it massed to attack within Korea. Thus, General MacArthur gave this airy promise to President Truman at Wake Island on October 15, 1950: "Now that we have bases for our Air Force in Korea, if the Chinese tried to get down to Pyongyang there would be the greatest slaughter."[48]

This faith in the efficacy of air power—and, more importantly, of the vulnerability of the enemy to its application—had firm foundations in intelligence analysis. In the initial fighting in Korea in the summer and fall of 1950, U.S. Air Force, Navy, and Marine fighters and bombers had not only devastated North Korean factories, railroads, and bridges but also had slaughtered the invading North Korean People's Army (NKPA) by the thousands and smashed the long columns of trucks that supported the attack, as well as the tanks that spearheaded it. Far East Command (FEC) intelligence concluded the following in a mid-November report: "Based entirely upon prisoner of war reactions this study indicates that there can be no doubt that the impact of UN air efforts in the tactical support of UN Ground Force probably has been the greatest single factor contributing to the overall success of the UN Ground Force scheme of maneuver."[49] This was not surprising, given that the NKPA was a fairly modern, Soviet-style army. This point was noted in a casual aside by FEC intelligence analysts, who observed that the average North Korean division had some two hundred vehicles (the average Chinese division had none) as well as large complements of artillery, signals, and other supporting branches (also lacking in the PLA), all of which required large amounts of road-bound transport.[50] Intelligence noticed the differences between the NKPA and PLA but did not ponder them; rather, it concluded that the Chinese divisions were merely inferior versions of the North Korean ones.

In fact, the PLA was a different enemy with a different concept of operations, tactics, and military culture. Sun Tzu and Mao Zedong, not Lenin and Stalin, provided the intellectual foundations for its doctrine. Its peasant infantry, unaided but also unencumbered by tanks or even artillery, quickly disappeared off the roads into the hills, forests, and villages of North Korea. Its forces infiltrated and attacked suddenly at night, using large quantities of grenades and close-quarters machine-gun fire to overwhelm the enemy. Eluding aerial reconnaissance, the Chinese closed in on spread-out UN forces with frightening speed. They suffered huge losses to be sure, but an exaggerated fear of implacable Chinese hordes abruptly replaced the fecklessness that had beset U.S. commanders and troops.

It was left to a reserve lieutenant colonel and historian-journalist, S.L.A. Marshall, to provide the first systematic view of the enemy's otherness at the tactical and operational levels.[51] By the simple expedient of interviewing as many U.S. frontline troops as possible, Marshall assembled a clear picture of Chinese methods with a view to defeating them. Chinese grenades were largely ineffective and Chinese ammunition supplies limited, so a stout defense within large perimeters would usually stop them; a tactical retreat under pressure, however, was often fatal. Accidentally ignited grass fires, threw the Chinese off their plans and even led to suicidal attempts by attacking units to stamp them out under UN fire. More systematic attempts to illuminate the battlefield could similarly throw the Chinese off their plan of attack. Their lack of communications gear such as radios made it difficult for their tactical units to adapt to unforeseen battlefield events. The absence of logistical support (after several days of fighting, Chinese divisions had to move to the rear to restock on food and ammunition) meant that the Chinese could not maintain a prolonged offensive; a panicky flight to evacuation ports, therefore, was unnecessary. Stout leadership by a new U.S. commander, General Matthew Ridgway, who imposed tougher discipline and shrewder tactics (based in part on Marshall's reports) soon turned the tide of battle. By March 1951, UN forces had begun a series of successful counterattacks.

The Challenge of the 1990s

It is no coincidence that our two extended examples of the problem of the otherness of the enemy come from wars between Western and Eastern powers. The British in Burma and the Americans in Korea confronted opponents whose differences from themselves—differences in culture, tactics, and even physiognomy—were glaring. Yet, even in those cases, it took years to comprehend fully the enemy's otherness and develop operational concepts accordingly. In the ancient world, the differences between one side and the other could not escape attention. No matter how stolidly parochial, the Roman legionnaires deploying in orderly lines opposite thousands of milling, half-naked, war paint–bedaubed Picts could not help but suspect that their enemies approached war differently than they did. Today, however, armies tend to resemble one another on the surface. One nation's tanks and airplanes look pretty much like another's. Most powers use roughly similar organizational forms (company, battalion, and division) and ranks (major, lieutenant, colonel, and general). In fact, however, these resemblances deceive the strategic analyst. As Solzhenitsyn and others have remarked, the seeming homogeneity of the world with respect to blue jeans, tape recorders, and soft drinks conceals great, and perhaps growing, divergences in far more fundamental areas of belief and behavior.

In the 1990s, the problem of crossing the cultural divide in strategic intelligence will worsen. Hitherto the intelligence community's overwhelming concentration on the Soviet Union has, willy-nilly, ripped a hole or two in the curtain of cultural myopia, although that curtain has hardly become transparent. If someone focuses on one object long and hard enough, he cannot help but see some of its peculiarities. But henceforth the United States will no longer have the luxury of concentrating its intelligence assets overwhelmingly on its chief target, the Soviet Union. Over the next two decades, the United States can expect three major trends to multiply the foci of its intelligence.[52] First, because of the Soviet Union's economic and demographic stagnation, it might become a relatively (and only relatively) less pressing threat. At the same time, the United States can expect a continued rise—on both absolute and relative scales—of intermediate powers such as Japan, China, India, and other smaller, considerably less friendly states. This will come about not only through the economic development of these countries and the continued diffusion of military technology and organizational ability in the Third World[53] but also through the gradual shrinkage of the shadow of U.S. power. As a result, the multipolar world prematurely envisaged in the early 1970s seems likely to emerge at the beginning of the next century.

Consider the case of India, which has a remarkable capacity for realpolitik in diplomacy and ruthlessness in the use of force. India has displayed these qualities by using fifty thousand troops to crush its fractious, erstwhile clients among the Tamils of Sri Lanka. Meanwhile, the Indians, unnoticed by many in the United States, have developed their military in many directions. They have upgraded its weaponry, deepened its industrial base, and forged new operational capabilities. India's uniformed military, two-thirds the size of the United States', operates sophisticated weapons, including a nuclear-powered submarine, Harrier jets, MiG-27s, and, possibly, nuclear weapons. How well does U.S. intelligence understand the workings of the Indian armed forces? Does it have a firm grip on their peculiar strengths and weaknesses, their tactical preferences, and their organizational routines? Does it know the structure of their cliques and their internal squabbles, the formative experiences of their leaders, and their relationship to civilian authority?

In the next two decades, the United States will face Third World states armed with some weapons comparable to its own: The Iraqi Exocet missile slamming into the hull of the USS *Stark* was but a portent. The slow and seemingly irreversible spread of nuclear weapons—surreptitiously acquired in most cases—will present terrible choices to U.S. leaders concerning the preemptive use of force. The more rapid, more open, and only slightly less scary proliferation of chemical agents, the means to deliver them over long ranges, and the will to use them without subterfuge poses a different but no less serious set of threats.

This growth in military potential in the Third World is occurring at a time when these societies are not looking to become more solid and peaceful. The experience of the Philippines, Iran, and the Central American states suggests just the reverse. On the whole, the two decades from 1945 to 1965 saw a relatively smooth transition to a post-colonial era. The Third World has now entered a post-postcolonial era (for want of a better term) in which many of the sources of even feeble international norms—international groupings such as the Non-Aligned Movement, for example—no longer function. At the same time, forces such as Islamic fundamentalism, heterodox communism (for example, Cambodia's Khmer Rouge and Peru's Shining Path), and inflamed ethnic and religious chauvinisms are creating societies that the United States will find extremely difficult to understand. Yet unless the United States chooses to abandon global power—and perhaps not even then—it must make the attempt.

In the next twenty-five years, the United States might see emerge a new and by no means more peaceful world order. In the past, the penalties the United States paid for misunderstanding its opponents through mirror imaging of one kind or another might have been more controllable than they will be in the future. The Chinese intervention in Korea was a severe blow, but U.S. firepower could compensate for it. In the future, this might not be the case, as Third World countries might match the United States in certain areas of military potential. At the same time, the advent of new conventional military technologies may, if properly handled, enable the United States to exercise its power in new ways, such as through long-range, unmanned, highly precise strikes with cruise missiles. Yet such technical possibilities will mean nothing if the United States is not informed by strategic intelligence capable of understanding an enemy's vulnerabilities.

Remedies: "Managing/Teaching New Analysts" Revisited

A problem of the dimensions sketched above does not lend itself to neat solutions. Indeed, I have not described all parts of the problem fully, including the danger of analysts becoming servants of a torrent of data generated by technical systems and government reporting, ignorant in some cases of other sources of information. Another equally disturbing possibility stems from the intelligence community's apparent emphasis (reinforced by Mr. Z's injunction to new analysts about the importance of deadlines) on short-term analysis rather than long-term research projects. Nonetheless, some broad measures do come to mind, particularly in the area of training new analysts.

Analysts do need extensive formal training, particularly if their basic education has left them the intellectual cripples portrayed by the author of "Managing/Teaching New Analysts." William Langer, one of this century's more distinguished diplomatic historians and the head of the wartime research and analysis branch of the Office of Strategic Services, has argued that a competent intelligence analyst requires training every bit as rigorous as that provided in a first-class doctoral program.[54] He hastened to observe that a Ph.D. is no prerequisite for intelligence work, and he argued that intelligence managers cannot assume an innate ability to perform research on the part of new analysts.

What might go into a serious training program for analysts? Again, I can only sketch out some possibilities, but I would suggest that a long period of both apprenticeship and formal education—rather than just the former—has strong merits. Obviously, one part of the curriculum should include language training, which must, at the very least, leave trainees able to read a foreign language easily. A system that rewards analysts more for learning two languages only passably rather than one really well defeats its own purposes. It would, indeed, be a good thing for intelligence analysts to read regularly not only the usual U.S. newspapers but also at least one superior foreign newspaper (*Le Monde*, the *Neue Zuercher Zeitung,* or *El Pais,* for example), even if his or her area did not include a French-, German-, or Spanish-speaking country.

In addition to language skills, the ideal strategic intelligence analyst would know a great deal about history, particularly military and diplomatic history. Graduate-level instruction, tailored to the needs of the trainee, would help provide what one wise writer calls "antidotes against cultural poisoning, credulity, homogenizing, and over-intellection."[55] More narrowly, however, the trainee would benefit from immersion in case studies—the more recent usually, though not always, the better—of intelligence gone awry. Among the merits of the case study method, particularly when it examines interesting failures, is the prick it administers to hubris. A readily available compendium of faulty assessments by eminent analysts, contrasted, where possible, with more accurate judgments by journalists, businessmen, academics, or other analysts, would be useful. Among other things, it might diminish the tendency of those "who live day by day in a rarefied atmosphere of secret information . . . to be patronizing of outsiders, even those who are given most of the security clearances."[56] More importantly, a thoughtful examination of such cases (including those where internal analysis cannot be matched against comparable external views) can help trainees—particularly those who emerge with a bachelor's degree in one of the natural or social sciences—learn the pitfalls of intelligence research and judgment. A word of caution is in order, however. The case study method of instruction seems, at first, a relatively cheap and easy means of teaching sound procedure. In fact, as its best practitioners argue, it requires rare skill and costly time and effort on the part of both the case writer and instructor.[57]

Large impediments to the creation of such graduate-level educational programs in the U.S. government no doubt exist.[58] The word *education* is critical. Although the government can and does run many superb training programs, the problem here is one of education. Although government educational institutions frequently have a quality of student and an overall level of funding competitive with those of good civilian institutions, they suffer from bureaucratic routines and prejudices that hamper sound teaching. The largest, though not the only, problem has to do with personnel practices affecting teachers and students. In the military, for example, operators view teaching assignments as either dead ends or tickets to be punched. The organization as a whole frequently treats teaching as a sideline (and a peculiar one) rather than as a critical expertise for its survival. No civilian academic institution could succeed if its presidents, deans, and faculty rotated out of their jobs or retired after two- or three-year terms, yet such turbulence is the norm in many government schools. Another difficulty concerns the length of time for which U.S. government agencies will release talented individuals for schooling. In the United States, a senior military officer will attend a war college for one year; in the Soviet Union, officers may attend prestigious graduate-level military schools for three times as long.

Of course, education is by no means the only problem and improved schooling not the only solution. One hopes that the turbulence in the analytic branches of intelligence referred to by many authors can be diminished and that analysts can make long-term careers in the study of particular countries. Innovative measures, including easy lateral entry by capable men and women in other walks of life (not just the university) can build the kind of long-term expertise required. Many analysts, however, will come from the same pool of people who do in fact become academics. To attract the best ones, the intelligence community must give them the opportunity to get what many seek in the academic world—time and license to publish in their particular field of expertise.

No doubt these measures have been thought of before and, in some cases, implemented to a greater or lesser extent. But consideration of debacles such as our assessments of Iran for nearly a decade past and examination of articles such as Mr. Z's leads one to doubt that they have been implemented with vigor and consistency. The patterns of thought and behavior that inhibit sound strategic intelligence analysis have deep roots, formidable obstacles impede the creation of true educational institutions (as opposed to competent training facilities) in government, and policymakers will continue to handle dissatisfaction by dismissing intelligence or harrying its producers. Nonetheless, the stakes are sufficiently great to merit a bold attempt at reform.

Notes

1. Hans Heymann, "Intelligence/Policy Relationships," in Alfred C. Maurer, Marion D. Tunstall, and James M. Keagle, eds., *Intelligence: Policy and Process* (Boulder, Colo.: Westview Press, 1985), 62.

2. Arthur S. Hulnick, "The Intelligence Producer—Policy Consumer Linkage: A Theoretical Approach," *Intelligence and National Security* 1 (May 1986): 215.

3. In this category, I would put Richard K. Betts, "Analysis, War and Decision: Why Intelligence Failures Are Inevitable," in Klaus Knorr, ed., *Power, Strategy, and Security: A World Politics Reader* (Princeton, N.J.: Princeton University Press, 1983), 211–39.

4. See Mark Lowenthal, "The Burdensome Concept of Failure," in Maurer, Tunstall and Keagle, *Intelligence*, 43–56.

5. "Managing/Teaching New Analysts," *Studies in Intelligence* 30 (Fall 1986): 1. Sanitized version of article released under the Freedom of Information Act. Author's name not released.

6. Ibid.

7. Ibid.

8. Ibid., 4. When this indeed holds true, it suggests that the student has received second- or third-rate instruction, no matter how august the institution that has provided it. Personal experience and Allan Bloom's *The Closing of the American Mind* (New York: Simon and Schuster, 1987) lead me to think that the author has a point, albeit one pressed too far.

9. Ibid., 2.

10. Ibid., 3.

11. Roger Hilsman, *Strategic Intelligence and National Decisions* (Glencoe, Ill.: The Free Press, 1956), 106–7.

12. Henry Kissinger, *Years of Upheaval* (Boston: Little, Brown, 1982), 464.

13. "Managing/Teaching," 2. Emphasis in the original.

14. Personal communication to the author.

15. "Managing/Teaching," 3.

16. The use of the term *madman* suggests not.

17. Hilsman, *Strategic Intelligence*, 105.

18. Ibid., 103. For a critique of this view, see Adda B. Bozeman, "Covert Action and Foreign Policy," in Roy Godson, ed., *Intelligence Requirements for the 1980's: Covert Action* (Washington, D.C.: National Strategy Information Center, 1981), 15–78.

19. "Managing/Teaching," 2.

20. Ibid., 3–4.

21. Ibid., 4.

22. See Edward S. Muskie, John Tower, and Brent Scowcroft, *Report of the President's Special Review Board* (Washington, D.C.: Government Printing Office, 1987), B6–B10.

23. NSC Working Group on Vietnam, "Intelligence Assessment: The Situation in Vietnam," 24 November 1964, *The Pentagon Papers,* the Senator Gravel edition, vol. 3 (Boston: Beacon Press, 1971), 650.

24. Reproduced in part in U.S. Congress, House Select Committee on Intelligence, *U.S. Intelligence Agencies and Activities: The Performance of the Intelligence Community, Hearings before the Select Committee on Intelligence, U.S. House of Representatives,* pt. 2, 94th Cong., 1st sess. (Washington, D.C.: Government Printing Office, 1975), 639.

25. Kissinger, *Years of Upheaval,* 465.

26. Discussant remarks of Ray S. Cline in Roy Godson, ed., *Intelligence Requirements for the 1980's: Analysis and Estimates* (Washington, D.C.: National Strategy Information Center, 1980), 77. Emphasis added.

27. Wesley Wark, *The Ultimate Enemy: British Intelligence and Nazi Germany, 1933–1939* (Ithaca, N.Y.: Cornell University Press, 1985), 35–38.

28. Ibid., 54.

29. Ibid., 237–38.

30. See Hans-Erich Volkmann, "Die NS-Wirtschaft in Vorbereitung des Krieges," and Wilhelm Deist, "Die Aufrustung der Wehrmacht," in Wilhelm Deist et al., eds., *Das deutsche Reich und der zweite Weltkrieg* (Stuttgart: Deutsche Verlags-Anstalt, 1979), vol. 1, *Ursachen und Voraussetzungen der deutschen Kriegspolitik,* 177–534.

31. See David S. Sullivan, "Evaluating U.S. Intelligence Estimates," in Godson, *Intelligence Requirements: Analysis and Estimates,* 49–84; Albert Wohlstetter, "Is There a Strategic Arms Race?" *Foreign Policy,* no. 15 (Summer 1974): 3–20; Albert Wohlstetter, "Rivals, But No Race," *Foreign Policy,* no. 16 (Fall 1974): 48–81; Albert Wohlstetter, "How to Confuse Ourselves," *Foreign Policy,* no. 20 (Fall 1975): 170–98.

32. John Erickson, "Threat Identification and Strategic Appraisal by the Soviet Union, 1930–1941," in Ernest R. May, ed., *Knowing One's Enemies: Intelligence Assessment Before the Two World Wars* (Princeton, N.J.: Princeton University Press, 1984), 418. Emphasis in the original.

33. Colonel Lloyd N. Cosby et al., "Net Assessment of Soviet and American Tank Crew Training" (U.S. Army Training and Doctrine Command, Fort Monroe, Vir., 1977).

34. In particular, Soviet crews had as their priority in training selection of the proper target; U.S. crews were rewarded for precise long-range gunnery. It should be noted that U.S. tank training has improved since that time.

35. T.J. McKearney, "The Solomons Naval Campaign: A Paradigm for Surface Warships in Maritime Strategy" (M.A. thesis, Naval Postgraduate School, 1985), 52–56, 76–96, 117–19. I am grateful to David Rosenberg for bringing this study to my attention and for a discussion based on his manuscript "Thinking Red."

36. Reginald V. Jones, *The Wizard War: British Scientific Intelligence, 1939–1945* (New York: Coward, McCann & Geoghegan, 1978), 457–58 is eloquent on this point.

37. Thucydides, *The Peloponnesian War,* Crawley translation (New York: Modern Library, 1951), 46–47. Emphasis added.

38. Ibid., 80.

39. Aleksandr Solzhenitsyn, *A World Split Apart* (New York: Harper & Row, 1978), 3.

40. See, in particular, Charles H. Fairbanks, "Bureaucratic Politics in the Soviet Union and in the Ottoman Empire," *Comparative Strategy* 6 (1987): 333–62.

41. Charles Oman, *A History of the Art of War in the Middle Ages,* 2d ed., vol. 1 (London: Methuen, 1924), 172. See also pp. 171–228.

42. William Slim, *Defeat Into Victory* (New York: David McKay, 1961), 98.

43. Ibid., 192.

44. Ibid., 266.

45. See, for example, Ronald Lewin, *Slim: The Standardbearer* (Hamden, Conn.: Archon Books, 1976); Geoffrey Evans, *Slim as Military Commander* (London: B.T. Batsford, 1969); and the official history, S. Woodburn Kirby et al., *The War Against Japan* (London: Her Majesty's Stationery Office, 1962), particularly vol. 3.

46. See, for example, Far East Command, Daily Intelligence Summary #2977, 3 November 1950, Record Group 338, Washington National Records Center, Suitland, Md. X Corps, composed of army and marine forces, was operating on the east coast of Korea, independent of the Eighth Army, which controlled the bulk of U.S., UN, and ROK forces in the western and central regions. In December 1950, X Corps was subordinated to the Eighth Army. The overall commander was General Douglas MacArthur, who served as both Commander in Chief Far East (CINCFE) and Commander in Chief, United Nations Command (CINCUNC), based in Tokyo.

47. See, for example, National Intelligence Estimate 2, "Chinese Communist Intervention in Korea," 8 November 1950, in *Foreign Relations of the United States, 1950* (Washington, D.C.: Government Printing Office, 1976), vol. 7, *Korea,* 1101–6 (hereafter cited as *FRUS 1950*).

48. Notes compiled by General Omar N. Bradley, *FRUS 1950,* vol. 7, *Korea,* 953.

49. Far East Command, Daily Intelligence Summary #2988, 14 November 1950, Washington National Records Center, Suitland, Md.

50. Far East Command, Daily Intelligence Summary #2976, 2 November 1950, Washington National Records Center, Suitland, Md.

51. His two reports, "CCF in the Attack," completed in January 1951, are reprinted in William B. Hopkins, *One Bugle No Drums: The Marines at Chosin Reservoir* (Chapel Hill, N.C.: Algonquin Books, 1986), 233–65. It is not clear that a comparable improvement in strategic intelligence occurred; witness the belief on the part of U.S. commanders that the beginning of truce talks argued a quick end to the war.

52. See Fred C. Ikle and Albert Wohlstetter, eds., *Discriminate Deterrence: Report of the Commission on Integrated Long-Term Strategy* (Washington, D.C.: Government Printing Office, 1988), especially pp. 5–12.

53. See Eliot Cohen, "Distant Battles: Modern War in the Third World," *International Security* 10 (Spring 1986): 143–71. More generally, see Stephanie Neuman and Robert Harkavy, eds., *The Lessons of Recent Wars in the Third World* (Lexington, Mass.: Lexington Books, 1986), vol. 2, *Comparative Dimensions*.

54. William L. Langer, "Research and Intelligence" (Lecture at the Main State Building, State Department, Washington, D.C., 31 May 1946), 11–13. In "Papers Relating to CIA and OSS Activities, 1945–1971," William L. Langer Papers, Harvard University Archives.

55. Jacques Barzun, *Clio and the Doctors: Psycho-History, Quanto-History, & History* (Chicago: University of Chicago Press, 1974), especially pp. 89–150.

56. Stansfield Turner, *Secrecy and Democracy: The CIA in Transition* (Boston: Houghton Mifflin, 1985), 116.

57. See C. Roland Christensen with Abby Hansen, *Teaching and the Case Method* (Boston: Harvard Business School, 1987).

58. I draw here on several years of teaching at the Naval War College and an unclassified study I performed some time ago for the Army War College.

II. PAUL SEABURY

> The test of a first rate intelligence service is the ability to hold two opposed ideas in the mind at the same time, and still retain the capacity to decide.
>
> —adapted slightly from F. Scott Fitzgerald, *The Crack-Up*

This essay examines analysis (and collection) perennials that will continue to bloom in the 1990s, together with new varietals likely to turn up. Some readers may deem the following recommendations politically unrealistic. Considering the unpleasant alternatives, however, I regard them as necessary.

Foreign policy analysts in the United States disagree about many things. However, there seems to be a general consensus about two aspects of the shape of things to come: first, that the 1990s will see a significant loosening of Eastern-Western bloc cohesiveness; and second, that there will be increasing nationality restiveness, particularly in the East, which already has many parallels in other parts of the non-Western world.

With respect to the collection and analysis of political intelligence, such anticipated developments are bound to strain the resources of the best intelligence system. The resourcefulness and vigor of both collection and analysis must be accompanied by talents of cultural understanding on a very wide scale.

The broad theme of this essay is that political intelligence for the 1990s must shift into active gear, more aggressively pursuing tasks of an inherently political nature. This will occur in a political world of greater complexity for which the analytical intelligence community is currently unprepared. This essay takes for granted, without discussion, the primacy of human intelligence, to which technical intelligence must always be subordinate.

The following is a summary of recommendations:

1. Analytical intelligence should not crave for itself a puristic, aloof independence akin to academic freedom in university scholarship. Analysts are servants of policy, not merely objective observers of events and trends.

2. In a sense, analytic intelligence should be composed of both watchful and activist components. The former is more of a passive

occupation than the latter. Both should at all times be highly sensitive to the needs of the executive branch. However, the activist component must be strongly represented in the intelligence community to aid policymakers in positive foreign policy actions. There are indications that this mind-set is currently out of fashion.

3. In recruitment and training for the 1990s, great care should be taken to obtain new cadres that are linguistically and culturally able to understand esoteric political cultures. It should be borne in mind that the United States is a multiethnic, multicultural society with vast resources of talents. Intelligence leadership cadres should exploit these assets. Although university training in area studies may be useful, all too frequently it can be counterproductive. Cultural training may best be gained from intense exposure to the political cultures themselves. Analysts bereft of such knowledge may be ineffective.

4. The bureaucratic organization of intelligence knowledge into sections, divisions, and branches may structure information so as to ignore key networked political phenomena, such as Soviet proxy operations, that cut across familiar lines, notably regional ones. Analysis should always be sensitive to this. Low-intensity wars, likely to continue in the 1990s, involve the cooperation of many U.S. adversaries. The interconnections must be understood.

5. Contrary to some now conventional views, the raison d'être of intelligence is not the substitution of intelligence for force. Intelligence is a form of force, but force without intelligence is blind, and intelligence without force is impotent.

Analysts and Policymakers

I am sure many well-informed, civic-minded people will agree that what this country needs is an intelligence service that, in collection and analysis, is honest, flexible, objective, devoid of arrières-pensées, open to contradictory and conflicting estimates, unbiased, and intellectually competent: "Ye shall know the truth, and the truth shall make you free," as the saying goes. Some would go further. They argue that this precious institutional ethos should be shielded from outside political attempts to bend or twist tasks, judgments, and estimates to correspond with preconceptions, particularly those of the foreign policy leadership (that is, those of a particular administration). Of course, who would argue oppositely—that a service should be dishonest and biased with its own hidden agenda, suppressing dissenting analytical conclusions?

Many subscribe to this ideal Weberian model of rectitude and excellence. Speaking as an academic, I note the obvious—that this model resembles an equally idealistic one for a great university, which should be the place for learning and teaching and the pursuit of truth by dispassionate scholars and scientists. The two—the university and the intelligence community—have very standoffish relations today. Both nevertheless aspire to analogous general goals as far as knowledge is concerned. Allen Dulles had the famous biblical text about the pursuit of truth engraved in the main hall of the CIA; it could as well be engraved on the portico of any American university. Great CIA directors have shared the yearning for learning, and William Casey very much resembled Dulles in his enjoyment of the life of the mind and the life of action.

This model has led some exponents to make the case for great institutional autonomy. Ideal academic freedom suggests that the pursuit of knowledge is best carried on in conditions under which investigators, scholars, and scientists can ply their trade with as little outside intervention as possible. Some CIA officials hold similar views. The defense of the life of the mind in either case can be accompanied by a contempt for philistines who from time to time come in to mess things up.[1]

Freedom from outside intervention means that the atmosphere of learning remains uncontaminated. Both the university and the intelligence community, according to this version, should be particularly on guard against political interventions that bend judgments to preconceived perceptions of reality, especially to bind analysis and knowledge to the procrustean bed of predetermined political action.

But leaving the university aside, it is clear with respect to the intelligence community that this purist ethos should be rejected. The practitioners of collection and analysis, after all, are servants, not masters. The craft has no other justification than its charge to furnish policymakers with what is needed (or not needed) to take purposive action. The responsible executive leadership has the constitutional responsibility to task the community with its conceptions of purposes, policies, and goals, as well as its intelligence requirements. In this, as in the military establishment, the key to effective performance must be command, control, and communications (C^3).

To repeat, the intelligence community has no raison d'être other than that of furnishing information, reasoned judgments, and estimates on which rational action is possible. In this the intelligence community differs greatly from the ethos of the academy. There must be a continuous interplay between the political/strategic leadership and the intelligence community, including, in particular, matters of priority. The president bears the ultimate responsibility for the superintendency and deployment of intelligence assets. It goes without saying (although I will say something of this subsequently) that the intelligence community should not be in the position of serving two equal masters or of trying to do so.

Watchful and Activist Intelligence

Let me here turn to a subtle version of this matter of intelligence subordination, as it can profitably be compared to an analogous activity within the university. Major universities, like the intelligence community, engage in very important scientific work that is essentially monitory. Seismology, public health, and meteorology come to mind. The main aim of such work is to scan the horizon for signs and portents of future trouble—earthquakes, plagues, and storms—and to sharpen the skills needed to forecast, diminish, and possibly prevent the catastrophes that nature can inflict upon human beings. Analogously, the intelligence community is tasked in part to scan the horizon for signs of possible or real human threats to the nation from the outside. Intelligence failures, like public health failures, can lead to catastrophe.

As Pearl Harbor reminds us, such intelligence activities at times can be of cardinal importance to the safety of the nation, if not its survival. But having said that, one also can say that this aspect of intelligence, whether human or technological, alert or lazy, is what I would call from a strategic perspective *watchful intelligence*.

Even when such observant collection and analysis is conducted with daring, vigor, and brilliance, it is essentially passive in its posture like the sentinel on the walls of Rome. What is going to happen? Where? When? What are *they* up to? What are *their* intentions? What have *they* got? Whatever the catalog of threats, such monitoring is based on a defensive strategic mind-set, a defensive calculus, sorting out real toads and toadstools from imaginary ones.[2]

Of course, from a strategic perspective such tasking, which is absolutely necessary, is not sufficient. Vigorous leadership can and should demand down the line that collectors and analysts alike search for the intelligence that is needed for strategic action. Assessing political developments in peacetime is a far more exacting task than analyzing adversary economic and military developments. Political collection and analysis requires knowing and judging not only the inner mind-sets of political leaders but also the nature of cultural and psychological trends. Here, the question of what should be important politically to policymakers involves a keen respect for tendencies and occurrences that bear upon policy. Thus, the indifference of analysts to questions of high policy may result in a deafness to events that in themselves may seem trivial or uninteresting but in a political context are of fundamental importance. A *Fingerspitzengefuehl* (intuitive sense) for such matters requires innate and acquired intimate knowledge of which a novice in comparative politics may be devoid. In this regard, it may be hazarded that CIA Directorate of Operations (DDO) intelligence gained from covert action operations and the fruits of DDO collectors may produce far more important knowledge and insight than that gained from in-house analysts.

A primary question to be asked about intelligence requirements for the 1990s is whether the intelligence community then will be favorably disposed, as in times past, to engage in active intelligence— namely, the scouting of opportunities in pursuit of the active foreign policy goals of senior policymakers. Another way of putting the matter is to ask whether such an activist ethos in the collection/analysis realm may be actually distasteful or even repugnant to professionals who are uncomfortable with the politicization that such activism necessarily entails and who might be content with what might be called objectivist passivity.

It is hazardous to speculate about the atmosphere of the nation, Congress, or a new administration in the 1990s. But as for the CIA, one way to avoid trouble might be for it to stay away from new, controversial tasks and have it be a kind of data processing university dedicated to gathering and analyzing information about allies and enemies alike.

Obviously, this is a very serious question having to do with institutional responsiveness to political tasking of a positive and perhaps highly adventurous nature. It has to do with the nature of an institutional ethos as well as with an all too possible instinct to exercise caution and prudence based in part on past traumatic experiences. To invigorate activist intelligence work in the face of institutional foot-dragging might mean the appointment to key CIA positions of outsiders whose views correspond to the strategic views of the presidential leadership. When and if this occurs, is this, as some would argue disparagingly, politicization? As Pontius Pilate might ask, "what is politicization"? One person's politicization is another person's wish to have an institution serving as an arm of a very purposive foreign policy. (It might be said that even objective empiricists may have their own personal political agendas.) Even some even-keeled moderates go crazy over the possibility that the CIA, responsive to such activist tasking, might revert to older bad habits in which analyses simply support the domestic political objectives of the administration in power (or, for that matter, the objectives of an administration out of power). As one observer has written: "It is only a very short step from there to a return to CIA counter-intelligence staff interference in domestic US politics, a potential secret CIA 'empire' that awakens nightmares in the minds at home and abroad."[3]

The problem is compounded further when the agendas of the two political branches of government are at odds with each other; then the temptation of insiders may be to gravitate toward one or the other. The present standoff between the two masters of the intelligence community, the president and the Congress, might pass into history. The simple point, however, is that no person should be compelled to serve two masters, no person should play the game of insubordination, and those who play at insubordination should do so at their own risk. Such a situation is an invitation to disaster; it invites a novel form of inner politicization in which the CIA becomes one of divided loyalties.

This, some argue, becomes a parade of the horribles, a slide from the notion of bureaucratic accountability into the nightmare of a police state. It may be, of course, that the umpire of these matters will be the ironhanded intervention of future events as they affect the nation's mood. If the national mood in the 1990s moves out of its present isolationism to a more activist disposition, the issue might simply go away.

With respect to more activist and positive administration policies, it is necessary to say that those disposed to respond eagerly to tasks of advancing, rather than cautiously protecting, national interests might need to be brash in risking bureaucratic reputations and careers by acting as eager beavers. I assume that after "Contragate" everyone knows what I am alluding to. Otherwise, the lesson learned is our task is to scan the horizons, not steer toward them; to predict earthquakes, not make them. This is a very incomplete bureaucratic ethos indeed.

A nice way to resolve this issue for the 1990s is, as Franklin Roosevelt once told two of his speech writers who had diametrically opposed drafts, to "weave them together." The CIA in its recruitment policies should attract those who by both temperament and training are equally at home in both watchful and active modes, who are risk takers without being rogues.

Recruitment Priorities and Procedures: The Understanding of Esoteric Political Cultures

One way to resolve the question of watchful versus activist propensities is to conclude that future recruits should be people who by background and temperament are adaptable to both observant and active modes. These recruits would be risk takers who have immersed themselves in foreign cultures and are attuned to the political forces at work in them. Further, they would not be overly impressed with current trends and fads in academic area studies.

Leaving aside this watchful/active dispute and focusing on other attributes of new agency personnel, it seems to me that attention should focus on an often neglected, crucial aspect of recruitment and training. This has to do with analysts' ability to know and understand the things they investigate. The late William Casey was hardly alone in complaining that many CIA analysts neither knew the languages of the countries they watched nor had traveled to them. In this regard, an advanced degree in comparative politics from even a great university may not be an asset. In fact, it might be a grave disability.

In the 1990s, this problem of judgmentally ineffective analysts will increasingly plague the intelligence community. Older, experienced area specialists will continue to fade from the scene, and new regional developments (perhaps in Mexico or the non-Slavic regions of the Soviet Union) will demand expertise that is in very short supply. This occurred recently in a situation where the CIA was urgently tasked to assign collectors and analysts to a nearby country of considerable importance to the United States. In this case, very few otherwise qualified personnel were able to speak the language.

An important question is whether some analysts, by temperament and aspiration, are frustrated academics keenly sensitive to social science approaches to comparative politics or to biases, as in Latin American studies, that are overwhelmingly left-oriented. The pluralist orientation to Soviet studies by trendsetting American scholars might result in a downgrading of concern with unpleasantries such as systems of political control, the KGB, disinformation, the militarization of primary and secondary school training, and the like. A reviewer of Bob Woodward's book *Veil* notes the absence of any references to the KGB, apart from absolving it of any responsibility for terrorism or the attempted assassination of the pope. The CIA, he suggests, "that spoke so freely to Woodward no longer sees the Soviets as a potential enemy."[4] This mind-set is characteristic of many prominent academic Sovietologists in the United States today.

The excellence of some foreign intelligence organizations—which might be based on brilliant past performances and previous, yet not automatically renewable, qualities—is worth looking at. One example is the Israeli Mossad. As Colonel William Kennedy has noted, there are important lessons to be learned from it. In Israel's first twenty years of independence, he remarks, "the Israeli services were organized and led . . . by a collection of brilliant and daring men assembled from the very top levels of advanced societies throughout the world. . . a truly exceptional group."[5] A recent decline in quality, he suggests, is due to the fact that "advancement has come to be based to a considerable extent not on performance but on acquisition of advanced degrees. In short, a process of bureaucratization set in." He goes on to say that CIA assessors of the Israeli services (in noting some important Mossad intelligence failures) themselves failed to heed the casual connection between bureaucratization and failure. Why? Because the CIA itself may be one of the world's best examples of bureaucratization.[6] (The CIA, incidentally, may have a larger proportion of Ph.Ds in its rank than any other U.S. agency.)

Who then should be the analysts of the 1990s? During the 1980s, when the CIA began an energetic program of cadre recruitment under William Casey, its most vigorous actions were results of widespread advertising in journals, newspapers, and so forth. The extraordinary response to these advertisements testified to the revived drawing power of this recently morale-stricken agency.

To recruit capable analysts for the 1990s, however, recruitment officers and other searchers must actively go out on the streets to look for people who from experience and background already have qualities enabling them to understand political cultures and move easily within them. The Israeli experience mentioned above shows the possibilities of creating a service with truly cosmopolitan skills. Because of past life experiences, these people are able to pass within and judge the nature of widely different political cultures. If this has been so for the Israelis, it should be said that it is more than possible for the United States. With regard to linguistic talent, it might be suggested that recruiters actively search for deep linguistic expertise. The United States is a truly multicultural society,[7] but I would bet that there are far more Farsi, Amharic, and Arab linguists driving taxicabs in Washington, D.C., than there are in the entire U.S. intelligence community.

These many linguistic and cultural attributes in our society need to be tapped by means of active, rather than passive, recruitment. Anyone who knows how difficult it is for even extremely bright American students to learn either Chinese or Arabic may nevertheless have only a dim awareness of the greater difficulty of understanding the cultures of these languages. The fact that most U.S. college graduates are now virtually lacking in any foreign language competence is widely known. The decay of other essential knowledge in geography and history, for instance, is equally well known. In these respects, higher education, which one might think should automatically reflect the extraordinary cultural pluralism of the country, does precisely the opposite.

It may be true, as some have argued, that recruiting good people might be less of a problem than seeing to it that those recruited can be supplied with good in-house leadership and an environment conducive to high performance, but I doubt it. An overreliance on, say, highly homogeneous, young, inexperienced Caucasians with top records of academic performance coming from good, middle-class families may be the consequence of selection procedures that winnow first for generalized academic excellence and performance and only then seek special competencies.

Serious searches by CIA recruiters must already have impressed them with this difficulty. Still, a friend of mine with a long CIA career hypothesizes that despite the increasing cultural pluralization of the United States in the past forty years, the cadres of U.S. intelligence analysts today may be far more culturally parochial than they were in the 1950s.

The Bureaucratic Organization of Knowledge

A further observation concerning analysis needs to be made. In addition to a demand for operators and analysts who can understand particular cultures, there is now an urgent requirement that analysts be able to recognize interconnections among particularly aggressive covert political forces and movements. Much of the dynamism of the adversarial forces that the United States now confronts arises from purposive interconnections that regional specialists may not recognize or attend to. Covert interdependence is best recognized in Soviet proxy operations, which might be called the Red Orchestra. This can be seen not only in some terrorist operations but also in complex orchestrations of offensive forces that operate and cooperate in many regions of the world, including Central America, Africa, Southeast Asia, and the South Pacific. The nature of cooperation among the Soviet Union; its bloc satellites; proxy forces and movements; states such as Libya, North Korea, and Communist Vietnam; and front organizations presents a complex and not easily understood network of dynamic activities.

A bureaucratic mode, by which knowledge is organized into sections, divisions, and branches and which is hierarchical in nature, may so structure information as to ignore profoundly important interconnections among geographically separated tendencies and events. An understanding of interconnections may require far more than area expertise. What purely Libyan expert, for instance, would understand the interconnections between, say, Colonel Qaddafi and Vanuatu in the South Pacific or between North Korea and East Africa?

Today, the socialist division of labor among bloc states, fronts, and violently anti-American organizations is such that it operates in many theaters, particularly where the United States' principal adversary, the Soviet Union, prefers not to be up front. Journalistic accounts appearing in outstanding foreign newspapers, such as the *Neue Zuercher Zeitung*, about Soviet activities often show greater insight than reports from U.S. intelligence sources. Furthermore, the hierarchical organization of knowledge collection may actually discourage senior superintendents of analysis from actively engaging in the composition of analyses. Perhaps too much analysis is based on information gleaned from combing the files and summarizing available reports rather than on information and judgments gathered by people with a feel for their subject gained through residence, travel, acquaintances, and long-time study.

Intelligence as a Substitute for Force

A conjectural comment must be said about likely general tendencies in world politics in the 1990s. Such conjecturing is always hazardous, but nevertheless necessary. I would guess that, at least in the non-Communist world, the standard postwar blocs will be much less cohesive in the 1990s than they have been since the 1950s. It may very well be that collecting human intelligence (HUMINT) on friends—a delicate and sensitive matter at all times—may be of far more importance than it has been in recent years. A lack of cohesion also might be apparent in the Eastern bloc, but I would guess that NATO might be far less cohesive as a strategic military alliance than the Warsaw Pact. There is also the prospect that if *glasnost* continues, the Soviet Union might be far more porous than it has ever been. Even if it is not, it is probable that means of collection concerning heretofore esoteric problems will be greatly improved. Obviously, this observation would be true of the Soviet bloc as well. Thus, collection tasking in the non-Communist world is likely to increase, while opportunities for improved collection are also likely to increase in the Communist world.

Several years ago, when the Consortium for the Study of Intelligence devoted a session to analysis and estimates, one published paper by Angelo Codevilla titled "Comparative Historical Experience of Doctrine and Organization" contained some thoughts so permanently valid about the mind-set of academically trained Americans that it is necessary to repeat them here, nearly ten years later. Codevilla noted a deeply ingrained trait of empiricism in our culture, and he made some criticisms of it. "Empiricism," he said, "provides the intellectual means for substituting comfortable concepts for uncomfortable ones and for indulging fond illusions." He went on to say that

> [a]nalysts who subscribe to the conventional wisdom of empiricism also tend not to take seriously such nonquantifiable phenomena as love, hate, devotion to God, lust for vengeance, the cruel joy of conquest or political ideology. . . . Its influence may even atrophy a function essential to the survival of any organism—the ability to distinguish between friend and foe.[8]

Contrary to recent observers' pronouncement about the mission of the CIA, its raison d'être is not the substitution of intelligence for force. Force without intelligence is blind, and intelligence without force is impotent. In one respect, intelligence obviously can be force; the power of understanding should guide any type of strategic activity. Active intelligence on some occasions may obviate the use of instruments of violence. This is especially true of that most essential feature of human intelligence—the assessment of an adversary's intention. One of the great triumphs of such intelligence was that of Soviet spy Richard Sorge in Tokyo in 1941. Sorge gained authoritative knowledge of the Japanese strategic decision to strike south into the Pacific rather than north against the Soviet Union. This enabled Stalin to shift Soviet Siberian forces westward to the European theater in order to bolster his troops against a possible German attack.

The accurate assessment of intentions at all times is one of the most challenging and difficult of all intelligence tasks. Properly used in statecraft, it can strategically preempt potentially grave crisis circumstances and allow diplomacy backed by force to deter actions that might otherwise result in war. The assessment of intentions makes possible initiatives and responses designed to change them beneficially. Conversely, intelligence failures of a high order of magnitude may actually lead to disaster.

The seemingly benign description of intelligence as a substitute for force raises a key question as to future self-perceptions within the intelligence community—the very ethos of the profession. Self-delusion aside, it is conceivable that some professionals might actually internalize such a view. To do so would enhance a propensity to distance the community of analysts even farther from enterprises smacking of adventure. In addition, such a self-definition could serve as a pretext for bureaucratic caution and even self-protectiveness: Ours is to know, not to act. For bureaucrats fearful of public leaks and aware of political perils, such an ethos could become an excuse not to get involved.

It is obviously very difficult for an outsider to assess the inner ramifications upon the intelligence community's self-regard of recent press and congressional forays into the executive branch. To what extent have such forays intensified a propensity to caution? And what might be the longer-term consequences of these for inner morale and effectiveness? I regard this as a problem, but as an outsider I cannot assess its full impact.

What will be the reputation of the U.S. intelligence community among foreign intelligence communities in the 1990s? Can U.S. intelligence be trusted by the United States' friends? To a considerable extent, the quality of U.S. analysis has relied on the judgments of seasoned services in friendly countries. As an outside observer watchful of traumatic episodes in Washington, D.C., as veils of secrecy were torn aside, I wonder about the future of such delicate relationships. If confidence is greatly flawed, cooperation among national services might be fatally impaired. Thus, the United States would of necessity fall back on its own resources.

This question of institutional integrity applies with greater force to the future quality of clandestine collection and analysis. George Washington, founder of this country's intelligence service, had this to say about such operations: "For upon Secrecy, Success depends in most Enterprizes of the kind, and for want of it, they are generally defeated, however well planned & promising a favourable issue."[9]

Notes

1. The following hyperbolic observation from John Horton, a senior CIA official contemptuous of unwarranted White House intruders, illustrates

an in-house cultural contrariness toward policymakers: "[A]ttempts to persuade the intelligence community to accept on faith, rather than evidence, doctrinal views of the world are repugnant. . . . [I]f intelligence officers are not jealous of the independence of the intelligence process, who then will stand up for it?" John Horton, "Mexico, the Way of Iran?" *International Journal of Intelligence and Counterintelligence* 1, no. 2 (1986): 91–102.

2. As for imaginary toadstools, Frantisek Moravec, the former head of Czechoslovakia's once excellent spy service under Presidents Masaryk and Benes, tells the following tale in his memoirs. When Benes appointed him to take control of the service in the early 1930s, Moravec recounts, it was almost exclusively obsessed with detection of plots in Vienna to restore Austrian control of Bohemia/Moravia, a *deformation professionelle* that he quickly remedied. The service soon became one of the top spy services in Europe for monitoring German capabilities and plans. Frantisek Moravec, *Master of Spies: The Memoirs of General Moravec* (Garden City, N.Y.: Doubleday, 1975).

3. William Kennedy, "The importance of coping with intelligence," in William Kennedy et al., eds., *The Intelligence War* (London: Salamander Books, 1983), 201.

4. Edward J. Epstein, "Gripping Struggle for Power," *Insight* 3 (26 October 1987): 63.

5. Kennedy, "The world's intelligence organizations," in Kennedy et al., eds., *Intelligence War*, 26.

6. Ibid., 27.

7. A recent book on the linguistics of the espionage profession recounts a strange story from World War II to illustrate the limitless potential of the United States' diverse languages. The U.S. Marine Corps in the Pacific allegedly used Navaho Indians as combat radio operators at Guadalcanal. In their native tongue, they confused Japanese monitors who "presumably thought that the English they had learned at UCLA would suffice for most military purposes." See William Hood, review of *The Dictionary of Espionage*, by Henry Becket, *International Journal of Intelligence and Counterintelligence* 1, no. 2 (1986): 177.

8. Angelo Codevilla, "Comparative Historical Experience of Doctrine and Organization," in Roy Godson, ed., *Intelligence Requirements for the 1980's: Analysis and Estimates* (Washington, D.C.: National Strategy Information Center, 1980), 33.

9. Letter from General George Washington to Colonel Elias Dayton, 26 July 1777, personal collection held by Walter Pforzheimer.

Discussion

Robert Gates

To a substantial degree, this chapter, although addressed to intelligence requirements for analysis in the 1990s, could have applied to intelligence analysis in the 1960s, 1970s, and 1980s.

In examining this chapter, my comments are divided into three categories: first, the relationship between the analyst and the policymaker; second, the analysts' background, recruitment, and training; and third, intelligence requirements.

First, the analyst and the policymaker. Paul Seabury writes that "intelligence should not crave for itself a puristic, aloof independence akin to academic freedom." I could not agree more. I recall during James Schlesinger's brief tenure as director of central intelligence his complaint that the people at the CIA had forgotten they worked for the U.S. government. It seems to me that support for policymakers also means, on a fairly regular basis, telling them things they do not like to hear. In fact, unless intelligence officers are down in the trenches with the policymakers, understand the issues, and know what U.S. objectives are, how the process works, and who the people are, they cannot possibly provide either relevant or timely intelligence that will contribute to better informed decisions.

I have spoken recently of a significant degree of institutional autonomy for the CIA, and Seabury's paper addresses this topic. Autonomy is positive in that intelligence analysis is not subject to the parochial views of one or another policy agency. By the same token, autonomy is negative if it somehow involves being aloof or apart from the policy process and from those who seek intelligence support. I am also very sympathetic to Eliot Cohen's concern over the concept of no-fault intelligence—that is, the idea that all the United States' problems somehow derive from the failure of policymakers or failures inherent in the intelligence issues with which they deal.

I agree with Cohen that in the past inaccurate intelligence analysis either contributed to faulty decisions or allowed policymakers to go on their way without having to deal with at least an alternative perspective. Some of these shortcomings have been due to inadequacies in the way the United States approached the analysis itself as well as the substantive advice of the analysts involved. In recognition of this, significant changes were made in the CIA's Directorate of Intelligence (DDI) concerning both its organization and approach to analysis in the early 1980s.

With respect to background, recruitment, and training, to which both authors devote considerable attention, let me first acknowledge Cohen's point about the large number of relatively new analysts in the CIA and in other intelligence agencies. The fact is that some (probably half) of the analysts in the CIA have on the order of only five to ten years of experience. The exodus of officers from the CIA's clandestine service in the second half of the 1970s has been widely commented on. It is less widely-known that at least as high a percentage of people also left from the analytical side of the house. They did so for three reasons. First, a generation that had come into the CIA in the late 1940s and early 1950s came to the end of their careers. Second, during the late 1970s the government made it financially very attractive for people to retire. Third, and equally important, many people in both directorates—operations and intelligence—found after the travails of the 1970s that the business was no longer very much fun. Therefore, many who could have stayed longer left. New analysts had to be hired to replace those who departed. Additionally, there was significant growth in the size of the analytical directorate. The result of all these factors was a substantial number of relatively new analysts with the attendant loss of experience and institutional memory.

Perhaps I reflect a certain generational difference in saying that there was a good side to this as well. These new people did not carry a lot of baggage from the past, including old fights with other intelligence agencies, did not carry scars from old wars with policymakers, and especially had backgrounds that were in many respects superior to those of the people they replaced in terms of area and language expertise.

Concerning recruitment, Seabury speaks of the overreliance on "highly homogeneous, young, inexperienced Caucasians with top records of academic performance coming from good, middle-class families." I share this concern that U.S. recruitment brings a heavy percentage of these people. In a 1973 article critical of U.S. intelligence work on the Soviet Union, I noted that there is "a wide cultural gap between a college-educated analyst in the West, and the Soviet leadership. The same thing might be said of Iranians, Chinese, and a variety of others."

This cultural gap can be overcome in two ways—first, by looking for people with intensive foreign studies backgrounds and languages who have lived abroad, and second, by looking for people immersed in the culture of a country for a long period. To the extent the United States is unable to hire immigrants from other countries for its own employees, it should look at them for insight in the analysis of other cultures. It seems to me the United States has been deficient in this respect in taking advantage of both émigrés and defectors.

I agree with both authors that the United States needs analysts with language skills, extensive knowledge of history, and significantly greater cultural diversity. I further agree that the cadre of not only U.S. intelligence analysts but also U.S. officials in general is considerably more parochial culturally today than it was in the 1950s. In fact, some of those who helped found the clandestine service probably could not get in the CIA today.

Now, let us look at training. The Cohen essay draws on an article titled "Managing/Teaching New Analysts." He cites the article as saying that "the manager's first task is akin to deprogramming—undoing habits formed in four to ten years of college-level work." Cohen suggests, "The remark about deprogramming reveals a disdain for . . . universities." In Seabury's essay, he observes, "[T]he intelligence community has no raison d'être other than that of furnishing information, reasoned judgments, and estimates on which rational action is possible. In this the intelligence community differs greatly from the ethos of the academy."

It seems to me there are three areas where academic training should contribute to the formation of an intelligence analyst. The first is in making the analyst understand that brevity is critical. Second is the amassing of detail according to a clear line of analysis and drawing clear conclusions. Third is ensuring relevance and timeliness so as to enable action. This is hardly what most graduate programs teach.

I agree that training and education in the interpretation of foreign cultures is critical. Cohen cites Abram Shulsky as saying that "the problem of penetrating another government's workings does not resemble the challenge of unraveling 'a hidden, but ultimately knowable process of nature.' Rather, it is a 'struggle between two human intelligences each of which is trying to outpsych the other. . . .' " I concede that in the past too many intelligence managers placed little value on the idea that people of other cultures have different habits of thought, values, and motivations. These managers apparently rejected the idea that somebody who presumably has an intimate knowledge of cultural differences has any particular usefulness. But that view—and that view did exist to a considerable extent—is largely a thing of the past, or least I hope it is.

Citing again my 1973 article, I said, "The fact remains that our perception of situations is widely divergent from the Kremlin's perception. The Soviet Union has a strange and idiosyncratic policy not to be dealt with without conscious effort." I added,

> An analyst trying to understand the Soviet leaders or their approach to problems is seriously handicapped without a background in Russian history and culture, and the importance of this can hardly be overemphasized. I recommend that intelligence agencies should take steps to insure that future analysts have training in Russian and Soviet history and culture, that analysts without such training should be sent to school to acquire it.

In 1973, I was a fairly lonely voice arguing for this. At that time, I was the only person in my unit in the DDI with an academic background in Soviet studies. My first branch chief was an expert on the Middle East, and the other chief under whom I worked was an expert on Southeast Asia. Because of hiring policies in the last decade, this situation has changed dramatically.

Both essays speak of mirror imaging. I believe it is this lack of regional expertise that contributes significantly to mirror imaging. This problem has diminished in recent years, in part because of the changes in hiring practices and in the number of people who have area expertise and experience. I accept totally Dr. Cohen's emphasis on the importance of intelligence highlighting the otherness of the enemy.

With respect to training and education of analysts in the 1990s, I would like to quote Fritz Ermarth in dividing what the United States does not know into two categories: secrets and mysteries. Secrets are those things that are potentially knowable. Cohen's example is the physics underlying a Soviet barrage attack. Mysteries, again to use Cohen's point of reference, have to do with the interpretation of foreign cultures, with that struggle between two human intelligences each trying to outpsych the other.

In the latter, there are often no clear-cut answers, often because the other leaders themselves do not know what they are going to do or have not worked out their problems. Here our best contribution can be to help the policymaker understand the thought processes involved, the other person's approach to the problem and how it is consistent with his culture, the alternatives that are open to the other culture, and our estimate as to which alternative the other culture is most likely to choose.

We have taken a number of steps to deal with the need described in both essays for varied backgrounds and languages. In an ideal world, every analyst we hired would have specialized background knowledge and one or more foreign languages as a usable tool. In the real world of American education and people who can meet U.S. security qualifications, these two do not necessarily coincide. However, between 40 and 50 percent of all those hired as political analysts do meet these substantive qualifications, and we try to give the others additional education so they can do as well.

For example, over the years we have sent a number of people to Chinese and Russian studies programs to learn both language and history. We also try to educate our analysts to deal with problems not addressed in universities. For example, we have a deception analysis course on the techniques and practices of deception and the methodology for identifying them. For two years we have been teaching a seminar on intelligence successes and failures that uses case studies to illustrate causes of intelligence failures and how to encourage more effective analysis. It is one of our most popular courses. We have added other courses as well in an effort to help improve our understanding of foreign cultures and add ground truth to our analysts' views.

Let me close my discussion of training with several observations, beginning with Dr. Seabury's reference to Angelo Codevilla's paper discussing empiricism in American culture. It seems to me that intelligence analysis must combine an examination of empirical factors with a range of other considerations, including motivation, commitment, determination, history, logic, and motive. In those areas where empirical evidence or intelligence is ambiguous or even absent, there is always the danger of saying that because nobody heard or saw the tree fall, it must not have fallen. If a question arises about whether or not a foreign nation is doing something, and if the information is scanty, analysts must take into account the nation's past behavior, whether it had a motive for such activity, and whether that action would be a logical extension of the motive. I think the United States' experience with terrorism is an example. Thus, there is no question that the United States has to take into account nonempirical considerations.

Analysts must build a case regardless of the nature of the project. They must bring together both empirical data and subjective considerations in describing events that have taken place or policies as they have been developed. Only if analysts establish a presumptive and persuasive base of argumentation—a case, if you will—can they then bring the reader along when they begin to speculate about the future. It seems to me that analysts must persuade policymakers that they, the analysts, know what they are talking about, have mastered the material, and understand the culture with which they are dealing before they have the credibility to forecast the future.

In dealing with the so-called mysteries, analysts have to discuss the alternative ways events may develop. At the same time, the intelligence community owes policymakers a clear-cut best estimate. Analysts are not paid simply to provide an array of alternatives or options. Policymakers want to have some sense of what analysts think will happen. Analysts need to be honest with policymakers concerning the quality of their evidence and the degree of confidence they have in their judgments.

Today, a high priority is being attached to hiring analysts who have lived abroad and have area expertise and knowledge of foreign languages. We also are attaching a high priority to developing extensive contacts with experts in the academic community and think tanks in order to have people challenge the analysts' views and bring other information and perspectives to bear on problems. As for problems of deception and denial, thanks in substantial measure to the efforts of Senator Wallop and Angelo Codevilla, they have become a growing part of our analyst training curriculum. These and all other changes I have been speaking about proceed at different paces, but substantial progress has been made. We have to keep the pressure on to keep these changes going.

Finally, because both authors focus primarily on training—that is, the need for analysts to be familiar with foreign, and shall we say alien, cultures—there is very little focus in either essay on substantive requirements. Let me address what they do say and make a few observations of my own.

Paul Seabury focuses on the need for analysts who can see connections between widely separated trends and events. One of the disadvantages of a regional organization for analysis is that it tends to make the interconnection of such events more difficult. It was in recognition of this that we created several organizations to try to bridge these regional patterns. We created an insurgency center, an organization designed to track patterns of subversion, particularly of Soviet, Cuban, and Libyan involvement in insurgencies around the world. We have tried to establish some connections that will enable us to address these transregional phenomena.

One of the more important assets we have in connection with this is with academics and think tanks. The people in these pursuits can often give us the macro analysis that at least points us in the right direction or suggests the right questions to ask.

I think Dr. Cohen has put his finger on a larger issue with respect to requirements for the 1990s. He writes, "[H]enceforth the United States will no longer have the luxury of concentrating its intelligence assets overwhelmingly on its chief target, the Soviet Union." He then points to a number of other problems that are certain to become significant intelligence challenges. I not only agree, I believe that this trend began several years ago, and now only about 50 percent of the assets of the intelligence community are focused on the Soviet problem.

My principal worry for the 1990s is that the absence of intelligence guidance and priorities from the senior levels of the policy community will result in a continued diffusion of efforts as U.S. intelligence is pushed in the direction of satisfying an increasingly wide range of problems. In anticipation of the 1990s, the intelligence community itself is going to be forced to reexamine its priorities and at some point inform the policy community and Congress that it can no longer carry out an open-ended program of collection and analysis on every conceivable subject of interest to the U.S. government.

Beginning with the Soviet Union, the United States is going to have to identify the hard-core issues on which it will devote all the necessary resources to resolving the problem satisfactorily, knowing in advance that this choosing will withdraw an intelligence effort from areas that are peripheral to national security concerns but have influential bureaucratic and congressional constituencies. Identifying those areas other than the Soviet Union will be a difficult and painful task.

Although I am a strong supporter of the idea of specialized area training and having analysts who have not only lived in a foreign country but also have studied its language and culture and are steeped in its history, I must say that regional experts are often less competent in forecasting discontinuities. It is often forgotten that the CIA's analyst on Iran in the 1970s had worked on Iran for twenty years. That, in my view, was part of the problem. Although a deep understanding of a country's politics and history will help in understanding its actions and reactions, the fact is that in most countries actions are part of long, continuous chains of events. Thus, those most familiar with these long, slow processes are those who will find reasons to say that the warning signs of instability have occurred before, fit into a historical pattern, and therefore can be dismissed. Maybe they are right, and maybe they are not. For this reason, there must be a combination of people with area expertise and those who fly broadly, who ask hard and sometimes even simple questions. Also needed are those who have unorthodox views and challenge the conventional wisdom.

Dr. Cohen speaks of short-term analysis rather that long-term research. This was a significant problem until a few years ago. With the personnel drawdown in the 1970s, the CIA was forced to abandon its long-range research on Soviet defense industries and also on the Third World. The mail of the day always had to be answered. One of the principal benefits of the significant resources provided by both the administration and the Congress during the 1980s has been to allow the establishment of a significant foundation for a long-term research program in which the resources for carrying out these projects are protected. The analytical directorate of the CIA has been able to produce five hundred to seven hundred new billets for this purpose. Thus, this long-standing problem has been largely brought under control. Most analysts now understand that an inability to produce longer-range research could have a deleterious effect on their careers.

Finally, I would like to say that Robert Butterworth's paper on collection notes that collection and analysis are inseparable and that intelligence errs in making the division between them great, both bureaucratically and in other ways. In the abstract, I endorse this. But I would also say that in reality, from the management standpoint, it is difficult to avoid this division. Rather it is important to have many bridges connecting these two intimately related subjects.

Andrew Marshall

Both essays address basic issues regarding analysis and discuss how current analytical problems might change or be improved in the future. I would like to reinforce the view expressed by both Eliot Cohen and Paul Seabury that the next ten to twenty years are going to see major changes in world affairs. Some recent projections indicate that by 2010 the Soviet Union probably will have, at most, only the fourth largest gross national product (GNP) in the world. China and Japan will probably rise to be important powers. What China and Japan do with their industrial base and wealth is a key issue and will depend on factors about which the United States knows little—their strategic cultures and future resource allocation decisions. For example, Chinese military traditions and ways of thinking are very different from the United States'. For that reason alone, the intelligence community will have its work cut out for it as it tries to foresee likely evolutions of future Chinese military forces and operational concepts.

There is likely to be a world of three, four, or five major actors instead of only two major ones. Coalitions and interactions of these major players will create a more complex political-military world. Military technology and production of weapons will probably spread to a still greater number of countries. Further, a new wave of military technology will become available in the next twenty years, and some of the major powers may open up a gap relative to the others. These and other changes will require that major adjustments be made in U.S. intelligence analytic capabilities.

I share the view that the training of analysts has not received the attention it should have. Perhaps some experiments in the selection and training of beginning-level analysts would be useful. Why not select a group of well-recognized, outstanding analysts and study how they got that way and their characteristics or history. How do they differ from the average analyst? Perhaps these paradigms of success will help the United States discover and train other potentially superior analysts. Perhaps that will not work, but I believe that the United States needs to try some novel approaches.

One of the reasons I feel so strongly about the need for better analysts is, as I mentioned above, that I believe the analytic problem is likely to become more difficult. In intelligence, the data are often partial. In the future, perhaps even more than in the past, the United States is not going to have all the data it would like to have. That means that the analyst's knowledge and the general way in which he or she structures and thinks about things is very important. That is where the United States needs to focus its attention: Specifically, how career patterns, training, and selection can make it more likely that analysts will have the appropriate knowledge and intellectual frameworks to apply. This ought to drive the training and selection of analysts.

I also support the notion of trying to exploit other sources of analysis more widely, particularly articles appearing in the top newspapers in other parts of the world. Some years ago, when I was working on the NSC staff for Henry Kissinger, we conducted an assessment of the quality of the political and economic intelligence on a particular country. We used a panel of outside experts to compare the analysis of the intelligence community with the best writings in some of the leading German and Swiss newspapers that covered this country. A very convincing case was made that the analysis in the newspapers was better than that of the U.S. intelligence community. The intelligence agencies ought to have their people read such newspapers much more regularly and circulate them to the policymakers along with their analyses. This is especially true in the fields of business and economics. A great deal of information also is available from U.S. and foreign banks and other organizations whose interests are directly involved.

One of the things I most liked about Paul Seabury's essay was his concern about the parallel often drawn between academic research and the intelligence community. For one thing, the intelligence community is faced with real situations posing basic questions that cannot be ducked or that require judgments that cannot be put off until more data or new methods of analysis are available. A large part of academic research strategy is to avoid central issues until there is more promise of success and instead to focus on aspects where progress is possible. The intelligence community analyst cannot do this. Problems and schedules are set by the governmental processes these analysts serve. The intelligence community cannot say "it's too hard"—some estimate or judgment must be made. The analysts have to transform the question into something that can be answered intelligently. Otherwise, they might have to tell policymakers that they are going to have to fly by the seat of their pants.

I also agree that the United States is going to need regional specialists. But how can it find good ones? Many regional specialists become intellectually and emotionally co-opted by the countries they study, not just in the sense that they come to like the country and its culture. Some even seek to explain the country and its actions so as to gain understanding and support in the United States. Sometimes this affects what regional specialists write in their papers and say at public meetings. How to get knowledgeable but unbiased information and analysis can be a problem.

I was intrigued by Paul Seabury's conjecture about the decline of the Mossad. I have no idea whether the Mossad has declined or not, but it struck me that we should take into account the bureaucratization of intelligence organizations. Organizations seem to have life cycles. They begin young, energetic, and dedicated to one purpose or another. As they get older, they transmute into somewhat different organizations. What do you do about that? How do you get renewal and change in long-lived organizations?

Having been connected in one way or another with the CIA since the early 1950s, certainly through the mid-1970s, I have the sense that the intelligence analysis element and the whole of the CIA of the 1950s was very different than it is now. In the 1950s, the people in the CIA were quite active in trying to get outside people to help them in various ways. By the middle and late 1960s, they began to turn inward. Since then, they have again been opening up, which I feel is very positive.

It seems very important that intelligence organizations be as open as they can be—given the very real problems they have in doing so—to draw on the wider base of information and talent available in the

United States. Back in the early 1970s, one of the attitudes was "This is the best that we the people in the community can do." When I lectured occasionally at the CIA's mid-career training seminars, I used to tell the participants that that was the wrong objective. The objective is to determine the best this country can do.

Let me close by saying that one needs to be somewhat wary of many of the propositions put forth about the interface between intelligence analysis and policymakers. Most of this analysis proceeds from a far too simplified view of what actually goes on—that is, there is a tendency to draw on, or think of, the flow of information in terms of overly simplified organizational diagrams. The route by which information flows within or between organizations is not represented well in the usual diagrams. Most of these diagrams, for example, tend to leave out both personal networks and the staffs that support the top-level people. In some cases, staffs can be a barrier to the flow of information, and in many cases, they do analyses of their own. The real flow of information is usually far more complex and varies with the rotation and change of personnel.

Much of the discussion, particularly in academia, tends to proceed with a model in which people at the bottom of the organization have contact with the external world. The leaders are informed through the various layers of organization. I do not think that is the way it is in reality. The leaders of major nations have many other connections to the world than that model would suggest.

Another thing I find striking is that academic studies seem almost automatically to take the side of the analysts rather than the policymakers. Perhaps academics identify with the analysts rather than the policymakers. Perhaps American graduate students are trained in ways that are designed to make them good analysts and good staff members. Or perhaps they identify more with the staffs than with the policymakers.

General Discussion

The discussion at the colloquium focused on the types of analytical products the United States will need in the 1990s and the procedures and methods needed to produce this analysis. On the whole, the participants were highly critical of the quality of U.S. political and military analysis in the 1980s.

There was general agreement that ways must be found to make intelligence more responsive to policymakers' concerns. One suggested solution, which generated a good deal of discussion, was the call for more activism in intelligence analysis. An academic argued that analysis should be designed to advance policy. Hence, analysts should seek information to undergird political enterprises and accomplish specific tasks. A senior intelligence officer concurred, noting that policymakers often call for more opportunity-oriented intelligence—analysis designed to advance perceived U.S. foreign policy (i.e., vulnerabilities of foreign leaders, parties, or movements that policymakers want to affect). A participant cited a successful example of this in which the issue of technology transfer was forcefully brought to the attention of the policy community.

Another academic noted the reluctance of analysts to engage in this type of analysis for fear of getting involved in policymaking. A memo that addresses opportunities for U.S. policy might look like a policy option paper, which is not supposed to be produced by intelligence analysts. A number of participants felt that this problem would become particularly acute in the aftermath of the Iran-Contra affair. A congressional staffer thought that for the next few years analysts would tend to focus on safe, uncontroversial questions.

In discussing the training of future analysts, an academic argued that universities cannot turn out fully trained analysts because they do not normally deal with the specific subjects that secret intelligence must confront, such as deception. Thus, the intelligence community has no choice but to do its own in-house training.

Another academic raised the question of matching the selection and training of analysts to the kinds of topics they are most likely to have to deal with in the 1990s. He argued that for analysts to do a good job, they must have personal experience in the substantive field. If the field is deception, the analyst must have worked at deceiving or at seeing through deception. In military matters, the analyst must somehow be sensitive to the actual possibilities of military operations. Further, this academic contended that some of the topics that were intellectually most exciting in the 1970s (for example, whether the Soviet Union will abide by arms control treaties) will be settled by the 1990s, while topics that will be of great importance in the 1990s (such as the performance of Soviet strategic defenses and Soviet deception) are not currently "hot" and therefore are not receiving adequate attention.

A State Department official questioned whether analysts should be trained as generalists or specialists. An academic argued for having some who can do both. A senior intelligence official agreed, contending that this was necessary to solve "transregional problems," where an event in one part of the world (for example, a terrorist incident in the South Pacific) is linked to another region (such as the Middle East). He cautioned, however, that this approach can create bureaucratic problems. He explained that regional specialists are sometimes horrified when a generalist, focusing on a particular problem, dares to presume to know something about a particular region.

There was also a great deal of discussion about improving the relationship among collector, analyst, and policymaker. A senior intelligence official stated that today—and presumably even more so in the 1990s—the kinds of questions that policymakers often ask cannot be answered by machines or with facts. Policymakers take for granted that they will know Soviet capabilities, but what they want to know is what the Soviets will do in this or that field and why. It has never been easy to give such answers. Given the nature of the fields that will be of the greatest interest in the 1990s, this job will be even more difficult.

An academic suggested that the intelligence community should restrict the number of issues with which it must deal in order to do a better job. An intelligence official replied that because intelligence products are a free good to the executive branch, and increasingly to Congress as well, the intelligence community has come to be regarded somewhat as the Library of Congress. The CIA, then, is more often doing analyses that once would have been done by other government departments, such as the Commerce or Treasury Department. Properly, top officials should manage who in the government does what for whom. This person concluded that it is, to say the least, difficult to get top policymakers to set intelligence policy.

A former White House official strongly agreed. He noted that it had been nearly impossible to get senior White House officials to focus on what their intelligence needs were and on how they should be met. At times, policymakers even wanted information they were unable to identify. Although they were often impatient when they did not get satisfactory answers, they were unwilling to do the work necessary to ask the appropriate questions.

A conferee wondered whether the problem with analysis is excess information. An intelligence official disagreed. He felt that the problem is not excess information but rather insufficient breadth of understanding. He added that this problem is especially acute in U.S. intelligence because the relevant information on any given topic is divided into a number of security compartments. Few people, all of whom are too busy to take advantage of the privilege, are privy to all the information in the compartments. Hence, chances are not good that any U.S. intelligence analyst will have all the available information to deal with a key topic. Pearl Harbor was given as an example. The information necessary to realize when and where the attack was coming was available, but it was not put together.

There was general agreement that analysts in the future, as in the past, owe policymakers a full account of the factual and logical bases on which they draw their conclusions so that policymakers can judge the limitations of the information they receive. A senior intelligence official noted that at times analysts have presented as evidence their own assertions. To correct this problem in the early 1980s, generic indicators were developed to give policymakers a sense of the access and quality of the source. Since 1984, however, the number of leaks and the resulting fear of compromising a source have resulted in enormous pressure inside the intelligence community to back away from this identification system.

A further problem noted by a participant is that as technical collection systems become more and more complicated, it becomes harder for the analyst and the system operator to understand the other's world. Thus, more people are needed to turn the analyst's requirements into a form that a machine can handle. The result is that the analyst's questions sometimes are not answered fully or properly.

Finally, an academic asked how intelligence producers can properly support policies if they are either nonexistent or self-contradictory. All the coordination in the world will not make up for incoherence at the top. Several participants maintained that the trouble with the analyst-policymaker relationship seems to be that neither one levels with the other. Intelligence producers do not want to say how little they really know, while policymakers do not want to say how indefinite their own policy plans are.

4
Counterintelligence

Essays:

I. George Kalaris and Leonard McCoy
II. Merrill Kelly

Discussion:

I. Kenneth deGraffenreid
II. James Geer

I. GEORGE KALARIS AND LEONARD MCCOY

As we contemplate the postulated counterintelligence (CI) challenge of the 1990s and seek a CI structure and posture appropriate to that challenge, our outlook is inevitably conditioned by the discovery in the past several years of a devastating series of CI setbacks. To our knowledge, the United States' most sensitive intelligence agencies were penetrated seriously for the first time. Further, the United States suffered damage in the strategic national defense area, which has been professionally categorized as "threatening the very heart and existence of our freedom" in one case and, in another, of "jeopardizing the backbone of this country's national defense" in a manner that involves potentially "altering the course of history."[1] Costs of these compromises are estimated in the billions of dollars. Certainly there is a basis in these recent cases for forming a perception that the United States' national CI program has failed to carry out its mission in the 1980s.

Even though the quality of performance by the components of the government charged with CI responsibilities has improved substantially over the past decade, that has still not prevented severe damage from being inflicted on U.S. interests by hostile intelligence services. The whole CI system has proved to be inferior to the excellence of its component parts. With the intensified activities of hostile intelligence services against the United States that can be expected in the 1990s, the present structure of the CI community, which can be judged as having been inadequate to meet the threat in the 1970s and 1980s, will find itself overwhelmed.

Thinking in the late 1970s and early 1980s about the needs, direction, and requirements appropriate to the U.S. counterintelligence effort in the 1980s was for all practical purposes a straight-line projection of what was then in hand. All that was advocated was more of the same. Even before the mid-1980s, however, that thinking proved to be totally inadequate to the challenge faced. Therefore, we propose a radical change in the structure of the U.S. counterintelligence community (which should be debated by the community and its supporting infrastructure in government and the private sector) in order to effect changes in CI posture that will dramatically improve the U.S. counterintelligence capacity for the 1990s.

The Challenge of the 1990s

U.S. counterintelligence concentrates primarily, and appropriately, on the United States' major adversary, the Soviet Union. As witnessed in the 1980s, increased emphasis must also be placed on countering the intelligence services of the Eastern European countries, which have been acting on behalf of the Soviets or in their own countries' interests. These and other Communist intelligence services have scored major successes against the United States and its closest allies.

In the 1990s, the United States can expect to see even more such operations. These will be spurred on by the United States' opponents' success to date and by Soviet pressure for increased effort, especially in the acquisition of technology. Beyond the numerous intelligence services of the Soviet Union and the Warsaw Pact countries, we also project increased intelligence collection efforts against the United States on the part of Asian Communist countries and Cuba.

In addition to this increasing threat from Communist countries, the United States must expect to have to counter intelligence operations by a growing number of "criteria" and underdeveloped countries. Further, the United States will have to deal with operations conducted by friendly countries that are not satisfied with particular aspects of U.S. policy or believe that the most direct way to obtain information satisfying their own intelligence requirements is by penetrating U.S. intelligence agencies. Operations in these areas have been discovered in the 1980s and should be looked upon as examples of what the United States can expect in the 1990s.

Most such activities will be in the classical human source recruitment category. However, some of the countries most likely to be involved also have substantial technical intelligence collection capabilities. In several cases, the United States will find itself cooperating in intelligence and counterintelligence matters with these countries, while at the same time they will be operating against the United States (and the United States against them).

The United States' most crucial need in the 1990s will be a greatly increased unilateral human CI capability overseas. During the 1990s, the Soviet intelligence services are going to be forced by circumstances such as increased FBI capabilities and enhanced public awareness of espionage through the media—be it fact or fiction—to concentrate their recruitment activities against the American target outside the United States. An increasing burden, therefore, will be placed on those U.S. intelligence organizations charged with espionage and counterespionage responsibilities abroad. The United States also will need an increased ability to detect and counter technical intelligence collection by opposition services.

Definition

By the early 1970s, the definition of counterintelligence crafted in the mid-1950s had outlived its relevance to the realities confronting the intelligence community. By the late 1970s, that definition had literally fenced in the efforts that had to be made to counter the multifaceted threat directed against U.S. security interests. It had reduced counterintelligence essentially to a passive discipline concerned primarily with locking up the barn door after the horses had been stolen.

Finally, in the late 1970s, the United States officially recognized that the threat to its security was not limited exclusively to the human element. It became quite clear that collection against the United States by Soviet agencies using technical means was substantially greater and more significant than U.S. officials had generally believed. The Soviets were able to use their knowledge of U.S. technical collection capabilities to lessen their own exposure to them. Hence, the United States' understanding of operational security changed and heightened. In the 1980s, some U.S. intelligence organizations revised their CI components to analyze and contend with this multifaceted threat.

Fundamentally, counterintelligence for the 1990s should be defined as that discipline of the intelligence sphere that is concerned with the actions of foreign intelligence services and organizations, friendly or not, that employ human and technical means to gather information about the United States and that adversely affect U.S. national interests and goals. It naturally includes actions by U.S. counterintelligence agencies to negate such activities. Thus, counterintelligence includes, as component disciplines, counterespionage, counter–signals intelligence (SIGINT), counterimagery, and so on. Above all, it includes analysis of foreign behavior from the standpoint of counterintelligence. The instrumentality used by the foreign entity against the United States is what determines U.S. actions to counter the effort.

The substance of counterintelligence does not change with time, but its emphasis must inevitably shift to meet the nature of the attack on U.S. national security. Before we reach the 1990s, it is imperative that the U.S. counterintelligence community accept the concept of a multidisciplinary threat and the need for a multidisciplinary response. If counterintelligence remains limited to what is, in effect, only counterespionage, the United States will lose the intelligence and counterintelligence battle that is so vital to the national security program. In the 1990s, the CI threat must be redefined as the composite human and technical threat that it is, and appropriate cross-disciplinary countermeasures must be developed to defeat and exploit this threat.

Technology transfer and state-sponsored terrorism are not likely to abate. However, to the extent that these threats are susceptible to countermeasures, the foreign policy, security, and police mechanisms of the government will contribute the lion's share of countermeasures and defensive operations. Actions taken to identify, monitor, control, and neutralize foreign intelligence operatives will continue to constitute the major CI contribution to frustrating threats to U.S. national security by hostile services. As in counterespionage, one of the more significant sources of information on such hostile activities will continue to be the penetration of these hostile services.

Under our definition, personnel security of those elements of the U.S. government and its contractual components that are involved in activities that affect national security interests also falls within the purview of counterespionage as a discipline. The vetting of new employees, as well as those in more advanced stages of their careers in national security work, including contractor personnel, is a counterespionage responsibility. Our definition would also include the foreign manufacturer, under licensing, of classified U.S. defense equipment.

The Status Quo

The present CI response to the generally recognized multifaceted threat is fragmented, with each CI component (other than the FBI) focusing primarily on the threat to its own parent organization, component, or program. We are not suggesting that this is in itself improper. We are suggesting, however, that fragmentation and departmentally oriented efforts do not constitute in their sum an effective national CI program. This approach considerably impedes the formulation and execution of a national program, the development of universal guidelines, and the establishment of homogeneous national CI objectives. A more integrated approach is imperative for the 1990s.

The FBI counterintelligence program continues to expand and improve. It needs only to reevaluate its CI capabilities under the increased multidisciplinary concept for the 1990s. The FBI's involvement in Defense Department CI/industrial security operations and programs is the most important step necessary in the overall enhancement of the domestic CI program.

With primary responsibility for counterintelligence overseas, the CIA has the greatest challenge for the 1990s. Pressure for enhanced CIA capabilities abroad has reached irresistible proportions in the wake of revelations of repeated agent meetings overseas in all of the extremely damaging cases of the year (plus) of the spy. This effort will be crippled without the full integration of FBI, DoD, and CIA efforts, however.

It will not be sufficient for the CIA simply to monitor the Soviets overseas or for the FBI to do so in the United States. Both must have extensive knowledge of the primary Soviet target—the U.S. defense complex. Further, the CIA and the FBI must actively participate in DoD counterintelligence and security programs set up to identify, neutralize, and exploit opposition penetration efforts directed against the defense complex.

It is true that the greatest damage to national security has been in areas for which the DoD is responsible—that is, national defense— as this is the target of the United States' major opposition. All CI resources must be brought to bear in this area. The departmental and geographic CI boundaries that the United States has established are not honored by the primary opposition services, which use them to defeat us. Opposition services recruit in one area and run the case in another. Further, they move agents and operations officers about the map at will. This engenders among U.S. counterintelligence agencies a cumbersome, lumbering coordination process that seldom catches up with opposition actions. This bureaucratic weakness was cited in a recent legislative review as having caused a crippling delay in introduction of the FBI into a major espionage case.[2] The United States must eliminate the opposition's advantage in this area by bringing its three primary CI bodies together at the sources of its vulnerability.

New Look Overseas

The security of U.S. intelligence operations abroad, be they collection, covert action, or counterintelligence, is the paramount CI responsibility. These operations are the principal targets of hostile intelligence and security agencies. The goal of these agencies is to discover, compromise, expose, penetrate, neutralize, and deceive U.S. operations. The United States' goal is to protect them.

The critical need of counterintelligence today is to prepare both operations and CI officers for the challenge they face by providing intensive training and familiarization with the modus operandi of foreign intelligence services, whether they be friendly or not. New personnel configurations must be developed in overseas installations that take into account the shift in emphasis that the Soviets will place on their activities against the United States. The recruitment of Soviet intelligence officers should remain high on the priority list at each foreign-based U.S. intelligence installation. Further, the ability of U.S. intelligence organizations to monitor the activities of Soviet intelligence officers, whether they represent a recruitment target or not, must be substantially increased.

Tokyo, Vienna, Paris, and Mexico City are today, and are likely to remain in the 1990s, the favorite agent meeting places and walk-in locales of the Soviet intelligence services. Accordingly, U.S. coverage of Soviet activities in those cities, as well as in others that might be added as U.S. efforts are detected by the Soviets, must be substantially increased.

Technical Licensing

Extensive DoD licensing of foreign companies to manufacture U.S. weapons systems and technology has added another dimension to the CI problem overseas. The United States' unilateral CI capability overseas must be prepared to counter hostile collection action against these exposed targets. The United States also must develop effective local liaison relationships that will assist in protecting these weapon systems and technology from hostile intelligence collection.

Personnel

Staffing

A separate career track for CI analysts must be established for the 1990s as the core of the new CI component. Entry into the track must be competitive, requiring at a minimum four years of successful operational experience in the recruitment and handling of agents. To ask a CI analyst with no direct operational experience to analyze and judge developments in any agent case is tantamount to asking a premed student to diagnose gastrointestinal anomalies. Unless the analyst has experience in handling agents, he really has no sound basis for evaluating behavior and spotting discrepancies.

Sophisticated countermeasures will have to be developed, springing in large part from the United States' own development of technical collection systems. This threat will dictate CI recruitment of technically qualified officers who can keep counterintelligence abreast of technical developments and conceive defensive and counter operations to neutralize the threat.

The CI component of any intelligence organization cannot be the depository for has-beens. The component must command respect not only because of where it is placed on the organizational chart but also because of the quality of its officers and their individual records of achievement in the more traditional facets of the intelligence business.

Training

Regardless of whatever other training is given prospective operations officers in preparation for the 1990s, the curriculum must include heavy exposure to CI information. We believe that a minimum of fifty hours of appropriate training would be adequate. No intelligence officer should be allowed to venture into operations at home or abroad without a solid understanding and appreciation of the capabilities of the United States' principal adversaries. Doing otherwise is the equivalent of casting an innocent lamb into a wolf-infested forest: the officer's chances of coming out whole are slight.

The ultimate objective in exposing all prospective operations officers to intensive CI training is not to produce fifty-hour CI wonders but, rather, to ensure that all operations officers of the 1990s will be acutely aware of the lessons learned in the past sixty-five years as a result of encounters with hostile intelligence agencies. Unless the first echelon of defense—the operations officer—is aware of the possibility for fabrication, deception, and disinformation, the early warning signs of a bad case may be completely overlooked, misunderstood, and not reported.

The Ultimate Need for the 1990s

Responsibility for the establishment of a national CI policy, allocation of tasks to the various CI organizations, monitoring of progress, and resolution of interagency conflicts must be lodged in some entity or person. Continuation of the piecemeal and parochial approach to counterintelligence can be expected only to perpetuate the great national security damage that the United States has suffered to date.

Existing interagency coordination procedures, NSC interagency committees, and excellent personal relationships among the heads of the CI components have not and cannot produce and implement a national policy with teeth in it. It also cannot ensure that maximum effort will be applied to a particular national CI objective.

The present structure of U.S. counterintelligence is inadequate to fulfill the tasks posed by the CI challenge of the 1990s. A centralized authority is required that will be capable of, and responsible for, mobilizing all U.S. counterintelligence agencies and capabilities against the common foreign intelligence and security threats. Wherever this authority is placed, a newly constituted DoD counterintelligence office that is directly and vigorously involved in national CI management of service CI and security agencies should play a big role.

Counterintelligence must be raised to a level of authority that gives it command and operational responsibility across the entire intelligence community as well as throughout the CIA itself. The position of deputy director for counterintelligence—on a par with the deputy director for intelligence and the deputy director for operations—may well be too low for the holder to have such authority. Although such a position might be created temporarily until staffing and organizational complications are resolved, it will eventually be necessary for the CI responsibility to be placed in a deputy director of central intelligence for counterintelligence (DDCI/CI). Only then will the full integration of all interagency CI capabilities become feasible.

A number of the functions of other CIA components will have to be assigned to the DDCI/CI. This includes those elements concerned with personnel security, communications security, domestic intelligence elements working on strategic deception, and elements responsible for defensive measures against hostile technological attack. The DDCI/CI also must be acutely aware of the existence of the potential for the United States' adversaries to engage in strategic deception.

The intelligence and counterintelligence operations of all federal agencies must be subject to review, coordination, and operational direction for national purposes by a central CI authority. For example, if the FBI and army are jointly running a case with foreign and domestic ramifications, this case must be subject to coordination with the intelligence and counterintelligence activities being conducted in the same geographic, foreign, and substantive areas. The DDCI/CI would have to be placed in the chain of command for oversight of all operational matters concerned with CI and have responsibility for a portion of the performance evaluation and reassignment of all senior CIA officers.

One of the first tasks of this new CI leadership of the 1990s should be to define its area of responsibility—specifically, the elements of counterintelligence that are to be the focus of the CI community. This task is not the domain of lawyers, academicians, or dilettantes. It is the prime responsibility of those who have practiced the craft. No one understands the nature of this art better than they do.

Notes

1. U.S. Congress, Senate Select Committee on Intelligence, *Meeting the Espionage Challenge: A Review of U.S. Counterintelligence and Security Programs,* 99th Cong., 2nd sess., 1986, S-Rpt. 99-522.
2. Ibid.

II. MERRILL KELLY

The 1990s are just around the calendar corner. One could argue that most of the 1990s could be called "near term" as an estimate period and, thereby, see formulating CI requirements as a relatively easier projections problem. This is not so. Those who have participated in the intelligence estimates and national security planning process know that in many functional areas, the shadows can be awfully deep and the ground quite shaky under intellectual feet.

This essay is concerned with two particular aspects of the projection. First, I will examine the relationship between CI activities and defensive security programs—information, personnel, physical, industrial, communications, automation, material, security education, and all the subdisciplines of these programs. Second, I will identify key questions for CI planning in the 1990s. For many, even those in the CI trade, defensive security issues are somewhat boring, complicating, and generally undesirable. With limited exceptions, these issues are not romantic, dramatic, or loaded with the mystique of the intelligence professional. I believe, however, that the United States' national CI program is, and should continue to be, a servant of the defensive security programs.

Counterintelligence and Defensive Security

There would be no significant need for a separate discipline called counterintelligence if it were not necessary to support the defensive security function with offensive CI activities. Some of the components of counterintelligence would still be needed as elements of positive collection and analysis. But in that case, counterintelligence would be only a supporting element of estimates and threat intelligence. It would lose its own function as a direct counter to enemy activities. This emphasis on the defensive security support orientation of counterintelligence might sound like counting angels on the head of a doctrinal pin, especially to the operationally oriented intelligence planner. But for the purpose of planning national CI programs for the 1990s, the defensive security support requirements should be the dominant consideration.

An unclassified environment is not appropriate for a detailed national CI estimate projected through the 1990s. In my judgment, the United States already gives hostile intelligence collectors and CI services entirely too much free help for their plans and operations. We do this as a necessary side effect of the way we want to live our own political and economic lives and because we are not willing to pay either the tangible or intangible costs of giving hostile intelligence collectors less help. However, an unclassified discussion of the details of the most likely U.S. counterintelligence threat and defensive security requirements is not necessary to define the broader policy and program requirements. A general discussion based largely on open information and logic will suffice for our purposes here.

Threats and Vulnerabilities

What kinds of intelligence threats and defensive security requirements will the United States likely face through the 1990s? Will the United

States continue to face serious and continuing conflicts of interest with foreign powers or groups, requiring the country to have secrets (classified information) that themselves represent important elements of power or capability? Are there likely to be hostile governments or groups in significant scope and intensity whose goals and activities will ultimately damage the welfare of the people of the United States and who will try to penetrate the defensive security systems and acquire those secrets for their own advantage? Is the country likely to continue its international military and political alliances, with extensive overseas military commitments, through most of the 1990s, in much the same posture as it does now?

Barring the advent of an international utopia—a condition not generally accepted as highly probable by most reputable pundits and soothsayers—the answer to the foregoing questions is a clear yes. There are no indications that hostile governments are reducing their efforts to collect national security information about the United States.

Information about some of the high-tech sensor collection systems as well as the human intelligence (HUMINT) collectors that quickly come to mind are available to numerous foreign elements with long-term collection requirements about specific U.S. secrets—especially in the research and development, diplomatic planning (intentions), and military plans areas. In an international environment of political fragmentation and restructuring, small powers also will have their own collection interests in these areas. U.S. illegal alien, amnesty, and naturalization programs present hostile HUMINT collectors with an irresistible opportunity to insert or recruit agents. Predicted increases in the international flow of automated information, the continued internationalization of business and capital management, and the probable expansion of both international travel and communications to and from the United States also will contribute to the problem.

There is hardly any reason to foresee the development of a consensus for significant constraints on the free flow of large amounts of information on national security matters. Most indicators point strongly in the other direction. Only in narrow areas of interest, such as protecting the identities of U.S. foreign intelligence agents, highly critical military technology, and specific strategic or tactical military operations plans, is there a willingness to enact and enforce constraints. Recent national incidents have produced a new round of attacks on secrecy in government and strong public, confrontational debate about the role of secrecy and compartmentation in security sensitive government operations.

Current Situation

In historical perspective, the U.S. counterintelligence program has seen significant refinement and improvement during the past ten to fifteen years. Doctrinally, both in and out of the government, there is general acceptance that counterintelligence is a highly specialized subdiscipline of the intelligence and security programs of the government that warrants specialized subprograms, policies, management, and personnel within the overall system. There is solid public support and legislative consensus for the foreign counterintelligence and counterespionage subelements of the program.

Organizationally, the president and the National Security Council (NSC), with general congressional support and urging, have begun to put in place national CI policies, program staffs, and procedures. This is being done to maintain an appropriate level of emphasis and coordinated and disciplined interagency management of resources and operations for CI functions. The support responsibility of the various national CI organizations to the defensive security programs (especially classified military programs) is clearly recognized. A sophisticated concept of multidisciplinary CI threat analysis for decision makers, weapons developers, operational military commanders, and foreign intelligence collectors is a part of the national system. In terms of resources, until recently the trend (in both quantity and quality) has generally been quite favorable to the CI discipline.

In some agencies, development of a cadre of truly professional CI careerists has been a problem. As a discipline, CI requires a lot of skilled and experienced people. New budget constraints will probably affect the number of people in this area. As in numerous other national security fields, the use of advanced technology for foreign intelligence collection increases the demand for U.S. counterintelligence personnel with both a social science and technical education. This is not a new situation, but the problem will continue to grow.

Through the 1990s the U.S. counterintelligence system will have to continue to deal with the doctrinal, philosophical irrationality of the way in which the United States goes about protecting information.

Many such conflicts are at work in the national system. For example, an executive branch agency might classify a specific piece of information. A number of years later, a political or economic issue will arise in the executive branch or Congress calling for the unclassified handling of that information. In most cases, the political interest will probably prevail, even if the reason the information was originally classified has not changed. In another area, U.S. industry wishes to sell high-tech hardware to numerous foreign customers. The government, however, does not always want to help improve the military capabilities of some of these countries. Once again, there will be pressure on the government to back down on classified versus unclassified decisions.

Management logic indicates that the volume and nature of the information the country should protect—that is, keep out of the hands of those who could use that information to damage the welfare of the people of the United States—should have significant bearing on the extent and nature of the CI program designed to contribute to that protection. Any serious discussion of CI management should take note of two implications of the unresolved national debate on this subject. One is the organizational inefficiency of a system that tries to protect information in a given category on the one hand and condones or supports its open dissemination on the other hand. The second implication is a resource management question for a CI program. There seems to be a quantitative ratio between the volume and substance of information a country wishes to protect and the amount and nature of its CI activities.

Requirements for the 1990s

True national-level, coordinated, advance planning and development of CI programs is a relatively young idea in the United States. The conflicts of interest and ambiguities that are part of the current national CI and security fields can be expected to survive into the 1990s (and may well become more intense and confusing). The requirement for national CI policies, plans, and programs—with associated coordination—was clearly recognized and redefined in Presidential Executive Order 12333 and in the subsequent establishment of the NSC's Senior Interdepartmental Groups for Counterintelligence and for

Countermeasures. The national intelligence community also has long recognized the need for interagency cooperation in the development, coordination, and review of CI plans and programs. The existence of a coordinating and planning staff in the intelligence community fulfilled this need. It is basic to successful U.S. counterintelligence in the 1990s that these organizational elements be hard at work now.

In common with most other sensitive national security programs, the trend has been toward greater centralization of policy development, operations decision making, and organizational control in Washington offices. The degree of organizational and operational control, although an important factor in the 1990s, is basically a bureaucratic management question of admittedly great complexity. It is not a specialized CI issue.

For the purpose of this book, it is sufficient to note that the executive branch has at hand the resources and the basic organizational capability to develop national CI strategy, policies, and requirements for the 1990s. It will need to continue and improve that capability throughout the next decade.

The extent to which future administrations use these capabilities and resources will be dictated by the state of international tensions, domestic political pressures, and the attitude of the media concerning the news value of reports about hostile intelligence collection and U.S. security losses. Historically, with respect to leadership attention, this has been very much a field of "greasing the squeaking wheel." There are now reasons for optimism—insofar as leadership attention is concerned. The public is somewhat more aware of the issues involved; some members of Congress are also somewhat more sophisticated in their understanding of the discipline; and, barring a dramatic shift in domestic behavior, the media will continue to amplify any squeaking wheels they can find. Policy, strategy, and planning do not, however, necessarily imply a willingness to take significant steps to improve defensive security.

If my view that counterintelligence should be conducted primarily to contribute to defensive security prevails, then the nation's defensive security requirements become critical to planning CI activities for the 1990s. Although perhaps not as romantic as the "pure counterintelligence" requirements, the question of what the nation wishes to secure, and to what degree, is both complex and difficult to resolve. Notwithstanding complexity and difficulty, including heavy domestic political freight, an important requirement is a clearer, broader public consensus, as well as greater uniformity and precision in government regulatory designation of what should be protected, for now as well as through the 1990s.

It sounds easy, but it is not. Deciding what to classify and at what level is a sophisticated and complex task requiring concurrent consideration of factors from a number of disciplines. This process is especially demanding in the military security area, involving both substance and volume problems. Currently, the basic standard operating procedure is that the proponent of the information classifies, using classification guides from a higher authority when they exist. This means that the government has a large number of classifiers, who have no particular knowledge of how a hostile government or group could use the information, determining how much effort should go into protecting that information. This classification system must change. Anyone who stamps something classified should have a good idea of the harm the information could do in the hands of a foreign intelligence service, how that service will try to obtain the information, and how to protect it. This is a very tall order.

Some organizational elements in the national security community have made significant improvements in the classification management discipline in recent years, but there is still much room for improvement. One possible requirement for the 1990s is to specialize, or "professionalize," the process of classification determination. This would require a cadre of specialized security classifiers working in all organizations developing classified information. Some aspects of this type of system are already in place, but the basic concept that proponent (read "originator" or "developer") classifies is still the general practice.

Although a broader consensus on national security information policy and improved classification management could have a significant impact on military counterintelligence in the 1990s, there are other requirements of greater significance in this critical discipline. Probably the single most important requirement will be for both military and civilian agencies to stay the course on the following improvements already under way:

Increased national and field level interagency planning, coordination, and cooperation

Greater specialization, professionalism, career development, and advancement opportunities for CI operations personnel

Sophisticated CI threat analysis support

An increased and improved offensive counterespionage operation

More scientific and technical capabilities to deal with both technical collection threats and vulnerabilities

It is already accepted that the last improvement will pose a significant problem in the foreseeable future.

It is no secret that contingency plans and readiness for most probable threat scenarios depicted in long-range intelligence estimates are standard components of military planning at all echelons of U.S. military commands and the Department of Defense. Two aspects of such planning are CI and operational security programs. Hopefully, defense and military service planners have already projected CI and operational security requirements well into the 1990s, and their annual requests for resource support are designed to develop capabilities to meet those requirements as well as to accomplish near-term missions. The following are some other specific military CI requirements that may require special attention in the 1990s:

Timely recognition and dissemination to tactical commanders and their counterintelligence support staffs of nationally developed hostile collection information affecting the operational security of the tactical commander. This could be critical in virtually any tactical operations scenario, but it is especially important for low-intensity conflict (LIC) operations where the whole national system might not be completely involved in the specific LIC at hand. National intelligence agencies (such as the State Department, FBI, and CIA) not normally involved in direct support of such operations must recognize their responsibilities to support them when conflict looms.

Soviet scientific and technological intelligence collection specialists have demonstrated time and again how effective they can be when they focus their large-volume effort on particular problems. Their attack against the newly constructed U.S. embassy in Moscow is a recent example. Soviet military intelligence planners are well aware of the high-tech nature of command, control, and communications (C^3) and of the weapon systems U.S. military field commands might be expected to employ in the 1990s. U.S. counterintelligence agencies, especially the military CI support organizations, will have to be able to identify and describe the hostile collection threat, including the high tech as well as the more conventional, to these C^3 and weapon control systems. Also, the requirement for interaction among supporting U.S. intelligence systems, counterintelligence, and operational security becomes even more important in the high-tech tactical combat battle area, especially in ground warfare situations. There are some current indications that the United States and its allies may move toward increased reliance on conventional forces. Operational security for the conventional force can be a deciding battlefield factor.

Returning to the broader area of national counterintelligence in the 1990s, other requirements deserve special mention. One of these is resource constraints. Will there be a special problem about budgets? Probably. The rest of the national security budget is facing constraints and reductions that are likely to continue well into the 1990s, barring some dramatic turn of events in the national security environment. It is highly likely that the CI programs will face these same constraints, despite the public hue and cry that attends each revelation of new hostile espionage successes. It is therefore probable that tighter management—with the emphasis on identification and support of only the most effective techniques and operations—will be a dominant theme in the 1990s.

The most important management tool in this regard will be sophisticated national management analysis and assessment of the various CI strategies, techniques, and programs, looking toward continuing improvements in quality (in contrast to quantity) in resources. As the national CI and security operational agencies are unlikely to see much growth in resources, and they will continue to face a heavy foreign collection threat, more efficient priorities, determinations, and use of existing resources will be critically important. A typical strategy and priorities problem might be determining which operational program contributes more to ultimate security—special CI operations against foreign collection agencies or defensive personnel security background investigations.

For whatever reason, there is a tendency in the United States to turn to proposals to change the organizational infrastructure in order to solve difficult doctrine and policy problems. This is probably because it is easier to deal with organizational questions. No matter what the U.S. government does about its CI structure, the doctrinal and policy issues will still be at the heart of national management requirements in this discipline.

Discussion

Kenneth deGraffenreid

The recommendations of both essays in this chapter are well argued, timely, and generally right on the mark. That they have been made by distinguished former intelligence officers long involved in this discipline make them all the more welcome.

I am dismayed, however, that virtually all of these recommendations have been made before, most certainly at the beginning of this decade at earlier colloquia of this consortium. It is indeed remarkable that they have to be made again, in view of the frightening events that have occurred during the past decade to confirm the need for these reforms. I also find it curious that the unprecedented and sustained hostile intelligence successes against our most protected secrets have occasioned so little official consideration of how they might be stopped. It is particularly odd in this era of introspection about putative intelligence failures, increasing congressional supervision of the intelligence community, and the resulting detailed public discussions of the nation's most intimate intelligence issues.

For example, the 1987 confirmation hearings for the directors of the CIA and FBI were almost devoid of questions about the "years of the spy," even though the intelligence community repeatedly reassured the intelligence committees during previous years that all was well with U.S. counterintelligence. Compare, for example, the attention given counterintelligence to that received by U.S. efforts to counter terrorism, which received the highest level of attention throughout the administration and Congress. Yet in terms of actual damage to U.S. national security, even the most provocative and emotionally charged terrorist incidents the United States has experienced cannot compare to the magnitude of damage resulting from a single Pelton, Walker, or Whitworth.

In this book, our task is to look to the challenges of the 1990s. Let me quickly underscore the wisdom that is found in this chapter. I believe that there can no longer be any serious question that in the 1990s the United States will have to do many things that have not been done for so long largely because of crude bureaucratic resistance.

Both essays in this chapter confirm what is obvious to any observer: The threat is multifaceted and diverse. The United States must counter not only espionage but also hostile signals intelligence (SIGINT) and a variety of other techniques practiced against it at home and abroad. Resistance within the U.S. intelligence community to this elementary fact has been particularly strange, given that the same community often points with justifiable pride to the multidisciplinary nature of the United States' own efforts in collection and analysis. Why not admit that any competent positive intelligence service is multidisciplinary and that, hence, any CI service that is not multidisciplinary is unlikely to counter that threat? As one of the essays points out, fragmented departmental efforts do not constitute even in their sum an effective national CI program, however well each component may perform individually.

Next, because of the real (as opposed to postulated) limits on U.S. resources, there is a need to concentrate CI efforts in places of intense espionage activity, particularly abroad, as George Kalaris and Len McCoy point out. This includes increased emphasis on unilateral CI capabilities abroad, ensuring that the United States has the capability to conduct counterintelligence effectively without relying on local intelligence services. This is an eminently sensible and much-needed reform. It is also likely to show early results.

There is also a compelling need for CI practitioners to understand the location, nature, and sensitivity of the U.S. secrets and institutions that are to be protected. Only in this manner can counterintelligence effectively support the defensive security effort. How can CI officers carry out their missions if they do not know about the programs and operations they are protecting? A specific example, as Merrill Kelly points out, is that people who classify information have to have some understanding of hostile needs and requirements in order to know what to protect. I assume that we all agree that it does no good to classify everything in a free society because it debases the coinage.

I endorse other suggestions that have been mentioned: specified career tracks for CI officers; improved CI training for all intelligence operations officers (which I would expand to include all U.S. intelligence personnel); and, finally, creation of a centralized CI authority capable of mobilizing all CI operations and capabilities against the threat. Kalaris and McCoy recommend a DDCI for counterintelligence as this authority. Of all the reforms, I think this one's time has certainly come.

Now I would like to voice a couple of small disagreements. First, I do not agree that the greatest challenge necessarily will be abroad, even though that may prove a lucrative area for U.S. counterintelligence efforts. The United States needs to concentrate its CI efforts in regions where the threat is high. The foreign cities Kalaris and McCoy mention certainly fall into that category. But the "volunteer"—what one might call the ab initio spy—aspect of much of the espionage that has occurred in this country in the 1980s suggests that the United States has an espionage threat right here at home that is as serious as any we face. The Peltons, the Whitworths, the Walkers, and many of the other fifty-odd individuals who have been arrested in this country for espionage volunteered for foreign intelligence service. How does one mount CI operations against that kind of threat? This is a very difficult problem with which the United States must come to grips. Although some would suggest a variety of CI surveillance techniques that would come close to infringing on civil liberties, I think a great deal can be done without going in that direction.

Second, I strongly disagree that the United States has in hand the organizational capability to develop national CI strategies, policies, and requirements. Although it is true that both the Carter and Reagan administrations made small steps in this direction and at least recognized that counterintelligence deserves a place at the policy table, little has been done to follow through. Today the United States has no national CI strategy, and few CI entities have developed strategies of their own.

Third, I believe both essays are overly concerned with definition. The United States' problem is not primarily one of definition. After all, I do not think that it was the misleading definition of counterintelligence included in Executive Order 12333 that prevented enactment of the vast majority of recommendations for CI reform and improvement. Those things could have been done within the executive order definition. The problem lay elsewhere.

In any case, given the confusion engendered by the definition, as well as attempts to correct it, the United States can get around many of the conceptual problems by conceiving of countering the threat as the reverse of the way in which it approaches hostile targets. That is to say, the United States should think of the hostile intelligence threat as it is—in all of its multiplicity and manifestations. The United States should understand that the proper response to that threat should be the coordinated multiplicity of all the things it does to detect, analyze, and counter those activities. The U.S. response must be iterative and should include the use of the knowledge it gains as it deals with the threat. Such knowledge can be used both for operational purposes (that is, to foul up hostile intelligence services) and to help provide information and analysis for policymaking (that is, using CI information for positive intelligence collection and analysis). The United States can do none of this, however, if the information is kept fragmented behind a series of green doors.

Some other issues also deserve comment. Neither essay sufficiently treats the four key functional and procedural aspects of counterintelligence: (1) the analysis function, (2) the coordination of CI operations, (3) the policy formulation dimension of CI, and (4) the political support necessary to sustain CI activities in a democracy. These issues are critical to a successful approach to the hostile intelligence threat in the nineties.

First, CI analysis will be the key to the United States' success in the 1990s. Analysis is the principal element of counterintelligence because the United States cannot view the hostile intelligence threat in a piecemeal way. The United States does not attack foreign intelligence targets that way, and neither do foreign powers. Hostile services come at the United States in a multidisciplinary, sophisticated way. The U.S. response, logically, has to be to integrate all those things it does to protect its interests and, specifically, analyze what is going on in order to counter the threats.

But the United States must first know what it is trying to protect. What are those values, secrets, and institutions that it needs to protect? In a free society there are a lot of them. Because the United

States cannot give them all the same protection, given the finite nature of its CI resources, what are its most precious secrets? This requires analysis and decisions. Certainly this will require great care. For example, when the United States sets up secret military special access programs, at least potentially it focuses the target for the Soviets on its important secrets. If there is anyplace the United States needs to protect, it is where a hostile service believes the country's most precious secrets are likely to be located.

It is an interesting paradox that in the American democracy, which rightfully depends for its strength on things other than secrecy, the secrets the United States does have are relatively more precious than those of a totalitarian society where everything is secret and which, in one sense, draws its strength from its repressive governmental apparatus. For example, the United States depends on its technological advantage. It cannot afford to let that advantage slip away to the Soviets via espionage as it has in the past fifteen to twenty years. It is safe to say that a large part of the Soviet strategic buildup over the past few years was made possible by the U.S. taxpayer. Further, the United States pays twice. It buys its own secrets and then has to pay for the fact that it allows the Soviets to rob them through their intelligence successes.

After helping to decide what the United States needs to protect, analysis must deal with the specific nature of the threat. Which are hostile intelligence services? What is important to them? What is their modus operandi? Is it conceivable that a secret could be very valuable to the United States but not of that great an interest to a hostile service, and vice versa? What do the hostile intelligence services already know about U.S. secrets and intelligence operations? How could they use that knowledge to deceive the United States as to their intent or degree of success? In sum, the analytic function must be able to integrate many elements to know where to deploy the United States' limited resources.

Second, once the United States understands what it is trying to protect, it needs a coordinated strategy of how to approach the hostile intelligence threat. Otherwise, the degree of success will be random, serendipitous, or poor. The United States will be like the football team whose defense is preparing for the run while the opposing offense is preparing for the long pass. The defense might stop the long bomb, but chances are it will not. To field random defenses in counterintelligence is a disservice both to the professionalism of the dedicated personnel and to the goals they are supposed to serve.

Somewhere there has to be a method for sorting out where the United States should put its effort. For example, should it buy more FBI agents or more safes? Should it focus on denying entrance to known hostile intelligence officers or hire thousands of FBI agents to surveil them? Does it emphasize personnel security in a society where there are limits to the kind of intrusiveness it would want to use to vet people? Or does the United States come up with other schemes, such as removing individuals from control of sensitive cryptographic material and going to electronic keying systems?

It is beyond my scope here to go through the hundreds of such choices the United States faces. But somewhere in the government, the United States must decide where to best put its resources. Once again, its failure to do this is curious because in most other parts of the federal government, let alone in the private sector, this is one of the key things good managers do. For example, the concept of a senior executive service is to produce a cadre of people who have these qualities, who can weigh alternatives, and who know where to put these resources and how to respond to threats and opportunities. It is extremely strange that in the area of hostile penetration of secrets that are vital to the country, the government has not wanted to make these kinds of decisions rationally. I say rationally because decisions do get made as to where CI resources go, even if they are made willy-nilly.

Third, it is not just the countering of the hostile intelligence threat that is important. I think that national policymakers both benefit from good counterintelligence and need to contribute to the formulation of CI policy. Given that counterintelligence focuses on the activities of the KGB-GRU and the position of the KGB-GRU within Soviet society, there are many valuable things that policymakers can learn from an aggressive, expanded CI analysis capability. Because the Soviets place such emphasis on the KGB-GRU, these institutions become a window by which the United States can better understand the threats to U.S. national security. The United States must make much greater use of this opportunity.

The other side of the coin is that policy affects the way the United States does counterintelligence and the way it responds to the hostile intelligence threat. Today this comes in the form of the United States' inability, at times, to give counterintelligence a fair place at the policy table. That is not to deny that policies are made with regard to the hostile intelligence threat. Bureaucrats follow lines of action that, ex post facto, are called policy. But in my view, policy in this field is not being made by those at the top levels of the government—the people who ought to be making it.

When I was at the NSC, one example was the insistence of many State Department colleagues that little serious effort, diplomatic or otherwise, should be directed at the KGB threat within the United States. They argued that doing so would upset U.S.–Soviet relations. To my mind this was and is a highly dubious proposition. Whatever its merits, however, such a profound issue involves a serious policy choice. This choice is properly a decision to be made at the highest levels of government. Instead, it was made down in the bowels of the great engine of government. For the most part, the president did not make a decision on this matter, and neither did Congress. The State Department's bureaucratic position, unarticulated and unaccountable (and sometimes disguised), effectively became U.S. policy. That policy decision significantly affected the United States' ability to perform counterintelligence, to detect the threat and analyze it, and to do something about it. The policy may or may not be correct, but it was not made in a procedurally correct way. In the American democracy, there must be someplace in the government where adequate consideration of hostile intelligence threat issues can be presented in a fair and unbiased way to senior policymakers so that they can make the decisions that are properly theirs to make.

I would like to add that, whatever the policy during my years at the White House (1981–1987), the State Department, to my knowledge, opposed at least initially every one of the hundreds of recommendations for dealing with the hostile intelligence threat presented within the government. This even included the distinctive license plates that are now given to diplomats in this country. This type of resistance cannot simply be chalked up to the unavoidable bureaucratics of the Beltway culture; this is policymaking pure and simple.

In a democracy, there is a need for political support. That is to say, if the political leaders of the United States—Congress and the executive branch—do not understand that the hostile intelligence threat is important, or if they do not believe (and act as if they believe) that the hostile intelligence threat is important, then there will be no way that this issue will get the attention it needs relative to all the other demands on the government. For example, if the political leadership spends an enormous amount of time decrying the threat from a handful of foreign terrorists and does not comment on what I believe to be a much more serious threat from the KGB, it is not surprising that the American people do not petition their leaders for action in the area of counterintelligence. The seeking of political support, aimed at both securing the understanding of the American people about the nature of the threat and what needs to be done and executing the reforms and recommendations set out in this chapter, requires the attention of U.S. political leaders. Support for counterintelligence is not going to emerge unaided.

Finally, it is interesting to note that during the Reagan administration, some of the support for the improvement and reform of counterintelligence has come as a result of the popularity of fictionalized accounts of the threat. Many of these, of course, have been very well done, and I mean them no criticism. In fact, however, the threat is much more serious than the popular accounts, and it requires the United States' sustained attention.

James Geer

I would like to talk about counterintelligence as we define it today and later comment on the suggestions about the expansion of that definition.

About 1982, a study was conducted on the foreign intelligence threat as it exists in the United States and the ability of counterintelligence in this country to respond to that threat. The study established a baseline for looking at what is out there in many terms, including numerical ones.

At that time, there were more than one hundred foreign establishments in the United States. There were two thousand to three thousand officials in these establishments, with considerable fluctuation in their comings and goings. The United States came up with an estimate of what it would take to deal with these establishments and people.

But as the United States' capabilities were being enhanced to meet this threat, the threat grew. Today the U.S. counterintelligence community has more people than in 1982. I sincerely believe it has better-trained people and better equipment. The analytic capabilities are significantly greater than they have been in times past. But while this was happening, the threat of two thousand to three thousand people became four thousand to five thousand people. In 1982 a small number of students from countries that pose an intelligence threat to the United States were studying in this country, but since then that number has increased to twenty thousand. Thus, the net change in the threat and in the United States' ability to respond to it is not positive.

Nevertheless, I believe that during this period of buildup, U.S. counterintelligence forces witnessed significant improvements in professionalism and in the development of additional expertise. U.S. coordination efforts also were significantly enhanced. I know that the authors of this chapter are aware of this and have taken positions on issues that still need to be addressed. From my perspective, I have never seen a time when coordination was better. This has something to do with the people involved. The current CI managers and others involved in this process get along well, and I think that has contributed to the overall improvement. But it goes beyond that. I think everyone recognizes the necessity to institutionalize cooperation, as compatibility might not be extended indefinitely.

The United States also needs to enhance coordination between those who are charged with countering the effort of hostile intelligence services in this country or aimed against U.S. interests wherever they might be and those charged with collecting intelligence on behalf of the United States. The CI people must have a full understanding of this country's collection capabilities, just as the collectors must have a good understanding of what a well-equipped, well-trained U.S. counterintelligence service can do to enhance collection efforts.

Another factor that has made a significant difference in the status of counterintelligence today is that, unlike in the past, it now has a voice in a number of places in the U.S. government. Why is this so? The answer is the "year (or years) of the spy." If there is a positive aspect of these heinous espionage cases, it is a better awareness of the need for counterintelligence on the part of both the general public and government agencies. That awareness has given counterintelligence a standing it previously lacked.

For instance, in the past if a country wanted to open a consulate in the United States, the decision would have been made without bringing the CI people into the decision making loop. That does not happen today. When a country wanted to open a consulate in California, the CI voice was heard in discussions about this issue. Counterintelligence may not always prevail, but at least it is considered. I do not expect counterintelligence to drive foreign policy and all national security issues, but I do expect that the voice of counterintelligence will be heard at the outset and throughout the deliberations, whether the government is talking about the opening of a consulate or the negotiation of an arms treaty. Counterintelligence needs to have a voice. Now it has one in a way that it never did before.

In the past few years, a number of events have occurred that will change our focus and should drive many of our actions as we move into the 1990s. The most significant is the expulsion from the United States of a number of officials from the Soviet Union and other countries who were involved in intelligence operations against the United States. That was unquestionably a quantum gain, but it does not mean that the United States should stop there. There are a number of things the United States has to do. The first is to keep these countries from replacing the officials who were expelled with experienced intelligence officers. To do that, the United States must have a strong policy regarding visa review and denial.

Further, by dealing this kind of blow to hostile intelligence services, the United States has caused them to rethink how they are going to operate on U.S. turf in the future. If the United States has dealt a blow to one—in this case, the major—collection technique, then the foreign intelligence service must rethink what it is going to do to make up for those losses while it is trying to rebuild. Is it going to go to other services? What is it going to do?

Counterintelligence in the 1990s must address these questions, decide what means are going to be employed, and gear itself toward addressing them.

Ken deGraffenreid mentions the phenomenon of volunteers. This is a critical issue for U.S. counterintelligence, presenting a number of sensitive problems. What can the United States, with its form of open government, do to identify possible volunteers? Should it put a RAM car in front of the Soviet embassy as the KGB might do at the U.S. embassy in Moscow? The FBI is not going to do that, but where can the United States close the loop on volunteers?

The suggestion has been made that anyone who is having financial difficulty and who has access to sensitive information should be the subject of some sort of FBI investigation. That idea is not appropriate or practical. The FBI has said that the United States' focus can never be in that direction. The FBI cannot watch the financial standing of everyone who has access to sensitive information, what the person's drinking habits are, what his or her marital situation is at any given time, or what other things might make the person vulnerable. Instead, the United States must, as in the past, concentrate on those active foreign intelligence officers who are in this country attempting to recruit Americans. It also must focus on the volunteer phenomenon and close it down as much as possible.

The other side to this issue also has been previously mentioned. By creating an environment in the United States in which it is particularly hostile for foreign intelligence officers to operate, something the United States has tried to do, the U.S. government forces them abroad. Now when they want to meet, with a volunteer from San Francisco, for example, they might set up the meeting in Caracas, Venezuela. This has not cured the problem, just moved it from one location to another. It would be easy to say, "At least we've gotten it out of the FBI's turf and the CIA has the problem." But that is not the solution.

There is considerable public discussion about reducing the number of people with access to classified information. Personally, I do not think that we can significantly do this. This is not the source of the problem. The problem is that the intelligence community has lost the appreciation of the "need to know" principle. Too many people have access to sensitive information that they do not need.

One proposal that has been put forth for a number of years is that counterintelligence must be redefined. I do not think the definition is the problem. The intelligence community understands what the threat is and that the threat includes foreign signals intelligence (SIGINT) and imagery collection as well as human intelligence (HUMINT) on the United States and its installations. The focus should not be a matter of how the community defines things but of how it addresses them.

I come from the counter–human intelligence side, but I recognize that other hostile (technical) collection efforts must be countered. I also recognize that these efforts must come together somewhere if the United States is ever going to be in a position to protect itself. But I believe that no radical changes are needed to address these problems. Merrill Kelly mentions that we already have bodies charged with the coordination of individual disciplines, from HUMINT, SIGINT, and imagery to personnel and document security. What the United States needs to look at is whether the work of these coordinating bodies comes together, whether it comes together at the right place, and whether the point where it comes together should be elevated.

I do not believe that imposing bureaucracies over perceived and real problems is generally the best answer. From my own experience, I believe that establishing "czars" and creating bureaucracies are seldom the best solutions. I do believe that some of the problems are real, but that the government has the ability to solve them within the existing framework, given some modification and perhaps some elevation of where the process comes together. By this I mean that the United States might need an overall CI body to which these coordinating groups will report. But I think the United States is farther down the road in addressing these CI problems than many realize.

General Discussion

At the colloquium, the discussion of counterintelligence in the 1990s ranged from consideration of the specific problem of Americans who volunteer their services to foreign powers, to the identification of requirements not mentioned in the essays, to the general topic of organizing the U.S. intelligence community to meet these requirements. There seemed to be agreement that, with a few notable exceptions, identifying the things that must be done is much easier than achieving consensus within the executive branch for accomplishing them—despite bipartisan congressional support.

A former intelligence official began by explaining that the volunteer problem is anything but new. In the 1940s, Americans such as Alger Hiss, Elizabeth Bentley, and Whittaker Chambers eagerly donated their services to the Soviet Union. These individuals, noted the official, shared a common background. The FBI could get a handle on the problem by surveilling the organizations—mainly the Communist Party USA (CPUSA)—that spawned such volunteers. But today's volunteers do not seem to come from any identifiable place. He suggested that efforts be made to identify those parts of the American social fabric that now play the same role with regard to volunteers that the CPUSA played a generation ago. An academic suggested, however, that there may be no way to get the job done as it was in the past and that wholly new ways will have to be found.

A number of conferees agreed that any approach to the volunteer problem would have to go down two distinct paths: surveillance of possible spawning grounds and surveillance of known KGB officers to see whom they are seeking out and where. A government official said that both paths are difficult to follow. For example, the FBI noticed that KGB officers attempted to recruit ordinary students by hanging around public libraries and asking them to do unclassified research. Once the relationship with the student was established, the KGB officer could initiate the recruitment process. Such recruits are preferable because they do not have the problems—financial, drinking, or marital—that make other agents difficult to control and sustain in the long term. The official noted, however, that the FBI's mere observation of this process drew stiff protests from librarians.

Another aspect of the problem is the volunteer who provides nonprotected information. A conferee pointed out that about 40 percent of the KGB's foreign intelligence officers are assigned to "Line PR," the acquisition of political information and active measures. Many of the agents these officers recruit do not violate the laws of their own country. Rather they provide nonclassified information and attempt to influence specific situations. Yet these volunteers can do almost as much harm as the sellers of classified material.

A congressional staffer asked if it would be a good idea to station the FBI at the door of Soviet establishments in the United States, just as the KGB is stationed at the door of U.S. embassies and consulates in the Soviet Union, in order to deter some volunteers. A former White House official replied that there are so many other ways of making contact that such a step would not be worth the trouble.

In light of the volunteer problem, there was a good deal of discussion about the effectiveness of U.S. counterintelligence. A government official argued that the "year of the spy" should not be viewed as a scandal. Rather the increased number of spy arrests are a result of the increased commitment of resources to counterintelligence over the past ten years. Further, as a result of labeling each espionage arrest a "scandal" or "failure," senior government officials in the future might back off from arresting and prosecuting agents for fear of having a scandal occur on their watch. He cited the Walker family spy case as an example of a CI success, and argued that the case was used in a positive way to lay out a blueprint for counterintelligence in the 1990s.

An academic replied that U.S. counterintelligence had nothing to be proud of in the Walker case. An intelligence officer amplified this point. Walker was turned in by his wife. The tool for the discovery was a plain envelope with the FBI's address and a twenty-two-cent stamp. Little CI work was involved in the discovery, despite the fact that the ring had operated for seventeen years and had done tremendous damage.

A journalist questioned how analysts looking at the Soviet navy during the time the Walker ring operated could not have noticed that the Soviets were privy to U.S. secrets. Perhaps, suggested the academic, intelligence analysts were not looking at the Soviet navy from a CI standpoint and failed to notice what was happening because they had not been looking for it. The purpose of analysis, he said, includes counterintelligence, but the purpose of counterintelligence ought not be limited to putting people in jail after the fact. Another government official agreed that the United States should not view the Walker case as a success. He argued that counterintelligence, rightly understood, is an analytical discipline whose purpose is prevention of damage rather than an investigative discipline aimed at punishment.

A former intelligence official pointed out that there is little theoretical opposition to the proposition that counterintelligence is an analytical, preventive discipline. Every serious study of the subject in the past decade, whether coming from the Senate Select Committee on Intelligence, from commissions in the executive branch, or from the Consortium for the Study of Intelligence, has come to very similar conclusions and recommendations. A recent congressional study contained some two hundred recommendations in this regard, but the bureaucracy has failed to follow through, and senior policymakers have lacked the fortitude to ensure their implementation.

A government official suggested that there is so much to be done in the CI field that every CI officer could spend the rest of his or her career on it without getting close to impinging on U.S. civil liberties. The juxtaposition of counterintelligence with civil liberties proceeds in large part from a faulty understanding of how to do effective counterintelligence.

An academic wondered why top policymakers have spent so little energy on educating the public about the complexity and seriousness of the espionage threat to the United States. He contrasted this with the high-level attention given to combating terrorism. A former White House official stated that the Reagan administration has in fact disseminated considerable information on the hostile intelligence problem. President Reagan himself has given at least four speeches on this topic. Yet, the official agreed, the administration's actions have belied its own message. While policymakers spoke dramatically about the damage caused by the year of the spy, much of the bureaucracy conducted its business as usual.

One possible reason, the official felt, is that there is a disagreement within the executive branch over how to deal with CI matters. Some State Department officials oppose taking any action that might damage U.S.–Soviet relations. For example, the expulsion of some eighty KGB officers from the United States at the end of 1986, through the reduction of the Soviet diplomatic presence, was first proposed many years ago. When it finally happened, it happened not because of national security considerations but as a result of the Daniloff affair.

An FBI official agreed that, despite its rhetoric, the executive branch has been reluctant to implement a number of CI reforms. Further, although terrorism was a major problem, he said that he does not believe it threatens U.S. national security to the extent that the hostile intelligence threat does.

A congressional staffer noted strong bipartisan support in Congress for improved counterintelligence. He explained that even members of Congress who are strong supporters of improved U.S.–Soviet relations are also leading advocates for controlling the hostile intelligence threat. For example, the House and Senate called for a restructuring of the State Department's handling of foreign missions in the 1988 State Department authorization bill. They even mandated that the attorney general inform the intelligence committees whenever the State Department grants visas to Soviet diplomats against the advice of the FBI. The president was not supportive. The staffer cited this as an example of how the executive branch is in a weaker position than Congress to take strong action in this area.

Another academic raised an issue not treated in the essays, namely, the kind of operational security required to protect the human and technical intelligence operations the United States will be conducting in the 1990s. Given the nature of these operations, he asked, what can the Soviets be expected to know about them, and through what channels? What can they be expected to do with that knowledge? And how can U.S. counterintelligence both restrict the Soviets' knowledge and turn what the Soviets do gain to the United States' own benefit? Two former intelligence officers said that somebody had to be given the job of watching over and judging the United States' own positive intelligence operations. To do this well, the overseers must have a number of attributes. First, they must be technologically skilled in the substantive matter of the operation and understand what the KGB can and cannot do. Second, they should approach the job analytically—that is, as hypotheses to be tested. Third, they must be organizationally independent of those whose operations they judge, which means having their own separate career tracks. Without this, they will lack the personal freedom to be intellectually vigorous. This independent CI review must be done at all levels of intelligence, from everyday operations, to the development of human operations, to the planning of large technical collection systems.

Another former intelligence official added that those who protect the United States' own positive operations must know those operations inside and out and understand the nature of what is to be protected. Only in this way can they imagine how the hostile services approach getting at them. The current organization of the U.S. intelligence community, however, prevents this thorough knowledge.

A current intelligence official remarked that awareness of the fundamentals of counterintelligence has been growing within the community in the past decade and that, in his opinion, the CI business in the United States today is the best it has ever been. Many participants suggested, however, that there is still a need for much better coordination.

Following this was an exchange between current and former officials of the FBI and CIA concerning which of the two agencies should be given the job of coordinating counterintelligence at the national level and performing central CI analysis. A former White House official added that it matters less who is in charge than that someone be in charge. The president, he said, ought to have someone whom he can hold responsible for success and failure in the field of counterintelligence.

A former CI officer, while expressing satisfaction that so many parts of the executive branch are now vying with one another for primacy in the field, cautioned that this will not amount to much until each of those parts acknowledges the role of counterintelligence within itself. Earlier, a journalist had said that the intelligence agencies had not yet come to terms with the role of counterintelligence. The former officer recounted how counterintelligence had had a tenuous but nonetheless real place in the minds of those who had started the CIA, but that since the mid-1970s this understanding had disappeared. He said that an understanding and appreciation of the CI mission by the top leaders of each agency is a necessary first step. To succeed, new initiatives must be based on that.

5
Covert Action

Essays:

Discussion:

I.   RICHARD H. SHULTZ, JR.

Covert action (CA) is employed to influence politics and events in another country without revealing one's involvement or at least while maintaining plausible deniability. Although relatively easy to define, it has become increasingly difficult for the American democratic regime to consider it as a strategic instrument of statecraft. From the late 1940s until the late 1960s, there was a consensus in the United States concerning the need for covert action. Strong opposition to such action began in earnest during the congressional investigations in the mid-1970s, and many people in Washington and throughout the country are still uncomfortable with it. Here I argue that as a result of the kinds of threats and challenges the United States is likely to face in the 1990s, policymakers will have to consider how and to what extent the instrument of covert action can contribute to the achievement of foreign policy goals.

Covert action is a generic term that describes a group or class of activities. It can be divided into the following five categories:

Propaganda. This is the dissemination of unattributable communications to alter the conditions under which governments act. Either gray or black in format, the materials circulated may contain either true or false information.

Political Action. This entails money, advice, and assistance to individuals and/or groups in a foreign country. Provided through secret channels, the purpose is to encourage those who are either friendly to you or hostile to your adversaries.

Paramilitary Assistance. This consists of furnishing secret military assistance and guidance to foreign forces and organizations. Paramilitary assistance may be provided to those either conducting or defending against an insurgency. In either case, the assistance is not to be directly attributable to the source.

Coup d'Etat. In its traditional form, this constitutes assistance to or backing of a faction within a foreign country that carries out a consciously conceived and swiftly executed seizure of government power through the removal of the current leadership. A less traditional and broader definition might include advice and assistance to a leader who, while friendly, is rapidly losing legitimacy and control, with his or her deposition clearly in sight. In such instances, the goal would be to assist clandestinely in the leader's safe departure from the scene, while helping those individuals and groups in the opposition that, if they come to power, will be either friendly to you or unfriendly to your adversaries.

Secret Intelligence Support. This includes the provision of security assistance and intelligence training to the leader of a foreign country to protect him or her and preserve the regime. Frequently, this is accomplished as part of the intelligence liaison process, which is generally carried out between an intelligence service and the leader the service seeks to help.

During the period from the late 1940s to the late 1960s, the United States employed each of these CA variants, frequently in conjunction with diplomatic and other instruments, to influence to its advantage the course of events in different parts of the world. In the 1970s, however, the use of covert action came to be increasingly questioned from both an ethical and operational perspective. Some took the position that it was morally wrong for a democratic government to be involved in such subterfuge. For instance, Morton Halperin asserts that covert action commits the United States to a policy initiative that has not been debated publicly and without giving citizens an opportunity to express their views. It is, therefore, wrong for a president to carry out operations that have not been tested in the public marketplace.[1] Covert action is inimical to democratic mores and, according to Halperin, "the United States should not conduct covert action."[2] This position has also been taken by a handful of former CIA practitioners of the art. Ralph McGehee argues not only that covert action and democratic values are incompatible but also that the CIA has "helped destroy democracy around the world" through covert actions. He believes that this will eventuate in the destruction of democracy at home.[3]

In addition to moral qualms, the propriety of covert action has been questioned from the perspective of operational effectiveness. It rarely works and often results in controversy and political embarrassment when exposed. Former Director of Central Intelligence (DCI) Stansfield Turner states in *Secrecy and Democracy* that "everyone involved [in intelligence] should be required to read the history of covert action to be reminded of how little it can actually accomplish. . . ."[4] In light of this, his recommendations are twofold. First, "hold it in readiness until the right conditions exist." In his view, this generally occurs no more "than once or twice during an administration."[5] Second, even in those rare instances, only carry out noncontroversial covert actions.[6] In other words, only do covertly that which if it is exposed will cause you little political harm.

These doubts and questions about covert action were part of a larger reconsideration of post–World War II U.S. foreign policy. The result was the dissolution of the bipartisan consensus that had existed for more than two decades. Since policy was questioned, it should not be surprising that the means employed to carry it out also were questioned. This was especially true of covert action. In fact, it could be argued that the attack on covert action served as a stalking horse for a broader criticism and rejection of the post–World War II United States foreign policy of containment. In many respects, covert action and secrecy were easier targets than taking head-on the issue of whether containment of the Soviet Union and its allies and surrogates was a prudent and legitimate policy objective. During the second half of the 1970s, the Carter administration, following the lead of Congress, greatly reduced CIA assets for conducting these activities. The impact of this is summed up in the words of two skilled former practitioners. According to B. Hugh Tovar, "Covert Action in the late 1970s showed all the hallmarks of a dying art form."[7] Theodore Shackley put it this way: "Budgetary pressures, particularly under Admiral Stansfield Turner's stewardship of the intelligence community, forced drastic personnel reductions and maintained equipment inventories at levels below what I believe are necessary to sustain the third option."[8]

By the end of the decade, as the political crisis subsided, many argued from inside and outside the government that the United States had pushed the legislative reform pendulum too far. This was particularly true with respect to the president's ability to employ secret means as an instrument of policy. A series of intelligence failures revealed the price to be paid for ignoring the requirements necessary to respond to hostile intelligence threats and challenges facing the United States. These included the inability to collect information on and to understand the revolutions in Iran and Nicaragua, misestimation of Soviet military power, various counterintelligence failures, and the nonexistence of effective means for covertly influencing politics and events abroad.

The Intelligence Oversight Act of 1980 was indicative of congressional concern over these failures as well as a recognition of the fact that in certain situations the president requires discretionary power to conduct covert action. During the 1980 presidential campaign, Ronald Reagan ran on a platform that recognized the weaknesses in U.S. intelligence and specified a series of measures to reinvigorate it. This included the resuscitation of CA capabilities.

During the 1980s, a number of initiatives followed, as the executive and legislative branches began to focus on strengthening the performance of U.S. intelligence.[9] In the midst of these developments, however, the Iran-Contra crisis unfolded. The initial impact with respect to covert action has been to reexamine the question of whether, and if so under what circumstances and to what degree, the United States should employ this instrument of policy. For example, Gregory Treverton has suggested that covert action be considered only within a set of guidelines "articulated a decade ago by Cyrus Vance." Under these strictures, a president should resort to covert action "only as an exceptional measure" and "when no other means would do."[10] Other observers, such as Allan Goodman, go further and assert that "Washington should no longer conduct secret political influence, propaganda, and disinformation dimensions of covert action. Such practices are ineffective instruments of foreign policy and spawn doubts about the moral character of the U.S. government."[11]

What both Treverton and Goodman either overlook or do not sufficiently address in formulating these arguments are answers to two important questions: First, are democratic values and covert action completely at odds with one another? And second, in the 1990s will the United States face diverse and serious challenges that will require the use of covert action as an instrument of foreign policy? A brief examination of each will serve as a preface to an assessment of U.S. covert action requirements for the 1990s.

Democratic Culture and Covert Action

Through the first two decades of the cold war, realists generally maneuvered around the question of democratic values versus covert action by asserting that in a hostile world, moral and ethical principles could not be applied to the international actions of states. The statesman acting on behalf of the national interest was to follow a standard of conduct substantially different from that found within a democratic regime. Realism opposed the introduction of values into foreign policy, regardless of whether it was cast in the rhetoric of universal human rights of the Carter administration or the moralism and universalism of the anticommunism of the Eisenhower years. For realists, statesmen must think and act in terms of interest defined as power and not values. Covert action as well as overt forms of intervention were not opposed as long as these actions were strategically compelling and not based on moralism.

Although it is unclear whether this democracy has ever been able to compartmentalize values and pursue a foreign policy based solely on pragmatism and power, the breakdown of the post–World War II consensus noted above ruled out this likelihood in the 1970s. Indeed, the second half of the decade saw ethical standards and moralism move to the center of the policy process. Sometimes referred to as liberal internationalism, proponents of this view advocated a non-aggressive and humanitarian foreign policy. International cooperation should replace competition and power politics. Military power was said to have lost its utility, and interventionism, including covert action, was rejected as inconsistent with U.S. values. According to Stanley Hoffman of Harvard University, the legacy of U.S. covert action is laden with "disasters and fiascoes abroad, and the bad habits of illegality, deception, and dishonesty . . . at home."[12] This view held that covert action seldom produces the results promised and consists mainly of dirty tricks and dirty wars. Therefore, covert action lacks any instrumental or moral purpose.

Cast in this way, liberal internationalism was able to seize the moral high ground and foster the conclusion that covert action relegates one to acceptance of the Doolittle standard: "If the United States is to survive, long-standing concepts of 'fair play' must be reconsidered. We must . . . learn to subvert, sabotage, and destroy our enemies by more clever, more sophisticated, and more effective methods than those used against us."[13]

During the 1970s, those both in and out of government who came to oppose the use of covert action presented the options in the manner just described. In the aftermath of the Iran-Contra hearings, many have once again raised the issue of whether or not to make use of this policy instrument. Academic specialists, including Ernest Lefever and Roy Godson as well as former senior U.S. intelligence officials such as Cord Meyer, have argued that these are not the only alternatives.[14] They argue, and I concur, that there is a theoretical basis for the exercise of covert action that is not inimical to democratic norms.

The instruments of statecraft, whether overt or covert, can be used in the service of objectives that go beyond self-interest and power. Through prudential judgment, U.S. foreign policy can blend strategic interest and democratic principles. The two are not irreconcilable. The result would be three broad policy objectives: (1) assure the security of the existing democratic world; (2) keep off balance and contain the Soviet Union and its surrogates; and (3) promote democratic principles in places where they exist in embryo or not at all.[15]

With these objectives in mind, the use of U.S. power becomes more than the pursuit of self-interest (to be sure, one of the United

States' motivations). It also includes the promotion of pluralism, individual rights, and related democratic norms. The coalescing of self-interest and values through prudential judgment produces a sounder theoretical basis for foreign policy activism and intervention.

How does this play out in terms of covert action? In the first place, such action exists not as a substitute for policy, but as part of a process that seeks to get something accomplished that is compatible with the national interest and U.S. norms. What about the Doolittle standard? To be sure, stern measures are necessary against an implacable adversary who uses force and guile to create worldwide political conditions that are harmful to U.S. interests. Although this should not be construed as a moral equivalence argument, it would contribute to a policy that seeks to keep the adversary off balance, on the defensive, and unable to achieve expansionist goals. This would be even more compelling if the adversary had achieved the military advantage. In other instances, to borrow from the insights of one former practitioner, the covert actioneer's "stock-in-trade is not the seduction and manipulation of innocents, but the sub-rosa support and succor of peoples and institutions legitimately in need of such assistance."[16] In other words, covert action is the clandestine element of policies aimed at helping friends or potential friends in need of advice and support. Political circumstances may require that this be routed through secret channels.

How do values and interests mesh in such situations? The election in El Salvador in the early 1980s provides an answer. Recall that at that time both of the major candidates—Roberto d'Aubuisson and Jose Napoleon Duarte—asserted that they were allies and friends of the United States. Both stood in firm opposition to El Salvador's following the revolutionary path of the Sandinistas in Nicaragua, which was in line with U.S. strategy in the region. From the point of view of U.S. values, however, only Duarte was acceptable. Reportedly, covert political advice and support made an important contribution to his electoral victory over a better-financed opponent. Here we see secret means, in conjunction with overt measures, supporting a judicious policy that combines strategic interest and political norms.

A more difficult case involves the use of covert means to either bring down or drastically alter the behavior of another government. Even here, however, strategic interests and values can be reconciled. U.S. support for the resistance forces opposing Sandinista rule in Nicaragua can serve as an example. For many, this assistance is warranted solely on strategic grounds. In light of the fact that the Frente Sandinista de Liberación Nacional (FSLN) Directorate intends to encourage and promote the diffusion of their revolution throughout Central America, the United States has little choice but to use all means available to prevent this. An effective resistance movement would serve this purpose by forcing Managua to divert resources and attention to its own survival. In the world of the 1950s, this might have been sufficient. It no longer is today. What will it take for the United States to sustain its support to the resistance forces? Can the insurgents develop into a pluralistically based and politically legitimate alternative to Sandinista rule? Sub-rosa assistance and advice can contribute to this political transition and maturation, but it will take more than military assistance to help the resistance develop along these lines. Covert assistance focused on this objective would contribute to a policy that blends both strategic requirements and political values.

The change of government in the Philippines in 1986 is another example of the synthesis of interests and values. Although it should have been evident earlier, by the end of 1985, U.S. policymakers realized that the twenty-year reign of Ferdinand Marcos had run its course. The issues were who would replace him and how this would take place. In all probability, Marcos could have stayed on for the short term. The price would have been to turn the Philippines into bloody chaos. Out of this disorder, the possibility of a Communist seizure of power would have increased, even though the opposition to Marcos was broadly based. In the midst of this situation, the United States helped ease Marcos into exile, and Corazon Aquino assumed the presidency. It was in the strategic interest of the United States to prevent the Communist party from seizing power in the Philippines. Further, from the point of view of political values, Marcos was no longer a viable ally. Apparently, covert political action contributed to at least a temporary resolution of the situation. However, much remains to be done if stability and political development are to take root.

In sum, if U.S. presidents are to consider the CA option in the 1990s and identify appropriate requirements and capabilities, they will have to resolve the issues explored above. During the latter part of the 1970s, and again today, those who oppose covert action have successfully seized the moral high ground. This does not have to be the case. However, it will take effective executive leadership to articulate how the instrument of covert action can be used in support of sound policy objectives and within the context of democratic principles.

The Environment in the 1990s: Threats, Challenges, and Covert Action Options

The international environment and political terrain of the 1990s will influence where and what kinds of covert missions are to be considered. Although estimating future threats and challenges is always tenuous, some general observations can be made. An examination of the past decade provides relevant clues. One can envisage several major threats to U.S. interests in the final decade of the twentieth century. Related to each will be opportunities growing out of the vulnerabilities and weaknesses of those who challenge the United States. In the sections that follow, I identify those regional threats that might be exploited through covert action, then examine the kinds of CA missions that could be considered to, in part, address these challenges. Although not all are achievable within budgetary, political, and other constraints, what follows can serve as a guide to policy options. Taken together, they are suggestions that are directional in nature, not a list of specific plans.

The Soviet Union and Eastern Europe

Over the past two decades, Soviet power has expanded in a number of ways. Strategic and conventional military capabilities are only the most apparent. There is little to suggest that Soviet research and development, procurement, and deployment patterns will drastically change in the next decade. The result may be that the United States will find itself in a position of military disadvantage vis-à-vis the Soviet Union. Given the Kremlin's Clausewitzian view that military advantage converts into coercive leverage in both crisis and normal international competition, it is quite possible the United States will face unattractive political choices.

During the 1970s, Soviet power and influence also expanded in the Third World. Boris Ponomarev, former head of the Communist Party of the Soviet Union's (CPSU's) International Department, called the 1970s the decade of "progress of the world revolutionary process," the result of the "merciless objective laws of social development."[17] He cited as examples Vietnam, Laos, Kampuchea, Ethiopia, Angola, Mozambique, Zimbabwe, Afghanistan, South Yemen, Iran, and Nicaragua. In a number of these cases, the Soviet Union and its surrogates contributed to the shift in political power. During the period, the Kremlin implemented an integrated strategy of political and paramilitary measures to assist insurgents and political factions in seizing power through revolutionary warfare, coups d'état, and other forms of protracted conflict. Eastern European, Cuban, and other surrogates made important contributions to these efforts. While not without accompanying costs, which the United States could more effectively exploit, these developments contributed to the Soviet Union's geostrategic position in the Third World. Will the Kremlin continue to pursue this policy in the 1990s? Unless the United States exploits the Soviet Union's cost of maintaining gains, there is little reason to expect a significant change.

In the recently published *Chekisty: A History of the KGB,* John Dziak observes that, while the tradition of Soviet active measures and strategic deception dates back to the days of Feliks Dzerzhinskiy, the contemporary period began at the end of the 1950s. At that time, the senior leaders of the CPSU set new policy goals and established the organizational means for accomplishing them.[18] The latter included the security and intelligence services as well as an array of CPSU and state organs. This apparatus was then augmented by its counterparts in the Eastern European states. The strategic objectives included undermining U.S. foreign policy, weakening and splitting NATO, and destabilizing other U.S. alliances. During the 1970s and 1980s, a significant body of evidence has become available on the operational aspects of major active measures campaigns.[19] Soviet and Eastern European defectors have provided insight into the importance Moscow places on these activities.[20] In the 1990s, the use of this stratagem is likely to continue in a more streamlined and professional form, a process set in motion in the mid-1980s by a series of personnel changes in the active measures apparatus.[21] Consequently, countering these actions will be increasingly difficult, as Soviet sophistication allows for greater entry into Western Europe and the Third World. *Glasnost* may be only the initial phase in what will transpire in the years ahead.

Over the past two decades, the Kremlin has used its security and intelligence services quite effectively in acquiring Western scientific knowledge and technology. This has, in turn, contributed importantly to the Soviet development of advanced military capabilities and related national-level industrial and technological programs. Defectors from the Soviet scientific community have pointed out that technical acquisition is a major element of the research and development process coordinated by the Soviet Union's Military-Industrial Commission (VPK).[22] As with other parts of Soviet strategy, the Eastern European intelligence services also are integrated into this activity. The 1990s will likely see no reduction in Soviet efforts, a problem with strategic implications for the United States. Countering it will require increased attention and greater imagination.

Finally, 1985 was marked by a series of revelations, most notably the Walker spy net, that pointed to the extent of the Soviet bloc espionage threat to the West. More recently it was discovered that the KGB was able to carry out operations inside the U.S. embassy in Moscow. Many specialists agree that in the 1990s, the United States will continue to face "a large, if not massive, hostile intelligence threat, particularly from the Soviet bloc."[23]

Although this assessment is disquieting, each of these categories is accompanied by vulnerabilities that can be exploited. This is also true of other weaknesses (such as economic decay and political discontent) within the Soviet Union and its weak underbelly in Eastern Europe. Each of these targets could be reached through various covert measures to keep Moscow off balance.

In light of this, United States policy should, at a minimum, concentrate on preventing the Soviet Union from using the full range of military and other instruments of power to become the dominant player in the international system of the 1990s. The military imbalance will require the United States to use other means of keeping Moscow off balance and on the defensive. Psychological and political action, special operations, deception, and related tactics should be considered. This is ironic in the sense that the Soviet Union has proven to be more skilled at these activities. Indeed, one could argue that Soviet active measures and deception made an important contribution to the situation the United States will face in the 1990s.

Nevertheless, Soviet achievements over the past two decades are accompanied by potential vulnerabilities. This is even the case in what must be considered Moscow's major success—its massive buildup of strategic and conventional forces. This was made possible only at the great expense of the nondefense parts of the Soviet and Eastern European economies. To offset this, Soviet leader Mikhail Gorbachev has proposed a new course that is summed up in the terms *glasnost* and *perestroika*. The proposed goals are twofold: (1) a political thaw and opening of the system to allow for dissent and (2) a productive and efficient economy that includes more plentiful consumer goods and services. The latter presumably is to be accomplished by channeling resources away from the military sector. In light of the fact that *glasnost* and *perestroika* are currently being propagated inside the Soviet bloc, one can imagine a rise in expectations among various elements of the population who have had to bear the brunt of the past, both economically and politically.

In the West, disagreement exists over how to interpret these developments. Skeptics suggest that there is misunderstanding about what is taking place on two levels.[24] Directed inside, *glasnost* and *perestroika* are not intended to transform the foundations of the Soviet system. The goal is to reform what exists to make it more efficient and productive. The core elements of the regime remain unchanged. The result will be a more formidable threat to the West, with fewer economic constraints. Directed internationally, and particularly against the Western alliance, *glasnost* and *perestroika* are seen as the latest phase of an active measures and deception tradition that dates back to the early days of the Bolshevik regime.[25] This latter interpretation is by no means predominant. In fact, many Western specialists view the Gorbachev initiatives as the first steps in a process that will transform the entire Soviet system. Whitney MacMillan and Richard Ullman, for example, assert that, if Gorbachev succeeds, the Soviet Union will be greatly changed, having an increasing "stake in a moderate international order." Further, they believe Gorbachev's current efforts to modernize Soviet society "are among the most encouraging developments of our era."[26]

Although little evidence currently exists to substantiate Mac-Millan and Ullman's prognosis, perhaps it is just too early to tell. By the 1990s, however, the situation should be clarified. During the interim, an essential part of U.S. policy vis-à-vis the Soviet Union must be the monitoring of Gorbachev's new course. Collection requirements should include placing *glasnost* and *perestroika* under the microscope. Evidence collected should serve as the basis for a public diplomacy program that makes clear to the international community the relationship between what is said and what actually takes place inside the Soviet bloc. This would include communicating the findings directly to the populations of the Soviet bloc through Radio Free Europe/Radio Liberty (RFE/RL). Furthermore, until facts reflect words, drastic changes in the national security policy of the Western alliance would seem premature.

What if the skeptics are correct? If so, then the Kremlin is playing a potentially dangerous game inside its own territory. While they may not intend to do so, propagating *glasnost* and *perestroika* inside the bloc might further encourage the desires for religious, ethnic, and individual freedoms that already exist. In fact, acting on their own, movements demanding these rights may, in the next few years, call Moscow's hand and attempt to compel the Kremlin leaders to act on their promises. This has happened in the past under conditions that did not hold out the promises of *glasnost*. It will then be up to Washington to decide whether the United States wishes to encourage and assist those demanding real *glasnost*. If the United States chooses to do so, covert political assistance and advice could contribute to and intensify the activities of those inside the Soviet Union, Poland, Hungary, and elsewhere who are willing to take a stand.

What would the United States hope to accomplish? U.S. objectives would include intensifying cleavages, promoting opposition, and generally disrupting business as usual to forestall the Soviet Union from reaching the point where it believes it can prevail in a global confrontation with the United States. In other words, at a minimum the United States should introduce those fissures that would result in a negative Soviet calculation of the costs and gains of initiating such an action. Of course, this must be accompanied by a policy of building support for these popular movements on an international scale. If the United States is going to do this at all, it must take seriously what doing so is likely to engender inside the Soviet Union and Eastern Europe and be willing to follow up with other forms of overt and covert aid for those who undertake these actions. Such a policy would require the West to use public diplomacy, economic measures, and related instruments to pressure Moscow from inside and outside. During the past four decades, such policies have proven to be illusive or were rejected out of hand in the West. The consequences and responsibilities of pursuing such policies must be taken seriously or not at all.

A second area of vulnerability has grown out of earlier Soviet gains in the Third World. While the Kremlin could correctly point to a series of successes in the 1970s, maintaining socialist gains has been difficult and costly. A number of new pro–Soviet/Marxist-Leninist regimes that came to power at that time have proven to be vulnerable to indigenous resistance movements that oppose their form of rule. In many respects, as a result of the emergence of these opposition elements, conflict in the Third World has taken a new turn. Whereas in the 1960s and 1970s insurgency warfare was directed mainly against governments either aligned with or friendly to the West, by the early 1980s there emerged a number of resistance movements (outside the Soviet Union and Eastern Europe) opposed to the rule of Marxist-Leninist factions that are, to differing degrees, maintained in power by the Soviet Union and its surrogates. Recognizing these vulnerabilities, Moscow has sought to provide the means by which new allies can maintain power against armed resistance threats.

The Soviet goal is to ensure that regimes that come to power through Leninist means and with Moscow's support remain in control, but there are costs involved in achieving this. Charles Wolf and his colleagues at The Rand Corporation estimate the Soviet "burden of empire" in the Third World to have increased from roughly $18 billion in 1971 to $41 billion in 1981.[27] There is also some evidence of disenchantment in Cuba and the Soviet Union over the human costs in Angola, Ethiopia, and Afghanistan.

Although the United States has sought to exploit these situations only in a limited way, this has had an effect. Afghanistan is a case in point. For the Soviet Union, the invasion was the easy part. Despite Moscow's success in depopulating vast stretches of Afghanistan through firepower and terror, by 1987 the *mujhadin* were stronger, better organized, and certainly better equipped than at any time during the nine-year conflict. Limited, covert U.S. military aid played an important role in helping the resistance deny momentum to the Soviet army. Indeed, Soviet leaders have signed a peace accord and apparently began to withdraw their forces in May 1988. If this proves not to be the case and Moscow attempts to hang on, the United States could raise the costs considerably now and in the decade ahead through increasing covert paramilitary assistance. Such assistance would include advanced weapons, more effective training, and a sophisticated logistical network. Covert aid, if it is to attain maximum impact, should be part of a larger policy of building international support for the resistance and diplomatic and economic opposition to Moscow. The overall objective would be to end Soviet occupation of the country.

In the case of other resistance movements, the Reagan administration has not created a unified policy and strategy to help them develop political and military structures to achieve legitimacy and support—that is, to become a broadly based and meaningful political alternative. This is not surprising given the fact that the United States apparently has no corps of experts knowledgeable about the interrelated political and military elements of such an approach.[28] Current policy is not based on well-developed strategy or assistance programs that provide appropriate political and military training and advice.

What has been the result? In the case of Nicaragua, this lack of strategy has handicapped Reagan administration policy. It has resulted in organizational mistakes and tactical errors that have been politically costly to the resistance program in both the United States and Nicaragua. The fact that the United States seems unable to progress very far past the military side of resistance support reveals the extent of the problem. Political assistance, training, and advice have been, at best, ad hoc. This is evident in the lack of unified commitment to a program aimed at widening the base of support.

In the 1990s, if the United States is compelled to look for ways to keep the Soviet bloc off balance, covert paramilitary assistance to resistance forces outside the Soviet Union and Eastern Europe might become necessary. While the United States can secretly supply these forces militarily, if they are to raise the costs of and divert Soviet bloc resources, they must become more politically sophisticated and broadly based. The United States can provide such advice, support, and assistance only through the development of expertise it currently appears to lack. Such a program will require a different attitude toward resistance movements. Furthermore, if the United States is going to consider this option in the 1990s, it must begin to develop the necessary assets and capabilities today. Currently, covert paramilitary assistance—be it in Nicaragua, Angola, or elsewhere—is not part of a fully articulated and defensible policy.

As I observed previously, in the years ahead the United States will face increasingly sophisticated active measures campaigns, growing out of Moscow's current effort to streamline the apparatus for conceptualizing and implementing these activities. The United States will have to be able to expose and/or undermine major Soviet campaigns focused on splitting the Western alliance and discrediting and isolating the United States in the developing world. Covert action, in cooperation with active counterintelligence, has a role to play in defending against this aspect of Soviet strategy abroad. An essential mission of counterintelligence operations now and in the years to come is to penetrate and learn about the targets and patterns of future active measures campaigns. The collection and analysis of this information will present the United States with the opportunity to counter and undermine these efforts through overt and covert means.

With respect to the latter, both propaganda and political action should be considered. For example, once the United States has identified a foreign agent of influence, knows his or her operational activities, and can link the individual to a foreign intelligence organization, covert action can be used to manipulate this situation. Black propaganda abroad could be employed to unmask the agent's activities, or the agent might be used as a channel through which the United States could deceive Soviet intelligence. One can imagine several related examples of how the United States could counter Soviet active measures in Western Europe and the Third World.

In the 1990s, as the KGB and Soviet bloc services continue to undertake major efforts to acquire scientific information and strategic technologies, U.S. intelligence will be presented with numerous opportunities to deceive and undermine these efforts. Once the United States understands what the Soviets want and how they intend to acquire it, the door is open to use false companies, "foreign" intermediaries, and related operational techniques to frustrate Soviet plans. In my view, the United States should concentrate on this area, given the fact that Moscow depends heavily on technology transfer as a critical aspect of military-focused research and development. Consequently, covert action will not only help neutralize KGB operations but also directly affect Soviet military developments.

Finally, we come to the issue of factionalism among the Communist party elite in the Soviet Union and Eastern European regimes. While this is one of the more intriguing areas of Sovietology, the subject has generated significant disagreement and confusion. Although most specialists would agree that factions continue to persist in the CPSU leadership, differences exist over how to define the outlook and world view of each. Often there is an attempt to apply Western political distinctions, which entails labeling Soviet leaders as either hard-liners/hawks or moderates/doves. Other Sovietologists assert that, while a closed system by its very nature generates factions, it is incorrect to apply Western distinctions. The literature on succession struggles in Communist regimes supports this assertion.

While factionalism exists and often is played out with deadly seriousness, is it possible for the United States to influence this process? The answer is yes, but with a major caveat. In the first place, the United States must understand what different factions stand for, the policies they are advancing, and their strengths and weaknesses. Only by developing such a data base is it possible for the United States to consider how to intervene in the process. It could be argued, however, that more than at any other time in the history of the Soviet Union, the capacity to do so will be critical for the United States in the 1990s. As the Soviet Union reaches the zenith of military power, the United States' ability to take advantage of cleavages among leaders is yet another way of keeping Moscow off balance and preventing it from dominating the international system of the 1990s. Covert action can contribute to a broader policy of helping one faction or undermining another. This will take a level of sophistication and understanding of the Soviet Union that no post–World War II administration has possessed.

The opportunity to undermine Communist party leaders in Eastern European regimes is more attainable. This strategy would not pit one leader against another but confront party chiefs with societal opposition. There are many religious, ethnic, and political tension points that could be encouraged through both open and secret channels. Weaknesses that exist within Warsaw Pact armies also could be targeted. As noted previously, however, undertaking these steps requires a commitment to a long-term policy of weakening major parts of the extended Soviet system.

Latin America

In the 1990s, a number of states in Latin America will continue to experience instability, crisis, and revolutionary conflict. This will be a region of high priority for the United States. It is one of the largest loci of U.S. foreign investment and trade. Imports from the region include large quantities of oil, strategic minerals (such as manganese and aluminum), and a growing variety of manufactured goods.

Since the latter half of the 1970s, Central America, in particular, has been highly unstable. The 1979 victory of the Sandinistas was the initial manifestation of what has developed into internal crises in several states. Since then, the major threat to the region has taken the form of potential Cuban–Sandinista domination. El Salvador currently faces the most serious insurgent challenge in the region, with Guatemala not far behind. In these cases, as well as elsewhere in Central America, underlying social, economic, and political instability are at the base of the insurgent challenge. In each instance, however, Cuban and Nicaraguan assistance to the guerrillas has exacerbated the conflicts.

Will Cuba and Nicaragua continue to threaten the region? Under the present leadership, which is revolutionary in outlook, it would seem that the current pattern will continue. Indeed, revolutionary instability on a large scale might spread to Panama (already undergoing a major political crisis), Mexico, and Honduras. These developments could result in serious economic problems for the United States, including mass immigration. Terrorism and related security problems also might result from this scenario. In formulating a response, the United States might consider not only how to help friendly regimes survive but also ways to exploit the weaknesses of Cuba and Nicaragua.

In the 1970s and 1980s, other parts of Latin America also experienced an upsurge of terrorism and extremism. Colombia is currently threatened by four radical factions, some of which cooperate with well-financed and extremely violent international narcotics syndicates. In Peru a brutal Maoist insurgent group operates with impunity in parts of the country. Finally, Chile remains in a state of siege, with the security services and radical opposition locked in a syndrome of escalating violence. Although not on the same scale of importance as Central America, these three situations will require U.S. attention in the next decade.

If the trends identified above persist in Central America, the United States should consider the following response options: (1) assistance to friendly governments directly challenged by a revolutionary insurgency; (2) actions directed against those states in the region providing armed support, training, and advisory assistance to the guerrillas. In each case, paramilitary covert action could contribute to a broader policy response.

The presence of an insurgency, particularly one in an advanced stage, is evidence that the situation has reached a crisis level in the threatened state. Such a government's counterinsurgency response requires a variety of integrated programs. The United States can contribute to this effort through assistance aimed at socioeconomic development, political reform and social mobilization, military reform and reorganization, security of the population, and isolation and disruption of the insurgent infrastructure.

How can covert action contribute to an integrated counterinsurgency assistance program? During each stage of growth, a revolutionary insurgency seeks to increase the size and activities of its infrastructure. The local intelligence service has a major role in the penetration and disruption of these activities. U.S. paramilitary assistance can contribute to the establishment and maintenance of the intelligence and security services in a threatened country. In many respects, an effective internal security system is the first line of counterinsurgency defense. It requires the ability to penetrate the insurgent organization or recruitment from within it to determine strength, disposition, and plans as well as vulnerabilities.

The CIA's covert action staff is the proper place for this element of U.S. counterinsurgency policy. Given the modus operandi of insurgent organizations, this is not, as some have argued, a mission that military special forces can perform. In many ways, an insurgent apparatus has the attributes or profile of an intelligence organization.

Within Central America in the years to come, El Salvador should be a principal recipient of counterinsurgency aid. Success in El Salvador is critical for the United States. A setback would have serious strategic ramifications and undercut the United States' international reputation and credibility. Farther south, Peru also is facing a serious revolutionary threat. Elsewhere, U.S. efforts should seek to detect potential insurgent threats in their initial stages. An early warning system would allow for a response that seeks to prevent a situation from escalating. The United States should be concerned with Honduras, Mexico, Panama, and Costa Rica today and should not wait until they reach the condition of El Salvador in 1981–1982.

If the United States chooses to respond to those regimes in Central America assisting revolutionary insurgent movements, various options can be considered. Currently, the major focus has been to provide paramilitary aid to the anti-Communist insurgency challenging the regime in Nicaragua. As I observed previously, however, the United States appears not to have developed a unified strategy to assist this movement to develop the political and military structures required to achieve legitimacy and mobilize support among diverse elements of the population. If the next administration intends to continue this course of action, the professional expertise within the intelligence community will have to be expanded.

Beyond paramilitary assistance, other programs might be examined. While Nicaragua has been moving in the direction of establishing totalitarian structures, various indigenous opposition elements continue to resist. In the years ahead, these elements could be encouraged in various ways, including assistance provided through covert channels. Once again, these recommendations should be considered within a broader policy to pressure Nicaragua to stop exporting insurrection.

What can the United States do about Cuba? Although Cuba is as involved as Nicaragua in promoting revolutionary insurgency in the region, concern over provoking a great power confrontation has constrained U.S. countermeasures. This reasoning was certainly at play in the early years of the Reagan administration, when Secretary of State Alexander Haig suggested that the United States go to the source of the insurgency (that is, Cuba). Other senior Reagan advisors overwhelmingly opposed this option.

There is little doubt that in the 1990s the Cuban Communist Party (CCP) will continue to play an active regional and global role, but it also will face internal economic and political hardships. Examples of this already are apparent. For instance, there is evidence of internal dissent over Cuba's role in Africa, especially in terms of the human costs. Modest efforts could be directed at providing more accurate information on this matter. Similarly, the Mariel boat lift of 1980 signaled that economic privation, lack of jobs, and political repression can result in spontaneous dissent. Each of these situations demonstrates weaknesses that could be exploited, overtly and covertly, if Havana continues to serve as a global surrogate of Moscow. Finally, in the 1990s, Cuba is likely to experience its first leadership succession. Is there evidence of serious differences among those likely to compete for power? Defectors have suggested that there are those in the CCP leadership who are disenchanted with the Moscow–Havana relationship, while others staunchly support it. The United States should now be exploring the ramifications of this and other cleavages and how they might affect post-Castro Cuba.

Elsewhere in Central America, the United States will need to pursue policies to ensure that the fragile democracies in Costa Rica and Honduras endure. Intelligence support is an important part of this. Responding to regional terrorist threats that may affect U.S. interests also will require an improved intelligence liaison.

Finally, if not before, then in the 1990s, a number of leadership changes will take place in Latin America. In Panama and Chile, this is not likely to be a tranquil process, and the United States will face difficult choices. It will be in the United States' strategic interest to try to ensure that those who come to power are either friendly to the United States or unfriendly to its adversaries. The United States also will have the opportunity to contribute to the establishment of democracy in these two countries. In Chile and Panama, covert action can contribute to a policy that reflects strategic interests and democratic values. This necessitates developing the means to be in contact with and influence certain individuals and groups. This program should be set in motion immediately, if it is not already under way.

Middle East/Southwestern Asia

During the next decade, this region will remain of major importance to the United States. In addition to keeping the oil flowing, the United States has significant geostrategic and political interests in the region. Over the past decade, major points of conflict and instability have included the protracted conflict in Lebanon and the Iran–Iraq war.

The region also is host to other, less immediate crisis points that involve U.S. national interests and will require attention in the decade to come. Five specific security-related issues are identifiable.

First, the United States will face a growing Soviet effort to gain influence in the region. In the recent past, this has taken the form of promoting instability through assistance to insurgent and terrorist factions and alliances with radical regimes, most notably Iraq and Syria. The new Soviet leadership of Mikhail Gorbachev might, however, adopt a sophisticated political stratagem in an attempt to bring Moscow into the peace process. Recent signs suggest that *glasnost* will have regional applications.

A second major problem will be the security and viability of moderate Arab governments friendly to the United States. They face threats from a number of quarters. Iran has made it clear that the Islamic revolution should extend throughout the region. To this end, it has provided assistance and training to radical Shia elements in Kuwait, Bahrain, and Saudi Arabia. Ayatollah Khomeini has called for the overthrow of the Saudi royal family, and events in Mecca during August 1987 suggest that these are not idle threats. Libya has sought to destabilize states in the region that, in Colonel Qaddafi's opinion, betray the Palestinian cause, serve as lackeys of the United States, or violate his interpretation of Islam. This has resulted in several apparent assassination or coup plots against Hosni Mubarak, King Hassan II, Hissène Habré, and Mohamed Siad Barre. Qaddafi likewise has backed guerrilla and opposition movements in Morocco, Tunisia, Egypt, Chad, and the Sudan. Finally, Syria has employed indirect means to threaten King Hussein of Jordan.

A third area of concern will be terrorism directed against the United States. This will not only take place in the region but also is likely to spill over into Western Europe. It will take two general forms, both of which have a state-sponsored dimension. Iran has been a major supporter of radical Shiite factions in Lebanon that over the past five years have directed terrorist actions against the United States. The key organization is the Hizballah, or Party of God. It is apparent that Iran has made use of it to indirectly attack the United States. In a related fashion, Syria and Libya use a number of radical Palestinian factions. Syria has employed the Abu Nidal group and Popular Front for the Liberation of Palestine, among others, to carry out operations against the United States, Jordan, Israel, and the Fatah elements of the Palestine Liberation Organization (PLO).

While the previous three points have included mention of the indirect threats and challenges Iran and Libya present to the United States in the Middle East, it is important to note that their actions extend well beyond it. From an operational perspective, Qaddafi has assisted insurgent and terrorist movements in various parts of the world and annually brings their representatives to Libya for consultation. Libya is a radical state that openly advocates the use of terrorism and related, protracted warfare tactics on a global basis. Until the U.S. air strike in 1986, it had created the impression that it could take the measure of the United States without any consequences. In a very similar manner, Iran has established the same impression.

Finally, U.S. interests will continue to be affected in the 1990s by the course of the Arab–Israeli conflict. The ongoing and increasingly volatile dispute over the West Bank and Gaza, together with the protracted conflict in Lebanon, enhances the prospect for yet another major confrontation.

In sum, in the next decade major U.S. interests in the Middle East shall remain unchanged, and the region will continue to experience various forms of protracted struggle, including terrorism, subversion, and war. In shaping an effective response to these multiple problems, the United States will have to employ all the instruments of statecraft. As I will discuss below, in light of the threat profile, the different aspects of covert action will have much to contribute.

I began this section by suggesting that in the years to come the Soviet Union is likely to pursue new ways in which to insert itself into the Middle East negotiations process. In the past, it has focused on destabilizing the process through assistance to radical Palestinian factions and insurgent movements, as well as by forming alliances with states such as Syria. Recent signs suggest that Gorbachev has initiated a new political stratagem. On the surface, the Soviet Union will seek to create the impression that it is disillusioned with the extremism of those it supported in the past and now wishes to play an active and positive role in the peace process. I have already discussed how covert action and counterintelligence, working in unison, can defend against active measures. This cooperative effort is also appropriate in the Middle East.

The security and viability of moderate Arab regimes in Saudi Arabia, Kuwait, Bahrain, Egypt, Jordan, and Morocco will be a major issue for U.S. foreign policy in the 1990s. These societies have been targeted for destabilization by Iran, Libya, and Syria. From a defensive perspective, there is much the United States can do through intelligence support. Over the years, there have been major successes in this aspect of covert action. A case in point is the long-term provision of assistance and training to the intelligence and security services of King Hassan II of Morocco. There also have been major setbacks, most notably the assassination of Egyptian president Anwar Sadat.

The radical regimes seeking to topple moderate Arab states in the region are also involved in supporting terrorist factions. Indeed, for Libya, Iran, and Syria, this is a form of indirect warfare. Available evidence reveals the increasing dimensions and degree to which those carrying out terrorist actions depend on their state patrons. Details now exist about the operational principles, infrastructure, and international and regional coordination of the network that exists among these states and numerous terrorist organizations. Statistics show that during the 1980s terrorist operations have been increasingly directed against U.S. citizens and property. Additionally, there is a rising pattern of lethality, with the bombing of the U.S. embassy and marine barracks in Lebanon being the most notable examples. Middle East terrorism also has spilled over into Western Europe, where approximately one-third of all terrorist acts are traced back to the Middle East. Here also the United States is one of the main targets.

Against this backdrop, it is necessary for U.S. counterterrorist policy to encompass more than defensive measures. An array of offensive means should be developed and used against terrorist organizations and the states that support their activities. National Security Decision Directive (NSDD) 138 called for an active response against terrorists known to have struck Americans or currently planning such attacks. It likewise laid the basis for counterterrorist options against Qaddafi. CIA-directed covert action was viewed as part of a constellation of measures, including diplomacy, propaganda, and economic pressures. All were required if the United States was to establish an effective counterterrorist policy. This included more effective coordination with allies and friends, most importantly in the area of intelligence liaison. However, the transition from the formulation of a counterterrorist policy to its implementation has proven to be exceedingly difficult, especially with respect to the CA component.

The root of the problem in large part lies in the human intelligence base required to support counterterrorist covert operations. To be sure, a great deal of material is available in various open sources on specific terrorist groups. This material needs to be exploited in a more effective way. Intelligence penetration or the cultivation of a source inside a terrorist organization or its support system is equally important. Neither of these are easily achieved. A network of such assets requires a long-term commitment of time and resources. Although this can be supplemented by intelligence provided through liaison arrangements with the intelligence services of states in the region, such measures should not be considered as a substitute for a human source network established by the United States. Such a network has been difficult to establish, however, and not all elements of the U.S. intelligence community are convinced of its value.

If the United States is to consider employing covert and special operations against terrorist groups and those states that sponsor them, it will require this kind of intelligence base. Once established, collection can focus on the weaknesses and internal vulnerabilities of PLO and Shiite factions. As with any radical movement, these groups are likely to have vulnerability points stemming from ideological divisions and competition among leaders; corruption, factionalism, and weak support services within the organizational infrastructure; and disillusionment among those who carry out operations. These and related weaknesses could serve as the targets for propaganda and political-psychological operations carried out covertly.

The states sponsoring terrorism likewise have weaknesses and vulnerabilities. Substantial evidence has pointed to disaffection within the officer corps of the Libyan military, who often pay the price for Qaddafi's adventurism. Similarly, it appears that disaffection is developing in Iran over the carnage resulting from the war of attrition with Iraq. Likewise, Syria has its own internal vulnerabilities. Propaganda and political action, as part of a broad program and in cooperation with other regional powers, could exploit these and other weaknesses. To do so in the 1990s, the United States will require, in addition to an adequate human intelligence network, the willingness on the part of states such as Egypt, Saudi Arabia, and Morocco to cooperate in these efforts. The latter will not be easily accomplished, given the perception that the United States cannot be counted on to remain involved in such operations and is unable to prevent them from becoming public. This was driven home during the Iran-Contra hearings.

In addition to propaganda and political action, the United States should consider special military operations for preemptive and preventive strikes against terrorist organizations and for coercive diplomacy against state sponsors. Depending on the nature and size of the operation, these forces might consist of paramilitary elements within the CIA or small units of foreign nationals under CIA control and direction. The operation also might involve special operation forces under the command of the Department of Defense working in liaison with the CIA. In addition to the intelligence base discussed previously, small-scale special military operations require highly sophisticated training of personnel, methods of transportation that permit clandestine infiltration and withdrawal, forward support bases, and the use of deception. Missions currently permitted under the law include harassment, destruction of specific installations, abduction of designated personnel, and the rescue of hostages. The option of special military operations provides for an effective mode to counter, respond to, preempt, and even prevent terrorist attacks. It also can serve as an instrument of coercive diplomacy against those states that persist in aiding and encouraging terrorist organizations. In comparison with conventional capabilities, special military operations are more flexible in that they allow for stealth, surprise, speedy infiltration and withdrawal, and deniability. Many argue that these attributes make this option more attractive than the normal high-profile conventional military response generally adopted by the United States.

To summarize, in responding to terrorist groups and radical states that support them, covert action has much to offer because it enables the United States to take offensive or proactive steps. A note of caution is necessary, however. Isolated propaganda, political action, or special military operations are likely to have little long-term impact. To be effective, they must be part of a broad program of pressures and actions.

Thus far, I have focused on those covert operations within existing guidelines that could be employed to disrupt terrorist organizations or coerce and compel those states promoting terrorism and other forms of indirect warfare to desist. In the 1990s, the United States might, out of self-defense, have to consider harsher measures. With respect to hostile states that persist in escalating the use of terrorism and related protracted warfare measures, the issue will be whether to pursue a course of action that, if successful, results in a change of leadership. Additionally, if hard evidence exists, the question is likely to be raised whether lethal measures should be taken against those terrorist leaders who have directed operations resulting in the death of Americans.

Currently, such measures are prohibited under Executive Order 12333. This stipulation was conceived in the aftermath of congressional revelations of prior attempted assassinations. However, are the assassination of a head of state (for example, Fidel Castro) and the lethal self-defense against terrorist leaders (such as Sheik Mohammed Fadlallah) responsible for the murder of U.S. citizens comparable circumstances? Both actions are highly controversial and difficult for the United States to entertain, but current positions may be reconsidered if the pattern of events experienced in the past decade continues into the 1990s. The question the United States will have to answer is "If the evidence exists, do democracies have the moral duty to place at risk those responsible for the indiscriminate murder of their citizens?"

Other Regional Challenges and Issues

Beyond the Soviet–Eastern bloc challenges and threats to U.S. interests in Latin America and the Middle East, a number of other regional issues should be noted. I will focus only on those in which a U.S. response might include covert action.

During the 1970s, a number of pro-Soviet regimes came to power in different regions of the developing world. Marxist-Leninist forces, employing revolutionary insurgent or other protracted conflict strategies, seized control in several countries. A number of these regimes have become bases for training guerrillas and terrorists from neighboring states. These developments have raised important security questions for the United States. Several of these states have also found themselves engulfed in protracted guerrilla challenges. In the 1990s, these conflicts will continue to fester, and the United States is likely to have the opportunity to put an adversary on the defensive. Thus far, however, U.S. support has generally been limited, and covert action appears to be a substitute for a fully articulated and politically defensible policy. Angola is a case in point.

In the 1990s, the continent of Africa will continue to experience political turmoil and crisis. Although not a high-priority region, it will nevertheless be important for the United States to stand by friends who are threatened by direct or indirect intervention. In these cases, because of the political atmosphere, assistance might have to be provided through discreet and clandestine channels.

A number of examples come to mind. Over the past several years, Chad has been threatened by Libya. Indirect assistance from the United

States has helped make a difference. Other states that could face problems in the years to come include Kenya. With a fragile economy heavily dependent on tourism, terrorist strikes could cause serious problems. Perceived as pro-Western, Kenya will need more counterterrorism assistance in the years ahead. Growing instability in southern Africa and the possibility of further Soviet penetration will be another important security issue.

Currently the Philippines is experiencing a serious crisis that includes an escalating insurgency. Thus far the U.S. and Aquino governments have not found a satisfactory channel through which to address a rapidly declining situation. To a much lesser extent, Thailand continues to face the threat of internal Communist insurgency. In each instance, clandestine counterinsurgency advice and aid is necessary.

Finally, in the 1970s and 1980s, several long-term friends of the United States came to the end of their rule. In two cases, the results were the seizure of power by individuals hostile to the United States. In Iran and Nicaragua, the Carter administration was unable or unwilling to try to influence the transition process. In the Philippines, we saw a much different result. In the next decade, other allies of the United States may find themselves facing the end of their rules. If radical factions come to power, U.S. interests might be seriously affected. How these situations are addressed will be of vital importance.

It would appear that each of the five dimensions of covert action could contribute to the advancement of U.S. foreign policy objectives in regions besides those already examined. First of all, increased paramilitary support to the resistance forces of Jonas Savimbi in Angola could present U.S. policymakers with the opportunity of reversing a major Soviet victory of the 1970s. Over the past decade, the Soviet bloc has made a major investment in maintaining its client in power. The strategic consequences of a Soviet setback in Angola would be consequential for Kremlin policy in the Third World. This would especially be the case if such a setback was preceded by a debacle in Afghanistan. Covert paramilitary assistance could help generate this outcome.

Likewise, paramilitary assistance to the resistance elements opposing the Kremlin's client government in Ethiopia would have an adverse impact on Soviet actions in the Horn of Africa. Assistance to the non-Communist elements opposing the Vietnamese army in Cambodia could have the same effect in that region. Beyond the strategic argument of keeping the Soviet Union and its clients on the defensive, the United States would be on the side of those seeking to free their countries from totalitarian rule and establish relatively more open political systems. It is this last requirement that leads me to reject assisting the opposition in Mozambique.

While anti-Communist insurgencies will provide the United States with strategic opportunities, regimes friendly to the United States also will confront insurgent challenges. In the years to come, the Philippines will face serious problems. Counterinsurgency advice and assistance can make a difference, but the United States should focus on preventive counterinsurgency and development assistance to head off situations before they reach the crisis level that currently exists in the Philippines. Where U.S. geostrategic interests are threatened, early warning can result in positive steps to influence the direction and pace of change before it becomes the demand of a revolutionary insurgency.

Several friendly governments in Africa will be threatened by direct and indirect intervention by outside powers. It will be important to anticipate these developments and, to the extent possible, provide security assistance, intelligence training, and related support. Earlier I cited Kenya as a case in point. Other examples might include Zaire, Nigeria, Chad, and Sudan.

It is also likely that several national leaders will pass from the scene in the 1990s. The leadership transition process, as is often the case, will be marked by violent factionalism and domestic strife. Earlier I suggested that standing outside these situations and waiting for the dust to settle is not a prudent course to follow. Although the United States owes old friends and allies support, that does not prevent it from becoming involved. At the present time, the United States should be identifying where succession crises are likely to occur and who will be involved. The goal should be to build linkages where possible. This will not be easy and requires understanding and sophistication. The United States' goal should be to help democratic/moderate elements come to power. If this is not possible, the United States should at least seek to keep out of power those who would align with its enemies. Assuming the country has the assets, various forms of covert political action could be employed to influence the course of events.

Organizational and Resource Requirements

How might the United States prepare for covert action in the 1990s? What kinds of assets, organizational and individual, will be required to carry out the missions described above? The recommendations that follow are predicated on two assumptions. First, covert action is not considered to be a special activity that is employed only in exceptional circumstances. Rather it is one of a number of instruments of statecraft. When it is appropriate, covert action should be employed with other instruments of power and influence to achieve policy objectives. Second, in the 1990s a number of the threats the United States is likely to encounter can be subsumed under the general heading of protracted warfare. Therefore, the capacity to respond to and preempt these challenges should be an important consideration for senior policymakers. Furthermore, the various CA products will constitute a vital weapon system on the protracted battlefield.

At the policymaking and planning level, organizational requirements should focus on the issues of coordination and integration of covert action into the policy process. Perhaps the best way to explain this is through an example. Recent congressional legislation has mandated that the executive branch initiate steps to become more effectively organized to respond to low-intensity conflict (LIC) threats, including counterinsurgency, counterterrorism, and support for resistance movements. It calls for the establishment of a board for low-intensity conflict at the National Security Council level. The purpose of the board is to plan and coordinate the LIC policy of the United States. This creates a single channel for integrating those bureaucratic elements involved in LIC policy and plans. Depending on the issues, this would include the military services, CIA, U.S. Information Agency, Department of State, and other agencies when appropriate. The LIC board could be subdivided into three branches to focus on the most critical LIC missions the United States is likely to undertake: counterinsurgency, counterterrorism, and resistance support. Each of the principal bureaucratic elements would have a representative on the LIC board. In light of the contribution CA assets can make to each of these LIC missions, it would seem that the CIA should play a key role.

Not every policy area in which covert action has a role warrants such an elaborate organizational structure. The point is that it is important to establish, at the policymaking and planning level, recognition and acceptance of the potential contributions of covert action as an instrument to be employed, in conjunction with others, to accomplish objectives. The LIC board is structured in a way that will allow for this development.

Of course, changing the "wiring diagram" will not necessarily lead to an understanding of the importance of covert action. Reorganization will accomplish little without reorientation or realization of what covert action has to offer. Perhaps the best way to begin to achieve this reorientation is through an executive order that defines and outlines covert action as a specific class of activities and spells out how each relates to policy.

What kinds of CA infrastructure need to be developed within the CIA? Whatever currently exists, it seems safe to assume that it is probably insufficient to carry out the missions outlined previously. If what is needed is not currently in place, perhaps the following should be considered as one way to prepare to meet the challenges of the next decade.

To begin with, the CA staff within the CIA's Directorate of Operations (DDO) will require senior managers with proven abilities and skills in planning and implementing operations. This may already exist and needs only to be tasked. If sufficient assets are unavailable to take on an expanded CA role in the 1990s, alternatives to develop this personnel will have to be pursued.

One solution would be to draw on the expertise of the intelligence and security services of friends and allies. A number of these appear to contain practitioners skilled in the planning, management, and implementation of the different kinds of CA missions discussed previously. Through liaison arrangements, their expertise could be used to help educate and train a new generation of CA managers. A second avenue might be to undertake a systematic analysis of post–World War II CA programs conducted by the United States and others. The objective would be to identify what kinds of organizational and managerial procedures worked effectively under different conditions. This could likewise contribute to the preparation of a new corps of CA managers.

Arrangements to facilitate interaction between CA managers and the area divisions of the DDO also should be established. Apparently this has been difficult to do even during the 1950s and 1960s, when it was agreed that covert action could make a big contribution to U.S. policy. Indeed, available evidence suggests that even then covert action was viewed as a stepchild by many in the DDO and other parts of the CIA, as well as in the larger intelligence and governmental communities. In light of the Iran-Contra crisis, there might now be a tendency to de-emphasize the role that covert action can play as an instrument of statecraft. Additionally, within the DDO, the old argument could again surface that covert action, while necessary, should be located outside the DDO. After careful consideration, I am not persuaded by the latter position. Indeed, the opposite would seem to be quite compelling.

The CA staff and area division managers can benefit from each other's activities and successes. Certainly those planning covert action can profit from interacting with and having access to the products of those in the DDO responsible for human collection. It seems equally likely that the positive intelligence by-products of a covert action might contribute to the overall understanding an area division manager seeks to realize. Consequently, CA staff personnel need to be assigned to each of the area divisions, if this is not already the case. The opposite also should be true.

There also appears to be the need for improved interaction among CA planners, analysts, and counterintelligence officers. Further, formulation of a comprehensive and forward-looking plan that specifies how CA options contribute to the achievement of U.S. policy objectives is desirable on a periodic basis.

A solution must be found to the current debate over whether the DoD or CIA is the appropriate place to maintain U.S. paramilitary capabilities for assisting anti-Communist insurgents. In light of the political-paramilitary nature of resistance movements, the CIA has been the best equipped to build and maintain support programs. Of course, DoD special operations forces can provide valuable military assistance to these operations.

What kinds of human resources will be required to carry out CA missions in the next decade? The agenda of possible options developed earlier suggests that U.S. intelligence officers will need to be prepared to implement CA missions in diverse and non-Western societies. To develop an infrastructure in these regions, personnel selection procedures might need to be considerably altered. To be sure, finding this kind of personnel is a complicated process, but such talent does exist in the United States and abroad.

Threats and challenges in the Middle East serve as a case in point. In the first place, there will be the need to identify and recruit into the CIA individuals who either are Middle Eastern in lineage or can pass for such in that region. One solution might be to look in the Middle Eastern ethnic communities that exist in many parts of the United States. Recruitment could be focused in part on these ethnic and religious groups. Similar communities that exist in Western Europe and elsewhere also should be considered. Within each body various age, occupational, and professional clusters might be probed. Among those recruited should be a select number of individuals who would be prepared to live and work for extended periods in critical parts of the Middle East under new forms of cover. Although not completely analogous, these individuals would have a deep cover profile similar to those of Soviet illegals. Their immediate task would be to ensconce themselves in the society and then begin to work their way into positions where they could contribute to the kinds of CA options specified earlier.

The same kind of infrastructure will be needed to address threats and challenges in Latin America. Where will the United States find such assets? It is unlikely that elite undergraduate and graduate schools will contain more than a few such individuals. Attention should be focused in part on ethnic communities in the United States and abroad. Additionally, experienced individuals from a wide range of occupations and professions should be targeted. Here also a special group from among those selected should be prepared for long-term missions. Their objectives will include development of contacts, penetration of organizations, and establishment of clandestine structures inside states and political entities of strategic importance.

Can the United States find individuals in these ethnic and religious communities who can be recruited? The answer probably is yes, but it will necessitate important changes in personnel selection procedures. What about those to be prepared for long-term, deep-cover missions? This will be more difficult. It is first necessary to develop a psychological and political profile of the characteristics such individuals should possess. Once specified, individuals with these characteristics will have to be identified, recruited, and trained, all of which takes time and commitment.

In terms of CA skills, each of the different types of covert action will require personnel skilled in these activities. In some cases, these people may already exist. In others, such as paramilitary expertise for assisting resistance movements, the United States appears to have few individuals with these skills. Training programs will need to be established to develop these skills.

In summary, I have suggested significant changes in organizational structures (at home and abroad) and personnel recruitment and training procedures. Is this too much to expect? Many would argue that, given the opposition and biases about covert action that have developed since the 1970s, this is not possible. However, threats in the years ahead may result in serious setbacks for the United States if it is not equipped with the means—both overt and covert—to respond to and preempt these challenges. This will necessitate recognition and acceptance within the intelligence and policymaking communities of the value of covert action as an instrument of statecraft that is not inimical to democratic norms.

Notes

1. See the discussion by Morton Halperin in "Should the U.S. Fight Secret Wars?" *Harper's* September 1984, 37.

2. U.S. Congress, House Permanent Select Committee on Intelligence, Subcommittee on Legislation, *Hearing on H.R. 1013, H.R. 1371, and Other Proposals Which Address the Issue of Affording Prior Notice of Covert Actions to the Congress,* 100th Cong., 1st sess. (Washington, D.C.: Government Printing Office, 1987), 90.

3. See the discussion by Ralph McGehee in "Should the U.S. Fight Secret Wars?" 35–36.

4. Stansfield Turner, *Secrecy and Democracy: The CIA in Transition* (Boston: Houghton Mifflin, 1985), 278.

5. Ibid., 177.

6. Stansfield Turner, "From an Ex-CIA Chief: Stop the 'Covert' Operation in Nicaragua," *Washington Post,* 24 April 1983, C1–2.

7. B. Hugh Tovar, "Covert Action," in Roy Godson, ed., *Intelligence Requirements for the 1980's: Elements of Intelligence,* rev. ed. (Washington, D.C.: National Strategy Information Center, 1983), 71.

8. Theodore Shackley, *The Third Option* (New York: Reader's Digest Press, 1981), 19.

9. Roy Godson, "Special Supplement: U.S. Intelligence Policy," in Joseph Kruzel, ed., *American Defense Annual, 1986–1987* (Lexington, Mass.: Lexington Books, 1986), 203.

10. Gregory Treverton, "Covert Action and Open Society," *Foreign Affairs* 65 (Summer 1987): 1013.

11. Allan Goodman, "Reforming U.S. Intelligence," *Foreign Policy*, no. 67 (Summer 1987): 131.

12. *New York Times*, 3 May 1987, A31.

13. John Ranelagh, *The Agency: The Rise and Decline of the CIA* (New York: Simon and Schuster, 1986), 277. In July 1954, James Doolittle was tasked by the Eisenhower administration to make recommendations on future CIA covert action missions.

14. Ernest Lefever and Roy Godson, *The CIA and the American Ethic* (Washington, D.C.: Ethics and Public Policy Center, 1979); Cord Meyer, *Facing Reality: From World Federalism to the CIA* (New York: Harper and Row, 1980).

15. My ideas in this section have benefited from a series of articles by Charles Krauthammer. These include "The Poverty of Realism," *The New Republic*, 17 February 1986; and "Morality and the Reagan Doctrine," *The New Republic*, 8 September 1986.

16. Tovar, "Covert Action," 80.

17. Boris Ponomarev, "Great Vital Force of Leninism," trans. in *JPRS/ USSR Report*, July 1980, 11.

18. John Dziak, *Chekisty: A History of the KGB* (Lexington, Mass.: Lexington Books, 1988), 145–50.

19. For current information and analysis of Soviet active measures programs, see the quarterly publication *DISINFORMATION: Soviet Active Measures and Disinformation Forecast*, the Institute for International Studies, Washington, D.C.

20. Currently, the International Security Studies Program of the Fletcher School of Law and Diplomacy is completing an oral history project that focuses in part on extensive interviews with former intelligence, foreign ministry, and military officials, as well as members of the institutes from the Soviet Union, the Eastern bloc, Nicaragua, Cuba, Ethiopia, and Afghanistan who are concerned with international affairs. The subject concerns Soviet decision making as it relates to the panoply of protracted low-intensity operations, including arms transfers, training and advisory support, intelligence, psychological warfare, disinformation and active measures, and the use of surrogate forces.

21. For an examination of these developments, see "Shake–up in Top Soviet Active Measures Personnel," *DISINFORMATION: Soviet Active Measures and Disinformation Forecast*, no. 3 (Summer 1986): 1, 6–7.

22. This is described in an oral history interview with Dr. Anatoly Fedoseyev, a former Soviet scientist and leading designer of magnetrons, a critical component of the most powerful Soviet radars. He was the recipient

of both the Lenin Prize for science and the Hero of Socialist Labor award. In the interview, conducted under the auspices of the International Security Studies Program of the Fletcher School of Law and Diplomacy, Fedoseyev described his firsthand experience in the research and development process coordinated by the VPK.

23. Godson, "Special Supplement: U.S. Intelligence Policy," 204.

24. For example, Flora Lewis observes that *"glasnost* doesn't mean human rights, it doesn't mean the end of censorship and control, it doesn't mean democracy in the Western sense. Mr. Gorbachev gave his definition in his recent Murmansk speech. 'Democracy is conscious discipline and an understanding of the need for everybody to participate. . . . It is not the claim to a right to do as you please.' " Lewis goes on to note that "it's better that we know what they mean by the words." Lewis, "It Isn't Only Glasnost," *New York Times,* 30 October 1987, A35. Copyright 1987 by the New York Times Company. Reprinted by permission.

25. Dziak, *Chekisty: A History of the KGB.*

26. Whitney MacMillan and Richard Ullman, "America's Self-Interest in Helping Gorbachev," *New York Times,* 7 October 1987, A23.

27. Charles Wolf et al., *The Costs of the Soviet Empire* (Santa Monica, Calif.: The Rand Corporation, 1983), 19.

28. Stephen Hosmer and George Tanham, *Countering Covert Aggression* (Santa Monica, Calif.: The Rand Corporation, 1986), 24–25.

II. B. HUGH TOVAR

Writing on this subject some years ago, one observer with a fair amount of experience in the field lamented that covert action (CA) in the latter 1970s showed all the earmarks of a dying art form. Clearly, at that time, in reaction to the Church committee's exposures and the unending adverse publicity of those years, there were many who would have been delighted to witness its extinction. Even among professionals, the CIA practitioners, there was a growing distaste for a type of activity that threatened exposure, encouraged public criticism, and, as they saw it, reduced career prospects.

Yet covert action did not die. If we can accept at face value the disclosures of recent years, covert action seems to have taken a new lease on life. How well, or how badly, it has done is very difficult to evaluate from the outside, and I hesitate to accept at face value the highly partisan contentions—both pro and con—that continue to reverberate in the media. However, since current experiences and capabilities offer a line of departure from which to proceed in addressing the 1990s, let us look briefly at the picture of covert action in the eighties to the extent that the record is available in the public domain. A substantial portion of that record may be visible in Bob Woodward's book, *Veil: The Secret Wars of the CIA, 1981–1987.*[1] This is not to suggest that Woodward's reconstruction of the record is either complete or accurate. Indeed, there is reason to question it on both counts. But for the outsider who is dependent on the public record for current information, the book is a useful starting point.

According to Woodward, the United States, drawing heavily though not entirely on the resources of the CIA, has undertaken (or attempted to undertake) covert action along the following lines during the period 1979/1980 to the present:

1. Propaganda directed against Communist countries, with the initial focus on smuggling books and literature and later expanded to treat specific issues often in support of NATO

2. Limited paramilitary support to rebel factions in South Yemen, including collaboration with British intelligence

3. Extensive paramilitary support to Afghan rebels following the Soviet invasion in 1979 involving collaboration with Pakistan plus the extensive clandestine involvement of Saudi Arabia

4. A hostage rescue attempt in Iran (Desert One), carried out by U.S. military elements with CIA participation

5. Covert assistance to Hissène Habré of Chad in the form of funds, arms, and technical support carried out in collaboration with France

6. Initiation under President Carter of covert support for Nicaraguan anti-Sandinistas, to expand geometrically as the overriding CA issue of the Reagan administration

7. Covert support—financial, political, paramilitary, and propaganda—for President Duarte of El Salvador

8. Covert support to the pro-Western government of Mauritius, threatened by Marxist militants (A media furor arose when the story was leaked with the name of Mauretania mistakenly substituted for Mauritius.)

9. Covert support for Bashir Gemayal of Lebanon, although planned expansion of the relationship was aborted when Gemayal was killed

10. Financial support to the non-Communist Cambodian resistance forces

11. Covert assistance coupled with overt aid to Prime Minister Eugenia Charles of Dominica within the framework of the Grenada invasion

12. Propaganda and political action supporting the new coalition government of Grenada

13. Security assistance and intelligence training to support many, though by no means all, friendly foreign governments; a good example, not necessarily representative, is the program undertaken in collaboration with President Anwar Sadat of Egypt

14. Covert action aimed at the ouster of Ayatollah Khomeini, which included support for Iranian exiles working against Khomeini, support for anti-Khomeini radio broadcasts from Egypt, and provision of intelligence to the Iraqi government in the latter's war with Iran

15. A secret military air operation using sensitive intelligence information to capture an Egyptian jet transporting terrorists

16. Training and support of selected groups of Lebanese nationals to conduct armed strikes against terrorists

17. Covert action designed to topple Muammar Qaddafi by supporting external opposition groups, possibly in conjunction with preemptive and punitive military strikes against key Libyan targets

18. Selective passage of intelligence information to friendly foreign governments for political purposes

19. Covert financial support (nonlethal) to opponents of the Marxist Ethiopian government

20. Covert assistance to Jonas Savimbi and UNITA following rescission of the 1976 Clark amendment

21. The covert sale of arms to Iran for the apparent purpose of effecting the release of U.S. hostages and developing contact with moderate Iranian factions (An added feature was the provision of intelligence for Iranian use against Iraq; this operation was con-

ducted largely by the National Security Council [NSC] staff, independent of normal policy mechanisms.)

The scope of activity thus encompassed is indeed formidable, and it reflects an operational capability that could not have been deployed ten years ago on anything approaching the current scale. Most traditional forms of covert action are included—the one exception being covert support to international nongovernmental organizations, which figured so prominently in CIA operations during the fifties and sixties.

It is almost impossible for the ordinary citizen to determine how effective these operations have been. Nor is it clear how many of them are still functioning today. For example, in the case of the training of the Lebanese counterterrorist group, the disastrous bombing in Beirut on March 5, 1985, might have terminated U.S. willingness to experiment with such volatile and possibly uncontrollable elements. Likewise, the NSC-directed efforts targeted at Iran and the attempts at "disinformation" against Qaddafi have, we assume, ground to a halt in the glare of exposure and publicity and cannot therefore be construed as representing an available capability.

Challenges for the 1990s

The Soviet Union will continue to challenge the United States for world leadership in the next decade. Relations between the two superpowers will alternate between sustained tension and limited relaxation. There is no reason to expect that the Soviets will refrain from pursuing their traditional objectives while talking peace and democracy. *Glasnost* will continue to titillate observers as long as Chairman Gorbachev can maintain his preeminence among Soviet leaders. Whether it is a reality or a facade, *glasnost* may improve short-term prospects for settlement of some issues. But it does not mean that the Soviet Union will lose interest in maintaining existing hegemonies while seeking to expand its influence at the United States' expense in key areas of the world. To illustrate the rather smooth manner in which the Soviets can occasionally perform such feats, we should note the way they responded to three attacks in the Persian Gulf during 1987. The attacks evoked no bombastic response or threat of retaliation. Instead, the Soviets quietly introduced three minesweepers, a supply ship, and a destroyer into a waterway that the czars had for years sought unsuccessfully to draw into their sphere of influence. The ships continue to operate there unhindered.

Worldwide trends, including population growth, political upheaval, and economic disruption, will continue through the nineties, offering the United States and the Soviet Union new areas of contention and competition, challenge, and opportunity. The United States can expect the Soviets to respond at least as actively and aggressively as they are doing today.

Against this backdrop of sustained stress on the international scene, the United States also can assume that future administrations will not be substantially less interested than their predecessors in at least considering CA options to supplement overt diplomatic, military, and other forms of power projection in pursuance of overseas objectives.

For the United States, the Soviet Union will continue to play its essentially adversarial role on the world scene. Aggressive and dynamic despite their internal stresses, the Soviets will seek to test U.S. resolve and capability under conditions short of armed conflict, and they will be at the bottom of most situations in world affairs that might call for CA responses or where CA initiatives might offer prospects of advantage to the United States.

The focal points of such interactions will not differ greatly from the following, which hold our attention today:

1. Western Europe, where the Soviets would like to split NATO and drive a wedge between the United States and its European allies

2. Strategic regions of the Third World currently under pressure or in some instances besieged, including the Middle East, southern Africa, and Central America

3. Other states or regions important to the United States, including the People's Republic of China, the Pacific Basin, the Philippines, Indochina

4. Central and Eastern Europe, now entering a period of change as the Soviet grip on the bloc shows tentative signs of relaxing and where there may be emerging a Central European identity distinct from both East and West

As the two prime competitors face each other and deploy their respective assets and capabilities, I discern a few similarities and some striking differences. The Soviets can exploit a massive overseas presence. Their diplomatic missions are large and are concentrated in or adjacent to what they consider critical areas. They are supplemented by ample military and commercial representations. Aggressive espionage and intelligence collection are hallmarks of all Soviet missions. Among other achievements in penetration of sensitive U.S. military and civilian agencies, they have had notable successes in effecting secret technology transfer in the face of strenuous U.S. efforts to stop it. Economic and military assistance programs are exploited in projecting Soviet power and enhancing political influence. If, as some contend, this is also the way the United States behaves overseas, there is an important difference: The Soviets all march to the same drummer. U.S. overseas operations are rarely as concerted and disciplined.

The Soviets have the enormous advantage of almost, though not quite, unlimited use of proxies to carry out many of their less agreeable missions. Cubans appear to be available in great numbers for deployment overseas, and they have displayed remarkable versatility in serving Soviet purposes, as well as their own, in territories far removed from Cuba. East Germans have done likewise, although on a much more limited scale. Libyans and Bulgarians are also said to be available on occasion to serve as Soviet proxies, as are Czechs, North Koreans, Vietnamese, South Yemenis, and sometimes members of the Palestine Liberation Organization (PLO). In the past, the United States also has drawn on Cuban assets as proxies, sometimes quite successfully. Today, given the U.S. distaste for anything that smacks of mercenary action, Cuban assets are less viable than they once were.

Underlying all Soviet operations is the concept of *active measures*. This is the integrating force in the broad array of tactics employed by the Soviet Union to accomplish its policy objectives. Within its framework, diplomatic activity, economic and military assistance, propaganda and disinformation, and a host of other political and military techniques are systematically brought to bear on a particular objective. Soviet support of Nicaragua is a notable case in point, and there are many others.[2]

There are a number of trends in today's world that not only lend themselves to Soviet exploitation but also represent serious threats to local stability with long-term consequences. Islamic fundamentalism stands out among these, and the example of Khomeini's Iran has already begun to affect Islamic society on three continents. The only element of encouragement in this generally worrisome development is that the Soviets themselves are susceptible within their own borders to the dangers of Islamic ferment. The Armenian–Azerbaijanian upheaval of early 1988 almost certainly reflects new muscle flexing among Soviet Muslims, and it would be no surprise if other such manifestations were to occur.

Ethnic and racial tensions seem to be on the rise throughout Africa, Southern Asia, the southwestern Pacific region, and parts of Latin America. Territorial disputes also are widespread. Many such issues are insoluble from the outside. Others lend themselves to adjustment and possibly to solution. Demagogues will exploit local tensions with undiminished zeal. They have already demonstrated skill in adapting modern communications to further their ends, with an obvious multiplier effect. To date, the Soviets have demonstrated a fair amount of skill in exploiting such situations for their own purposes, whereas the U.S. approach has generally been to react to Soviet intrusions rather than to seize the initiative early in the game.

Organized terrorism has become a prime scourge of the eighties and shows no sign of abatement on either the local or international scene. The United States continues to grope in vain for a viable and consistent counterterrorism policy, while the Soviets have largely been spared embarrassment in this connection. On the one known occasion when a Soviet citizen was killed by terrorists, Soviet retaliation was apparently immediate, brutal, and effective, uninhibited by the sensitivities that make it so difficult for the United States to deal directly with terrorists.

The subject of narcotics traffic does not usually arise in the context of covert action. It is already evident, however, that narcotics trafficking in certain regions—Colombia, Peru, Panama, possibly Bolivia, and maybe in the days ahead Venezuela—represents a force with enormous potential for disruption. The availability of funds in previously undreamed of amounts has corroded the moral fiber of those countries and begun to synergize, with political forces agitating for expanded military revolt. This is terrorism under a different flag, and as with terrorism, attempts to suppress it have failed. It would be folly to exclude covert military action as one way of dealing with the narcotics epidemic.

Other important forces at work are congruent with U.S. interests and will tend, at least in the long term, to inhibit Soviet action capabilities. Nationalism is definitely on the rise within the Soviet bloc. It is making itself felt in Hungary, Poland, Czechoslovakia, Rumania, and East Germany. These countries' willingness to assert their cultural, philosophical, and even political differences may in time significantly reduce Soviet leverage in the face of a new "Central Europeanism." Even within the Soviet Union there are tentative signs of self-expression among the ethnic minorities. These are coupled with indications that the Soviet leadership has begun to face the fact that nationalism cannot be suppressed by fiat. In Eastern Asia, similar forces are at work in Vietnam and Cambodia, and they may in time affect Soviet influence there.

The phenomenon of dissent in the Soviet Union has had, and will continue to have, its ups and downs. Gorbachev has made gestures that offer encouragement, but there is no assurance that they represent a trend. Closely associated with the issue of Jewish emigration, dissent unquestionably represents a problem for Soviet leaders that the United States hopes will not go away. Such efforts as the United States has made to date on behalf of dissidents and those seeking to emigrate have, we must assume, been confined to diplomatic channels.

As the United States searches for other trends likely to inhibit the Soviet Union's ability to challenge U.S. equities, it might not be premature to address the emergence of democratic governments in previously authoritarian countries. The number of countries reflecting such a felicitous trend is small, but it may be growing. One such country is the Philippines. Although Corazon Aquino's future is far from assured, there is reason to hope that she will survive and lead the Philippines out of the morass into which Ferdinand Marcos had let it slide. On the other side of the world, Argentina continues to defy the oracles under Raul Alfonsin. He may yet induce that country to rise above itself and set an example for the southern half of the South American continent. Hope springs eternal.

U.S. Resources and Their Viability

Covert action has long been a vexing issue in the minds of many observers. For some the issue has focused on intervention in the affairs of sovereign states. Others, less opposed in principle, have argued that covert action diverts needed resources from more important intelligence collection. They also contend that exposure, which they see as almost inevitable, will tarnish the intelligence image. There seems to be little doubt that in the wake of the 1987 Irangate hearings and the interminable Contra debates, covert action has even less respectability in the public mind than ever before. What does that mean in terms of future employment of the CA option? Probably not very much. U.S. presidents have repeatedly seen fit to use it when faced with problems that have not responded to other pressures. Once the dust settles over the Iran-Contra controversy, it is a safe bet that the next president will follow suit.

Clearly, though, the extent of public distaste for certain features of covert action is something that must be considered in weighing the question of risk versus gain and the political impact of exposure. Compatibility with democratic values is a serious matter, and U.S. policymakers must strive to ensure it in any contemplated covert undertaking. Reasonableness of purpose, decency of method, and the likelihood that results will satisfy public opinion at both the giving and receiving ends are still valid criteria against which covert action should be weighed.

Covert responses to acts of war pose different and often more difficult problems. Violence by a government against accredited diplomats is an act of war; so are acts of terrorism if they are sponsored or abetted by a government. In response, these may call for warlike acts or acts of violence. Such fighting of fire with fire may be distasteful to most Americans during peacetime. But when forceful action is taken, as in the case of air strikes against Libyan targets in 1986, public endorsement may turn out to be surprisingly favorable. Qaddafi might well have been killed in that bombing, yet assassination as an issue did not receive wide attention at the time.

Past experiences urge a more discreet approach than has traditionally been the case. This should be marked by a more common sense awareness of the applicability of Murphy's Law and, in the public domain, a better articulation of policy objectives against which the utility of covert action will ultimately be measured.

Overt Mechanisms

Before tasking components designed to operate clandestinely, the United States should first consider the feasibility of doing the job openly and publicly. U.S. overseas missions which include the embassies and the ancillary bodies that supplement them, are available in most parts of the world and, under proper direction and policy guidance, can play active and vigorous roles on the diplomatic front. The U.S. commercial representation abroad, which is anchored at home but attuned to local government at many levels, might offer useful channels for pursuing national objectives. Both multinational corporations and smaller concerns merit consideration.

Recent years have witnessed the emergence of overt mechanisms intended to accomplish openly certain aims once pursued covertly in the absence of alternatives. The National Endowment for Democracy and Germany's foundations—the Friedrich Ebert Stiftung and its counterparts—are examples. Looking further afield, we see U.S. universities and academic bodies maintaining close links to overseas counterparts, even to governments, in an effort to exchange ideas and experiences and concomitantly to exert influence. Many private bodies such as church groups, trade unions, and charitable organizations sustain ongoing overseas relationships and perform tasks of interest and importance when viewed in the context of U.S. foreign policy goals.

Covert Mechanisms

Without derogating the value and effectiveness of these overt mechanisms, sometimes they are simply not able to accomplish the desired objective. In such cases, clandestine techniques might be necessary, carried out under various forms of protective cover.

The most readily available form of cover, and the one that has been most widely used over the years, is official cover. The obvious alternative is nonofficial cover, the deeper the better. This latter approach offers many attractions, especially to those who have never had to cope with its vicissitudes. Today the U.S. business presence abroad has become so vast that it dwarfs official U.S. representation in many if not most countries. Business is supplemented by a host of other institutional entities—professional, educational, journalistic, athletic, and entertainment. This is a far cry from the days when embassies were isolated outposts in remote places. Clearly, these conditions ought to afford channels for both intelligence collection and covert action during the coming years.

I realize that there are obstacles to relying heavily on nonofficial cover. The comparative security of official status is important, and senior management of U.S. businesses, if consulted, might be wary of the risks involved in providing cover for clandestine operatives. Other institutions are likely to be even more sensitive. Statutory and other restrictions, such as those in the standing Executive Order 12333 governing the activities of intelligence agencies, also curb this type of activity.

One mitigating factor bearing on the cover problem is that the need for cover varies under different operating conditions. If an operation entails collaboration with a host government in some mutually desirable activity, cover might be very light, even of the fig leaf variety. If the activity is to be conducted independently, without the participation of a host government but for compatible purposes, then there is a need for an effective cover. In this case, there is still some room for flexibility. However, under conditions dominated by a hostile or potentially hostile government, good cover is imperative. If it does not exist, the only alternative is to rely on clandestine techniques in the operation itself . . . and pray.

Another consideration bearing on cover is that a situation might be recognized in the international system but not acknowledged or discussed. Nonadmission is one way to describe this condition. During the Indochina war, this situation generally prevailed with respect to CIA paramilitary operations in Laos. Pakistan and Honduras today are other examples. If we can believe what we read in the press, they serve as bases for support to Afghan guerrillas and Nicaraguan Contras. Sometimes if nothing is admitted, questions stop being asked and the operations under scrutiny can get away with being less than fully covert.

In the final analysis, cover for truly covert operations will be increasingly difficult to obtain in the nineties. Legislative controls are likely to become more rigorous, media attention will remain omnivorous, and U.S. control of private activities might intensify in the wake of the NSC-run Iran-Contra maneuvers. Host governments will probably feel impelled to tighten restrictions on foreign entities conducting analogous activities within their borders, giving journalists, missionaries, and students less and less freedom of movement.

Requirements and Opportunities for Covert Action

The first and most obvious imperative for undertaking effective covert action in the 1990s is an ability to operate clandestinely. Although the CA product is generally something that happens and can be seen, U.S. input should normally be shielded from view. Many think this is impossible under present conditions. Experience with the Nicaraguan situation buttresses that argument. Alternatively, although politically motivated exposure originating within the U.S. government is a continuing menace to certain types of covert action, it is encouraging to note the strides that have been made in rebuilding the CA infrastructure, which underwent systematic defenestration from 1974 to 1977.

There have, of course, been setbacks. The highly charged Iran-Contra investigation has damaged the CIA's covert action ability. Woodward described its impact on morale among professionals at the operating level in some detail, calling it an "identity crisis."[3] If such is the case, it must surely have been aggravated by what many observers saw as an unprofessional performance, of dubious legality, implemented by amateurs, with a disastrous impact on the intelligence community. There is evidence of this state of affairs in the flood of leaks, backbiting, and irresponsible storytelling among the sources exploited by Woodward. More recently, and against the backdrop of grand jury indictments of the Iran-Contra principals, the press has reported severe disciplinary action taken by the CIA against a number of its operations officers for their role in the affair. These events will doubtless have a somewhat chilling effect on the CIA's disposition to undertake energetic covert action, even when called upon to do so by higher authority.

All things considered, a period of quiescence would seem to be in order—a time to regroup, reintegrate, and renew commitments to discipline, clandestinity, and silence. These conditions will be difficult to bring about if the operating levels continue to witness a cavalier attitude toward these virtues on the part of some of their professional supervisors and political overseers. Let us hope for the best as we look toward the next decade. With that in mind, we may assume that the period of quiescence will be rather brief and that the types of activity we can expect to see conducted will probably resemble the following well-established patterns:

1. Agents of influence will continue to be important both as sources of intelligence and as channels through which U.S. interests can be promoted. The term *agent* has unfortunate connotations here because the relationship is more often than not likely to be collaborative rather than manipulative, and the interests promoted are generally mutual rather than one-sided.

2. Propaganda of the more subtle variety will be useful and on occasion important. This is not apt to entail sponsorship of propaganda outlets. In the past, that approach has been exceedingly difficult to manage. Insertion of themes will be the primary concern and should be pursued with care. *Gray* as opposed to *black* vehicles should be emphasized, with close attention given to the dangers of blowback in the U.S. media.

3. Political action should be confined to assistance given to independently viable leaders and, under some conditions, through them to the organizations they represent. Ideally, assistance would be designed to achieve a marginal but possibly decisive advantage, as opposed to complete sponsorship. This might entail support to a respected incumbent facing demagogic or subversive opposition. Also ideally, the United States would not be inclined to support military leaders against civilian opposition, although in some circumstances this would not make sense. For example, in the event of a major upheaval leading toward a coup d'état or some other form of overthrow, there ought to be ways to develop and maintain contact with the prospective new leadership, while at the same time helping to ease a failing leader out of office.

4. Paramilitary operations designed to assist friendly governments threatened by subversion and guerrilla action may take the form of material assistance—equipment, weapons, and medical supplies—or the provision of training, intelligence support, and other types of direct or indirect aid. To be effective, the paramilitary assistance should be combined with political action to win popular support for the host government's position. Under certain conditions, it might be desirable to employ U.S. paramilitary elements in direct support of a beleaguered friendly government. For reasons of obvious domes-

tic political sensitivity, this might never be viable, but the capability to do so should be developed and maintained as an available option.

5. Paramilitary forces should be created to conduct backup strike operations against terrorist groups when they are warranted and circumstances permit. The failed Desert One operation of 1980 is one example of the type, if not the modus operandi, visualized. U.S. combat-compatible elements, whether military or civilian, might be deployable independently or in concert with allied or friendly forces. The fact that the United States has had unfortunate experiences with such activity in the past should not prevent its consideration in the future. This also might serve as a weapon against major narcotics traffickers when the latter operate in concert with insurgent forces in critical areas.[4]

6. Support to a friendly government in the form of intelligence information can be an extremely effective channel of influence. It may enable that government to improve its own performance while encouraging it to act along lines suiting U.S. interests. It might take the form of direct passage of information, or it might focus on advisory assistance and helping the recipient develop and strengthen its own intelligence capabilities. There are obvious dangers in this procedure. Political relationships can change, and the intelligence sword can cut both ways, particularly if the assistance given has included security and counterintelligence methods.

The Policy Process

How is the policy process organized, and how can it be improved? What better structure and patterns of coordination are feasible within the executive branch? How is it possible to improve relations between Congress and the intelligence community? Does more congressional oversight promise better intelligence? Would a joint congressional intelligence committee, instead of the present House and Senate oversight bodies, be more effective? These and other related questions are a bit daunting to someone out of direct touch with the existing process.

Be that as it may, some pertinent considerations on the subject would include the following. Intelligence makes many people nervous these days, not because they do not agree that we need intelligence, but rather because they are leery of the action side of intelligence operations—the struggle to obtain it, which sometimes becomes unpleasant, and the business of using it to achieve a policy-related end. Covert action is especially unpopular. While public attitudes on the subject are hard to weigh and easily confused with the biases of those who mold and measure them, there seems to be a great deal of distaste for covert action even within the bureaucracy. This extends to the operating levels of the agencies that should have something to say about implementing it.

What this amounts to is that the inspiration for good covert action is less likely to emanate from within the bureaucracy than from outside it. It may have to come from the top, a phenomenon not without precedent in the U.S. intelligence experience. U.S. presidents have often taken the initiative in instituting covert action.

Let us assume that this will continue. A helpful first step might be the issuance of a new executive order on the subject of covert action. Inasmuch as no one appears to be entirely satisfied with what has been set forth thus far, and given that negative attitudes continue to surface, with a presumably negative impact on the practitioners of the art, the answer might lie in a new and more careful definition of covert action accompanied by an explanation of its relationship to foreign policy . . . as seen from the top. Writing such an executive order might be difficult. Even among the partisans of covert action, one faction would argue that it is a special activity to be used sparingly and selectively, while another would call it a normal instrument of policy to be used whenever the president deems it appropriate. At least one former practitioner would call it a normal instrument, but one to be used a bit more selectively than has perhaps been the case in recent years.

If a more balanced philosophical approach to covert action could be promulgated under presidential authority, the public would benefit from sharing the wisdom thus developed. Structures for planning, organizing, and implementing covert action are less important than creating an environment within which new ideas are likely to be generated.

There is no doubt that if the days ahead are to see any significant covert action, some hurdles, such as the denouement of the Iran-Contra investigations, will have to be surmounted. At the NSC level, steps are said to have been taken to tighten up procedures governing covert action. On balance, we may assume that existing mechanisms such as the National Security Planning Group, the Senior Interdepartmental Group, and others will continue to function. More important will be the way they function. The deluge of leaks in recent years, largely attributable to sources who opposed the action under study or implementation, can be prevented only if there is full consideration of differing views among the interested agencies. Lack of consensus bodes ill for any planned project. If it is not blocked at or below the NSC level, leaks or exposures can be expected to stop the project even if it has been approved at a higher level.

The same problems affect relations with Congress. Early soundings and systematic consensus building seem to be imperative under most circumstances. There are risks if a large number of people have access to sensitive information. A single joint congressional oversight committee might be less threatening, but for the present approval by both congressional intelligence committees is essential. Such approval is likely to result in the preservation of secrecy, while disapproval or strong opposition will surely guarantee exposure.

Covert action should be undertaken in support of some widely known and understood public policy, or at least it should be consistent with the parameters of public policy and never run counter to it. If such is the case, the likelihood of exposure will be reduced, and if exposure should occur, the effort and the implementing agency are less likely to be repudiated by the media and public. As noted earlier, the means employed in a covert action must be decent. This does not exclude the use of force under controlled circumstances. It must, however, exclude any connection, connotation, or association with proscribed activities such as, assassination ("neutralization") or the use of weapons or techniques prohibited by treaty or other legislation. These strictures raise tough questions about the feasibility of operations targeted against terrorists and narcotics traffickers.

Any consideration of a new proposal for covert action must incorporate a deliberate and methodical review of the risk–gain equation as an integral part of the approval process. The operation itself must be described in detail so that it is fully understood and the consequences of failure weighed in advance. Murphy's Law must figure in the calculation, with emphasis on ways in which the operation could go awry because of its own built-in limitations or weaknesses (for example, only eight CH-53 Sea King helicopters in Desert One) or the pressure of outside forces such as hostile intelligence or chance exposure.

As the objectives of the operation are weighed and measured against the risks, an intelligence appreciation of the entire operational milieu should be made. Careful counterintelligence scrutiny must also be brought to bear at every level. There will always be a tendency to treat these controls casually and to rely on the area knowledge and expertise of the operators. Although these operators may indeed know their business well, they will profit greatly from constructive analysis by disinterested components.

Implementation

The leading agency for all U.S. covert action is clearly the CIA. Although other departments might be assigned primary roles, the CIA should share responsibility to ensure coordination with other clandestine activities in the chosen area. The CIA also should facilitate contributions from its own intelligence capabilities, both analytical and operational. If the operation is essentially military in thrust, the CIA can and should contribute its own capabilities to provide a political element.

The Department of State will always play an essential role, ensuring that the operation is in line with established policy for the area and making certain that it does not run afoul of diplomatic efforts. This naturally involves the ambassador in the country affected. This person is best situated to assess the political contribution and risks to U.S. interests. The ambassador's stake in the success or failure of the operation will be particularly high if embassy personnel are involved.

Specialized components of the U.S. armed services—the Army Special Forces, Navy Seals, Air Force security units, or recently publicized Intelligence Support Activity—may undertake covert action under a variety of conditions calling for deployment of their unique resources. Policy-level officials in the Department of Defense, with full cognizance of the operation's implications for overall U.S. military interests, must share in the responsibility for approving these activities.

Allied governments and their intelligence services can be important vehicles for certain types of covert action and can provide independent assistance. The extent to which they can be used will depend on their overall relationship with the U.S. government, the likelihood that they will be affected by the operation in question, and the degree to which they would be sympathetic to its objectives.

This area might offer greater potential than has been previously exploited. There are pros and cons to collaborating in an operation. Collaboration means surrendering a measure of control and incurring risks. The allied entity might be penetrated by a hostile power or a domestic political faction. It might have to cope with conflicting internal political pressures and thereby face special dangers of exposure. It might share U.S. objectives, although possibly not entirely, and it might have its own preferences as to which leaders it would like to see come out on top. If intelligence support is required, this might entail complications over and above sources and methods.

Conversely, collaboration is one way to hide or at least reduce the visibility of the U.S. profile. If the environment is one that the allied entity knows intimately, it can bring special expertise to bear on the problem. If the operation fails or exposure occurs, the allied role may shield the United States from the impact.

How might such collaboration develop? One way might be in the development and deployment of paramilitary assets against terrorist or narcotics traffickers. A joint task force might be feasible in some situations, while the United States might remain in a supporting role in others. In the sensitive political environment of a former colony, the expertise of the former metropolitan power might be drawn on in, for example, a joint effort to shore up an emerging democratic government. Or, the United States might agree to recruit unilaterally individuals with special skills or political expertise in order to mount an independent effort in support of the government in question.

The involvement of private groups is less attractive today than it might have been prior to the Iran-Contra episode. The dangers of loss of control, difficulty of supervision, and differences in agenda are obvious. If the groups in question drift off course, the United States is left holding the bag for actions undertaken at its behest if not in its name. The United States need not exclude the idea of private involvement, but the degree of consultation or collaboration should be weighed carefully against the probability of real cooperation and, more importantly, against the need to involve these groups at all.

Other Elements of Intelligence

Covert action does not function in a vacuum. It cannot be divorced effectively from the other elements of intelligence, either organizationally or in implementation. Its practitioners must be able to draw upon intelligence collection on a continuing basis. Often the professional collectors of intelligence will be the same people who manage covert action in a given situation. There is room for specialization, but it is not always practical at a time of limited resources. Similar considerations apply to analysis, also a vital adjunct to covert action, although it need not exist under the same organizational roof. Planning for covert action would be well served by drawing not only upon government sources—the CIA's own Directorate of Intelligence (DDI), the State Department's Bureau of Intelligence and Research (INR), the Defense Intelligence Agency (DIA), and certainly the National Security Agency—but also upon academics and other scholars who may have special knowledge and area experience as well as good contacts in the area under scrutiny.

The counterintelligence aspect of covert action often poses difficult and worrisome problems. Because the action itself may take place in an open and comparatively accessible environment, it is more readily subject to penetration than, for example, a precisely targeted intelligence collection effort. Operational security should be a dominant consideration from the outset, with the primary focus on personnel and on the modus operandi. In the past, this procedure has rarely been followed. Counterintelligence analysis has fared no better. In the future, it will behoove the United States to assess CA performance and results with great care against the backdrop of its adversaries' behavior. If the area of competition is well defined, Soviet active measures will certainly come into play and will warrant close attention.

It will not be easy to achieve a balance of operational support cum analytical oversight that is sufficiently strong to have an impact without interfering, or seeming to interfere, in the operation. Professional pride is both an asset and a liability. The solution will lie, as usual, in the quality of leadership and direction emanating from the top. Absent any up-to-date knowledge of the way the CIA is organized for covert action at present, we may assume that there is a division of labor between the operating divisions and staff elements along traditional lines. One way to cope with the problems of achieving adequate analytical input might be to assign individuals from the DDI to work directly with the operations people. Cross-directorate assignments have worked well, in the case of counterterrorism operations, and a similar leavening in the CA process might be very beneficial.

The Infrastructure

People who manage covert action at the upper echelons ought to be interested in the subject and believe it can serve U.S. policy well. The impression conveyed by Woodward is that only two senior people in the CIA had any feeling at all for covert action, namely Director William J. Casey and Duane Clarridge.[5] In fairness to the others, their skepticism or lack of interest may have focused on particular covert actions rather than on the genre itself. Be that as it may, senior people who really understand covert action and can objectively weigh its pluses and minuses are not numerous—a condition that is likely to improve only if the message reaches them from a still higher authority.

This is important because both middle-level managers and operations officers naturally take their cues from their superiors. If there is no encouragement from above, the result will be a dearth of ideas and a diminution of effort. People in the intelligence business want, as much as anyone else, at least internal recognition and reasonable assurance of advancement. They are reluctant to pursue avenues of career development that do not appeal to higher authority or that increase the likelihood of their personal exposure and risk damaging their career prospects. The events of the past decade or more have cast a pall over covert action in the minds of many young professionals, although judging by the range and apparent vigor of recent covert actions, these events might have had less of an impact than one might expect.

There is no agreed-upon profile of the ideal CA case officer. If I were to try my hand at sketching one, I would call for an experienced intelligence officer of proven competence. He or she should know the area and have intimate knowledge of the country under scrutiny, including fluency in the language. The officer should know all kinds of people, be able to get around in a variety of local circles, and have a hands-on feeling for the political milieu. The officer also must be skilled in tradecraft, that is, be able to operate clandestinely. Junior personnel embarking on their first tour of overseas duty will rarely meet these criteria.

With respect to CA agents, I have already expressed uneasiness about the term *agent* as such. The word has a connotation that I consider unrealistic and unnecessarily pejorative. More often than not the so-called agent is a collaborator rather than a person doing someone else's bidding. The relationship with the agent, if it is to be effective, will usually be reciprocal, predicated upon a mutually compatible agenda and objectives. If the relationship is manipulated in one direction, it will probably be manipulated in the other direction as well. The extent to which it is based on exploitation rather than a reasonable level of trust and mutual understanding will often be an indicator of the likelihood of eventual rupture and exposure. The agent, or collaborator, must not be totally dependent upon his or her covert partner. In many if not most instances, the agent will have some organizational affiliation that is of operational interest or value, and the support given to either the agent or the organization should be limited to that needed to attain marginal advantage, perhaps only to achieve a catalytic effect. If subsidy is the only basis for survival of the organization or the person in question, the prospects for success are doubtful.

What are we talking about here in terms of numbers and distribution of assets? To extrapolate from my general observations on the human side of covert action and arrive at realistic figures would be unrealistic. At the same time, it seems reasonable to assume that the staff infrastructure of, say, the CIA as the lead agency in the field, has developed and been programmed along defensible lines for the next three to five years. Therefore, unless the public environment changes radically in the near future, that is what we are going to get in terms of people and resources. If the need for CA initiatives should burgeon during the next administration, a rapid and effective expansion of the infrastructure would be difficult to effect because the CIA is already locked into the current budget and personnel cycle.

I see no way to circumvent this problem except to begin to work into the system people possessing the special skills and knowledge that would allow them to cope successfully with current requirements and later rise to the occasion when new CA initiatives are in heavy demand. People like that are in short supply, however, even under the best conditions.

Let us speculate about the CIA's current recruiting patterns. How many of the new junior officers have ever worked in a domestic election campaign? How many of them have ever organized anything or run any kind of pressure group—labor, student, women's, veterans', trade, and so on? Do the recruiters ever make an effort to assess the recruits' ability to think politically? For that matter, do the recruiters themselves ever think politically? The answers to most of these questions would, I fear, be negative. That is unfortunate, because if the same young persons who are to function later as case officers in political action operations have had no such experience in their own lives, one should question their ability to play effective roles in foreign environments. Who, moreover, will give them the leadership and guidance they need when the middle managers to whom they report are themselves lacking in this type of expertise?

On the paramilitary side, the outlook seems brighter. If the U.S. military can continue to produce bright young lieutenants and captains and tough youngish sergeants who are made to order for follow-up careers in the CIA, it should be possible to supplement whatever internal development the CIA pursues with respect to its own junior personnel.

None of these programs can be brought to fruition overnight. They take time. That also applies to other skills, such as language. There are never enough language-competent people available. If a new intelligence officer must start from scratch to learn a foreign language, as the majority probably do, that is a very costly process in terms of time and money. Why not recruit more systematically from among the ethnic minorities, including those not yet fully assimilated? They have not only the language but possibly also a more thorough knowledge of their areas of origin. In the past, this has been done with fair success among Americans of Chinese and Japanese origin, and that experience should make it easier to expand the recruitment program to other groups. There is plenty of talent in the United States, and it would be a pity if the intelligence community failed to exploit it.

Training for covert action raises comparable problems that the United States must deal with today if it is going to be able to cope with future CA needs. It is difficult to visualize just how junior officers can be trained effectively for covert action when there are so few people left on duty who have been involved in operations of any real size or depth. Similarly, there are no Paul Linebargers left to provide the stimulus for what was once confidently described as "psychological warfare." But there are people close at hand who have run elections in the United States, who know the ins and outs of trying to get somebody elected to office. There are also political analysts whose observations and advice might be of great value to interested parties. (At one time, people like this were engaged to go abroad and convey their knowledge to people who badly needed guidance.) Today there are political consultants and public relations experts of every description. Why not select and engage a few of the better ones on a contractual basis to teach aspiring CA practitioners as part of a more comprehensive training program? These people also would be introduced discreetly in overseas environments where they might convey their expertise to people we want to assist.

Advice along these lines may well be considered gratuitous by those on the inside who are doing their best to cope with what they believe is the real world. I would hope that this is not the case. On purely technical questions, such as clandestine communications to support covert action, there is no point in trying to second-guess the experts.

There are two areas where questions arise regarding operational viability in the coming years. One has to do with the clandestine movement of funds, which is not a major problem on an individual basis but is often critical if organizational entities are involved. Many of the old techniques have been proscribed, and more recently developed techniques have evoked questions of legality. Large-scale funding is very difficult to carry out securely under any condition. Small-scale infusions, however, can be handled with relative ease. The second consideration involves the movement of equipment and material. At one time a remarkable organization called Air America was available to perform such tasks. Perhaps new channels have been developed, but even so, security factors will always be an important consideration. The bigger the operation and the more people and equipment involved, the greater the danger of leakage and exposure.

The Outlook

It would be easy to argue that covert action, following its recrudescence during the Reagan administration, has run its course and that, under pressure from the media and the more vocal sectors of society, the United States will soon revert to the minimalist environment of the late seventies. A 1987 PBS telecast depicting the actions of the "secret government" driven blindly by cold war imperatives, ever willing to circumvent both the truth and the law, illustrated this environment vividly. The director's undisguised bias was offset substantially by the almost religious fervor and utter conviction of his presentation. Like this director, many would like to end once and for all any transgression of the principle of nonintervention. Yet many others, myself included, do not believe that nonintervention is always for the best. For example, it is difficult to appreciate the sovereign right of a government such as the one ruling Haiti to brutalize its people in full confidence that outraged neighbors will never intervene to redress its outrages.

In actuality, intervention is practiced on a daily basis by most countries, including the United States. When the United States considers it necessary to intervene in the context of its current interests, it rarely hesitates to pressure its neighbors directly and indirectly to change their laws to meet what the United States considers its own needs. This also works in the opposite direction. Can anyone pretend that Japan does not intervene in U.S. affairs today? Or that certain proposals for trade legislation before Congress would not constitute intervention in Japanese life? If such intrusions are politically acceptable on the presumption that they are nonviolent, what about Panama and U.S. efforts to overthrow General Noriega by almost any means available? Why have public figures who have been vocal in denouncing U.S. efforts to overthrow the Sandinistas in Nicaragua been conspicuously silent in this matter? The explanation is obvious: Noriega emerged as an important figure in the narcotics trade at a time when the United States was declaring war on drugs. Most Americans agree that it is in everyone's interest, including that of the Panamanian people, to see an end to Noriega's rule in that country. It is interesting to note, however, that even the most ardent anti-interventionists have accommodated themselves to this turn of events.[6]

This is not to suggest that there are no rules, that the end justifies the means, or that presidents are above the law. Fundamental decency, legalities, and proprieties must be observed in covert action. In the circumstances that are likely to prevail in the 1990s—some of which will not be of the United States' own making—I would consciously concede to the president a certain latitude in trying to cope with intractable problems in the international realm. There is, and I think there should be, room for covert action in U.S. foreign operations and as part of the overall U.S. intelligence effort. Such actions should be handled by professionals who are disciplined and know what they are doing, and they should be undertaken when the potential gain has been weighed honestly against the danger of failure. We have seen that the price of failure is high. Thus the actions must be aimed at maximum levels of achievement that, if sustained, can make a significant contribution to the enhancement of U.S. interests and values in the 1990s.

Notes

1. Bob Woodward, *Veil: The Secret Wars of the CIA, 1981–1987* (New York: Simon and Schuster, 1987), 511.

2. For a detailed definition and discussion of the Soviet concept of active measures, see Richard H. Shultz and Roy Godson, *Dezinformatsia—Active Measures in Soviet Strategy* (New York: Pergamon-Brassey, 1984); and Uri Ra'anan et al., *Hydra of Carnage, International Linkages of Terrorism* (Lexington, Mass.: Lexington Books, 1986).

3. Woodward, *Veil,* 332ff.

4. Some insights into development of U.S. intelligence and paramilitary capabilities for these and related purposes emerge in Steven Emerson, "Secret Warriors: Inside the Covert Military Operations of the Reagan Era," *U.S. News and World Report,* 21 March 1988, 24–32. This summary of Emerson's book offers a rather heavy dramatization of U.S. efforts to build an effective antiterrorist force in the wake of the failed Desert One operation of 1980.

5. Woodward, *Veil,* 168, 212ff.

6. Intervention in Panamanian affairs is by no means without historical precedent. In 1903 Theodore Roosevelt used the threat of military force to intervene directly in support of dissident elements seeking to break away from Colombia. The result was Panama's independence and a quick start for the United States on construction of the Panama Canal.

Discussion

Eberhard Blum

This is very much a U.S. discussion in the sense that there is a deep urge to probe publicly into the last corners of complex and even shadowy issues, trying to solve every problem by finding solutions and rules, if not regulations. Yet, lest we forget, we are dealing with an art, not a science. The topic of covert action has been put at the end of the ladder of intelligence activities discussed at this colloquium. This symbolizes the fact that covert action not only combines the other elements—collection, analysis, and counterintelligence—but also goes beyond them deep into the realm of politics. No wonder its use is highly controversial in a democracy. It is Woodrow Wilson and not Machiavelli who represents the general U.S. outlook on the world and the way Americans want to be judged.

I certainly do not believe in the proposition put forward by some that covert action is immoral; this is as lopsided as saying war is immoral. The appropriateness of a given activity, overt or covert, must be judged by whether the ways, means, and aim are acceptable, as well as by its failure or success. This leaves enough room for a government to act according to specific circumstances but eliminates what might be called dirty and ugly plots (and certainly ridiculous ones).

I think these are the traditional Western standards for judging the justice of action in war. They are sobering, but they also offer a framework for the scope of covert action. Overstepping these boundaries has done more harm than good.

Coming back to my remark about the perfection of regulations, this business, above all, must be handled by "honorable men," who, of course, are highly qualified. This standard is the condition sine qua non. I therefore found the paragraph in the proposed U.S. legislation of the mid-seventies that said, more or less, "Thou shalt not kill" tasteless and at a level not befitting the leadership of one of the oldest democracies of the world. I use the words "honorable and highly qualified" because the art of intelligence in its many facets is much too difficult and important a duty to be left to the average government employee. One says that each country has the intelligence service it deserves; this lays a heavy burden on the shoulders of the executive and legislative branches.

The two essays in this chapter provide the following useful overview of U.S. covert action:

1. The heyday of the fifties and sixties

2. The change of climate following a change in perception based on the belief that covert action is a dying art, as Hugh Tovar quotes an old practitioner as saying

3. A look beyond to the threshold of the nineties

Both authors affirm the continuing need for using covert action as a necessary measure to achieve certain political results in a nonapplicable, if not clandestine, way. I could not agree more; covert action can be usefully applied only within the framework of an orchestrated political operation. It should not be started without a clear definition of what is to be achieved and a will to win.

Being part of the overall political strategy means that each measure and method must complement each of the others in the strategy. General Gehlen, the head of the Federal Republic of Germany's foreign intelligence service (BND) in the fifties, once explained to me why he would not initiate aggressive subversive action in East Germany while the overall Western policy was defensive. Actions that might have induced patriotic men and women to stick their necks out—prematurely at best, useless at worst—would only have offered a welcome target to the East German security forces. Such activities without political or military follow-up would, therefore, have been irresponsible. (In this context, I can empathize with the frustration intelligence officers must have felt in Vietnam, where the overall strategy was to escalate the war only to the level of the other side's buildup.)

Decisions about covert action must, therefore, involve the top policy people in the relevant departments of the executive branch, experts on the given region or target, and the people responsible for carrying out the operation. Because covert action is not a quick fix or an end in itself, its orchestration with overt and semiovert initiatives must be discussed, and everyone involved must know what is to be achieved. These procedures inevitably will widen the circle of conspirators at the top, but by reaching a consensus, they might prevent leaks by dissenters and will help ensure the cooperation of Congress.

For example, a change in government in Nicaragua is likely to be achieved only in the context of a sustained effort and eventual success in the entire region, including El Salvador. But where is the framework for such a forceful and comprehensive policy, including the neighboring countries and the Caribbean Basin area? I remember talk of a Caribbean Basin Initiative—what became of it? I have been impressed by the support of President Duarte in El Salvador and the land reform program. But a credible and successful policy with regard to Nicaragua would weave together the success in El Salvador with something like what was to have been the Caribbean Basin Initiative and a host of other plans. Thus, before deciding to undertake an operation, it is best to have all the instruments on the table. It is also important to monitor such a comprehensive operation continually. To do so, it may be healthy to bring in outside expertise, like the famous Team B during George Bush's tenure as director of Central Intelligence.

I agree with the authors that intelligence and covert action have much to offer in the 1990s. I also agree with the idea that more participation from allied or friendly countries is needed. Friendly services could help either as brokers or as independent, but related, actors in covert action. This would necessitate a change in the traditional attitude of the U.S. intelligence community to use covert action only when the chips are down and then to go it alone. It has struck me, through years of close and trusted association with American friends, that the idea of using our decades-old tradition of sharing secrets for policy matters—discreet and subtle—has never been fully discussed. Nor has our expertise or advice been asked for in operations concerning propaganda, influencing certain people, or deception. The exception has been technology transfer, which was born out of the CIA's Directorate of Intelligence, not operations. The tech transfer operation was very successful indeed because of West Germany's cooperation.

We are all afraid of leaks and the additional embarrassment it would cause if a foreign country were involved in a covert action. But the purpose of operations is success, so why voluntarily renounce the possibility of assigning tasks to those who can best do them? This practice is, of course, old hat to the Soviets. The long-established division of labor in the political framework of the Comintern and the Cominform has been adapted to the intelligence and security forces of the satellite states.

Maybe we should start discreetly giving each other advice on non-violent aspects of covert action, beginning with overt or semiovert ventures in the field of propaganda and information. The most auspicious and the least controversial aspect of covert action remains the "influence transfer." This should be done in a way that the good old principle of the action being deniable is honored.

Europeans are not without instruments in this field. For example, we Germans have our foundations. They were established as an ideal instrument for nongovernmental, overt assistance. They are an autonomous political transmission belt for each of the parties. The Konrad Adenauer and Friedrich Ebert foundations of the Christian Democratic Union (CDU) and Social Democratic Party (SPD), respectively, are the best known. There is also the Hans Seidel Stiftung of the Bavarian Christian Socialist Union (CSU). In the 1970s, the Friedrich Ebert Foundation succeeded, in concert with the social democratic politicians of Britain and Sweden, in dragging Portugal out of the quagmire of the Portuguese revolution with its hard core of communism. Unfortunately, the role of the Socialist International in other areas has usually not been as helpful. A lesser known example has been the impact of the Hans Seidel Stiftung's constructive (and therefore much challenged) policy in southern Africa.

It is important in certain situations that government funds not be used for an activity that cannot be kept clandestine. In the 1970s, for example, the leader of the Portuguese Socialist party, Mario Soares, reportedly refused to accept support offered by U.S. labor because, when asked, labor leaders had to tell him that the money was from the U.S. government and would just be channeled through them. This underlines the regrettable fact that it may be counterproductive to use the CIA if there is an alternative, not to mention the help of a third country. Here secrecy is of the essence. That is why it is really helpful to have available many, many channels in addition to those of a single government.

Nowadays, a discreet association may be more efficient than a clandestine one; the middleman should be neither tainted nor compromised and preferably innocent as to an intelligence background.

Despite any and all subtleties, the best underpinning for this sort of operation remains a forceful and credible foreign policy—a shining example of democracy in action—and reliable friends. Finally, in the future, as in the past, covert action will be at its best when its revelation makes everybody feel proud and happy and when it increases the numbers of "fathers" of the project.

Paramilitary actions are totally different—neither clandestine by nature nor covert in the classical sense. Yet the covert fig leaf sometimes offers a pretense that makes the enterprise bearable for all parties involved. I sympathize with those in the CIA who are unhappy about being involved or identified with these types of activities, but their expertise, experience, and the above-mentioned need for covertness make their involvement unavoidable. It is fair to say that the degrees of acceptability differ widely, as does the level of exposure. Afghanistan is popular, and the supply of weapons and equipment could be open if it were not for other considerations, such as the involvement of other countries, or making it easier for Moscow to accept. I do not, however, believe that Pakistan would have been compromised if more adequate weapons had been provided earlier in the war. Quite the contrary.

Let me come back to the question "What do we have to expect in the 1990s?" The hegemonic ambitions of Communist ideology combined with Soviet imperialism and the reckless use of their own and their proxy forces—with the whole spectrum of active measures available—will continue. Further, we can expect the Soviet Union to promote and exploit revolutionary situations and hold tight to their conquests. But let's face it, they have to try harder in using all their old and some new tricks because the system has lost its appeal; it has become crude and stale because of catering to the *nomenklatura,* and the Soviets have begun to realize this.

The main concern of the United States and its allies should be the controlled decline of the factors that have made the Soviet system such a threat to any peaceful, concerted, and balanced development of a pluralistic world structure. In the future, it will be important for the Western public to realize that the Soviet Union still remains a threat. In recent months, Gorbachev has been very successful in making the public feel too comfortable.

The emergence of other centers of power, mainly economic, in China, Asia, Western Europe, and maybe India will pave the way for a multipolar world in the next millennium. Issues will be less black and white, forces involved more complex, and actions more complicated and sophisticated. These fledgling regional powers should be given a greater responsibility for the stability of their less fortunate neighbors.

In a shrinking world, we are all neighbors. Europe should feel a special responsibility for Africa. This same feeling should certainly extend across the seas, supporting the activities of other strong nations.

Fundamentalism is one of the plagues of our time, and terrorism is one of its dragon teeth. The threat will grow not only within the Islamic world but also within societies where there happens to be a strong Islamic population. Western expertise in countering this is marginal, and the countermeasures employed thus far have been mostly postmortems. Closer cooperation with moderate Islamic governments should be enhanced—and the Israelis, I believe, will agree to this.

To sum up, covert action encompasses a variety of activities that are all part of external security in a wider sense. Therefore, they tend to be used by political leaders in times of crisis. But covert action is not a substitute for a sound policy, nor is it a pseudo–war game for dilettantes or zealots. The means and methods used should be acceptable in hindsight to reasonable people. In most cases, one can say the broader the orchestration, the better the chances to succeed. This includes, wherever useful, the cross-fertilization that only interallied cooperation can bring.

Stephen Engelberg

Gregory Treverton has written a book that says covert action should be used sparingly if at all.[1] I asked a veteran operator if this was the answer to the ongoing debate about covert action and, if not, what was. He answered, "We can't give up covert action. That's ridiculous. The answer is adult supervision." That is really what we are talking about. The authors here do not side with Mr. Treverton. Rather they argue that covert action is acceptable and useful. I think that is sensible, but I would like to raise a couple of points about what is appropriate adult supervision.

Operators should be inventive and bold and propose risky ideas. There is nothing wrong with that; in fact, there is everything right with it. But clearly the government needs a system for separating the wheat from the chaff.

For the past ten years, the United States has had both internal and external bureaucracies reviewing covert action. Within the executive branch there has been a standing committee overseeing covert action. First it was called the Forty Committee, and since the Nixon administration it has had various other names. The congressional intelligence committees also are considering covert operations.

I believe that these kinds of structures are by their nature at odds with deftness and elegance in covert action. It is certainly possible, although difficult, to write a speech by a committee. You can write a newspaper story using a committee, and I do that more often than I would like. One can even come up with daring ideas about tax reform and the budget using the cut and thrust of bureaucracy. But covert action is clearly, fundamentally different. It needs unity of conception and execution. A leak about a covert action is often fatal. This leads to a very natural temptation to tell fewer and fewer people about the proposed action. Thus, the nature of covert action seems incompatible with bureaucratic and congressional review.

We saw this quite clearly in the Iran-Contra operation. The frustration with leaks led to a desire to limit the activity to the smallest possible number of people. Yet in making the Iran initiative a reality, the White House ignored the formal system it had established for getting all the government agencies, all the experts, to review proposed covert actions and, most importantly, to keep on reviewing them to make sure they are doing what they are supposed to be doing.

In this chapter, we see the assertion that covert action must be consistent with policy in order to be effective. The United States had a structure to ensure this. And yet, despite this elegant structure, it ended up with a covert action that was not consistent with policy and not particularly well done.

It is evident that the system broke down. I think the challenge of covert action in the 1990s will be to find some way to make the structure work, to come up with a structure that ensures the action is consistent with policy and yet is able to produce imaginative operations to serve U.S. national interests.

Richard Shultz offers the broadest possible scope for covert action up to and including so-called preemptive strikes against terrorism. For Hugh Tovar, the story of covert action in the 1990s is more a tale of limits, how it can be made to work within the constraints of Murphy's Law and the concerns of the congressional oversight committees. I tend to agree with Mr. Tovar because I believe that for the next five to ten years the memory of Iran-Contra is going to be a major factor in how things are done in the CA field. I know, however, that it is easy, and perhaps natural, for journalists like myself who spent the better part of thirteen months obsessed with the Iran-Contra affair to overestimate its effects.

Let us look at a couple of other events of the 1980s that I think are going to affect the way members of Congress and the bureaucracy look at this issue. If we accept Bob Woodward's book,[2] we have to believe that congressional committees raised concerns in 1985 about the so-called preemptive counterterrorism capability the CIA was building up. This in turn led Director of Central Intelligence William Casey to seek funding from the Saudis for an operation that led to the car bombing in Beirut. About the same time, the congressional oversight committees questioned whether the CIA should be funding the Catholic Church in Nicaragua. A great fuss was raised, and it was decided to drop this operation. Oliver North apparently then stepped into the vacuum, getting around the intent of Congress.

Congress's intent is always arguable, but in the end I agree with former National Security Advisor Robert McFarlane that it is usually comprehensible. It is pretty clear that in 1985, when Congress passed the Boland amendment, it intended to end U.S. aid to the Contras. I do not think that any of the people involved in passing the Boland amendment imagined that they meant to allow Oliver North to enlist CIA field operatives to run a private resupply operation. Like it or not, covert action in the 1990s is going to be conducted against this historical backdrop. One may argue whether that is wise, but I think it is inevitable.

This means that there are likely to be many people urging caution almost to the extent of paralysis and inaction. The only to get around this is by coming up with a structure that can be adhered to and can be convincing. Again, whether people like it or not, that structure is going to have to involve Congress, and it is going to have to involve a sufficient number of experts in the government so that we never again have people going out looking for "moderates" in countries such as Iran.

I have two final thoughts. First, it is difficult to evaluate the success of some of these covert actions as vehicles for U.S. collection.

How does the United States decide whether or not the Angolan program is a success? It looks at what has been collected by Jonas Savimbi's UNITA. But by the very nature of the game, all the United States gets comes through Savimbi or his operatives. How does the United States decide whether or not the Nicaraguan program is effective? U.S. representatives talk to the FDN or collateral sources. How does the United States gauge these sources' success as tools of policy? It is going to be a real challenge in the 1990s to come up with ways to measure effectiveness. I think it would be useful to have some rational criteria for doing this because it is clear that henceforth covert actions are going to be regularly reviewed.

Second, at least one massive covert program that has been very successful, the Afghanistan program, shows the importance of covert action being consistent with policy. There is absolutely no disagreement in Congress about the need for this program, and there is no disagreement in the administration about it either. As a result, I think you can probably count on one hand the number of leaks, of which there were very few damaging ones. I think there is something to this idea of trying to keep the two elements in line.

Notes

1. Gregory Treverton, *Covert Action: The Limits of Intervention in the Postwar World* (New York: Basic Books, 1987).
2. Bob Woodward, *Veil: The Secret Wars of the CIA, 1981–1987* (New York: Simon and Schuster, 1987).

General Discussion

At the colloquium, there was a general consensus that in the 1990s the potential existed for covert action to play a major role in exploiting foreign policy opportunities and countering threats. For future administrations to be able to use a covert option, however, certain capabilities must be acquired and a consensus for using covert action developed within the country.

One major task discussed by a number of participants was the need to rebuild the CIA's cadre of professional CA officers. An academic supported the call for new personnel capable of meeting the challenges and threats of the 1990s. For example, better use should be made of the ethnic and linguistic diversity existing in the United States. An intelligence officer argued that people who have practical experiences relevant to carrying out covert action, such as participation in elections and labor unions, should be recruited.

There was a great deal of discussion about the acceptability of covert action and its place in a democracy. A conferee began by noting that there was general public confusion about the nature of covert action. Far too many people believe that covert action is basically paramilitary activity. In fact, there are many other types of covert action involving political support, propaganda, and technology transfer that do not involve guns at all. Before we can think seriously of using covert action as an instrument of policy, we will have to reestablish the distinctions between the types of covert action that were described in the essays.

An academic argued that the acceptability of covert action appeared to rest on either of two conditions—a consensus on the foreign policy the United States ought to pursue or, failing that, "abnormal" and foolproof measures of oversight. An academic replied that a foreign policy consensus was essential under any circumstance. Nevertheless, he said, even with such a consensus, it is very important for people to realize that covert action is a normal instrument of policy that is not inherently insidious.

A journalist asked whether covert action would be possible in the 1990s, given the press corps' worldwide presence and its increased access to instant communications as well as visual reconnaissance satellites. An academic agreed that in the 1990s it will be difficult to conceal large paramilitary operations. He pointed out, however, that much of the covert activities likely to be used in the next decade (that is, propaganda and political support) will be smaller in size and able to be carried out covertly. A former intelligence officer added that when these programs are implemented correctly, a journalist who sees what is happening will likely mistake its outward manifestations for something else. The American media's failure to uncover the Iran-Contra affair was pointed to as an example.

A government official complained that the authors somewhat missed the point in arguing that opportunities for covert action would exist in the 1990s but that better coordination with policy would be necessary. He argued that despite many calls for covert action to be consistent with policy, it has not happened. This is principally because policymakers often continue to use covert action not as a tool of, but rather as a substitute for, policymaking when a consensus for action is not present. As a result, opportunities for using covert action to enhance policy have been allowed to fade away, and there is no reason to think that this will not happen in the future. Several conferees agreed that suggestions for covert action should not normally come from the intelligence community because policy is so clearly the logical prerequisite for covert action. Proposals for covert action must be in response to policy decisions made by the country's elected leadership.

It was pointed out that covert action, like other aspects of foreign policy, should be based on sound analysis. For example, the Iran initiatives in the mid-1980s were conducted in an intelligence vacuum. There was no clear knowledge of whom the United States was dealing with—their motives or their true relationship to other Iranian factions. The original National Intelligence Estimate (NIE) on the basis of which the operation was initiated was wrong. A subsequent NIE corrected the faulty picture of Iranian politics. But by then the policy was rolling along, and its architects paid little attention to the new assessment. Clearly, covert action must be based on good analysis, including counterintelligence analysis.

There was also some discussion about the effectiveness of oversight. Several conferees suggested that the contention that the oversight system broke down in the Iran-Contra affair was incorrect. They argued that the system did not break down. Rather it was bypassed by people at the highest levels who wanted to pursue a certain policy, believed that the rest of the government would not support their designs, and were unwilling to deal with that opposition.

Another conferee added that fear of leaks is not an entirely satisfactory explanation for reticence to either win over or overrule other parts of the government. After all, the program of aid to the Afghan resistance was beset by leaks from the outset. But the leaks had little effect because policymakers had made a sound case that the Afghan resistance deserved assistance, and they created bipartisan support for the program.

A number of participants discussed the proper home for paramilitary activities. One conferee suggested that they be transferred from the CIA to the Defense Department. An academic and a former intelligence officer disagreed. They argued that unlike normal military operations, paramilitary activities require an understanding of the political situation in the target country. They are principally a political rather than a military operation. Thus, they concluded, CIA personnel are best able to carry out these activities.

Finally, there was general agreement that a strategy must be developed to secure increased assistance from friendly governments. An academic wondered about the likelihood of this type of cooperation, given that in the past the United States has proven to be an undependable partner, often shifting course midway through an operation. As an example, he cited the Sultan of Brunei's gift of ten million dollars to the Nicaraguan resistance, which Congress revealed. To get allies to cooperate in the future, he argued, the United States will have to demonstrate a reliable, persistent, and credible commitment to its policies. A former senior intelligence official added that it would be difficult to get future allied cooperation if the U.S. intelligence community had to report that assistance to Congress. Fear of having their involvement or secrets leaked would increase the reluctance of allied services to cooperate with the United States.

Appendix A
Consortium for the Study of Intelligence

Origin and Purpose

During the past decade, there has been a flood of material dealing with intelligence, particularly U.S. intelligence and its relationship to national security and to U.S. foreign policy. Some of this information has been made available in the writings of former intelligence officials. Other major sources include congressional documents resulting from oversight activities and documents released under the Freedom of Information Act.

As a result, it has become increasingly possible to undertake objective, scholarly, and unclassified research into the intelligence process and product, and to examine their relationship to U.S. decision making.

In light of these new circumstances, a group of social scientists from several academic institutions decided in April 1979 to create a Consortium for the Study of Intelligence (CSI). Its membership includes political scientists, particularly specialists in international relations and in U.S. foreign policy, historians, sociologists, and professors of international and constitutional law.

CSI set for itself the following purposes:

1. To encourage teaching on both the graduate and undergraduate levels in the field of intelligence as it relates to national security, foreign policy, law, and ethics

2. To promote the development of a theory of intelligence—what is it, and what is its place in U.S. national security policy? Comparative analysis with the practice and experience of other nations will be emphasized

3. To encourage research into the intelligence process itself—analysis and estimates, clandestine collection, counterintelligence, and covert action; and to determine the feasibility of measuring efficiency or of setting standards of efficiency so that the product can be improved

4. To study the tensions between intelligence activities and the democratic and constitutional values of our society, and to seek the development of principles and methods for reconciling the two

For various cultural and political reasons, the study of intelligence has too often been regarded by academicians as *ultra vires*. Their self-exclusion from the subject has inhibited an understanding of this significant instrument of the modern nation-state.

Appendix B
Colloquium on Intelligence Requirements for the 1990s

4–5 December 1987
Washington, D.C.

List of Participants

Professor Hadley Arkes
Professor of Jurisprudence,
Amherst College

Mr. Frank Barnett
President,
National Strategy Information Center

Mr. Charles Battaglia
Professional Staff Member,
Senate Select Committee on Intelligence

Dr. Arnold Beichman
Research Fellow,
Hoover Institution on War, Revolution and Peace

Honorable Anthony Beilenson
U.S. House of Representatives

Dr. Richard Betts
Senior Fellow,
Brookings Institution

Dr. Thomas Blau
Senior Research Fellow,
Hudson Institute

Mr. Eberhard Blum
Former Director,
Bundesnachrichtendienst,
Federal Republic of Germany

Dr. Robert Butterworth
Deputy Executive Director,
President's Foreign Intelligence Advisory Board

Mr. Thomas Callanen
Central Intelligence Agency

Mr. Vincent Cannistraro
Special Assistant to the Assistant Secretary of Defense

Mr. A.R. Cinquegrana
Deputy Counsel for Intelligence Policy,
Department of Justice

Dr. Ray Cline
Chairman,
U.S. Global Strategy Council;
Former Deputy Director for Intelligence,
Central Intelligence Agency

Dr. Angelo Codevilla
Senior Research Fellow,
Hoover Institution on War, Revolution and Peace

Dr. Eliot Cohen
Senior Research Fellow,
U.S. Naval War College

Mr. Eugene Coon, Jr.
U.S. Marshal Service,
Department of Justice

Mr. Kenneth deGraffenreid
Office of the Secretary of Defense;
Former Senior Director of Intelligence Programs,
National Security Council

Captain Fred Demech
Inspector General,
Naval Security Group Command;
Former Executive Director,
President's Foreign Intelligence Advisory Board

Ms. Diane Dornan
Professional Staff Member,
House Permanent Select Committee on Intelligence

Dr. John Dziak
Defense Intelligence Officer,
Defense Intelligence Agency

Dr. John Eliff
Professional Staff Member,
Senate Select Committee on Intelligence

Mr. Stephen Engelberg
The New York Times

Mr. Charles Fenyvesi
U.S. News and World Report

Mr. Randall Fort
Special Assistant to the Secretary (National Security),
Department of the Treasury

Honorable Robert Gates
Deputy Director of Central Intelligence

Mr. James Geer
Assistant Director,
Intelligence Division,
Federal Bureau of Investigation

Mr. Bill Gertz
The Washington Times

Dr. Roy Godson
Associate Professor of Government,
Georgetown University;
Coordinator,
Consortium for the Study of Intelligence

Mr. Samuel Halpern
Former Senior Official,
Central Intelligence Agency

Mr. Gardner Hathaway
Central Intelligence Agency

Honorable Chic Hecht
U.S. Senate

Mr. Raymond Hemann
Director,
Threat Analysis, Strategic Defense Center,
Rockwell International

Lieutenant Colonel John Hines
Office of Net Assessment,
Office of the Secretary of Defense

Mr. Max Hunter
Former Director of Strategic Studies,
Lockheed Missiles and Space Company

Mr. H.F. Hutchinson, Jr.
Acting Chairman,
National Intelligence Council,
Central Intelligence Agency

Mr. David Ignatius
The Washington Post

Honorable Fred Ikle
Under Secretary of Defense for Policy

Brigadier General Walter Jajko
Director,
Special Advisory Staff,
Department of Defense

Mr. Paul Joyal
Director of Security,
Senate Select Committee on Intelligence

Dr. David Kahn
Author;
Viewpoint Editor, *Newsday*

Mr. George Kalaris
Former Senior Official,
Central Intelligence Agency

Dr. R. Norris Keeler
Los Alamos National Laboratory

Mr. Merrill Kelly
Staff Consultant,
Senate Select Committee on Intelligence

Mr. John Kringen
Central Intelligence Agency

Dr. Carnes Lord
Director,
International Studies,
National Institute for Public Policy

Mr. David Major
Supervisory Special Agent,
Federal Bureau of Investigation

Mr. Andrew Marshall
Director of Net Assessment,
Office of the Secretary of Defense

Lieutenant Colonel Mike Mastrangelo
White House Military Office

Mr. Leonard McCoy
Former Senior Official,
Central Intelligence Agency

Mr. James Milburn
Supervisory Intelligence Research Specialist,
Federal Bureau of Investigation

Major General Robert Morgan, Retired
Professional Staff Member,
Senate Select Committee on Intelligence

Mr. Donald Nielsen
Former Director,
Special Advisory Staff,
Department of Defense

Mr. Michael O'Neil
Chief Counsel,
House Permanent Select Committee on Intelligence

Mr. John Rees
Vice President,
Mid-Atlantic Research Associates

Mr. Oliver Revell
Executive Assistant Director,
Federal Bureau of Investigation

Mr. Charles Roades
Vice Deputy Director for Attachés and Operations,
Defense Intelligence Agency

Mr. Raymond Rocca
Former Senior Official,
Central Intelligence Agency

Mr. Herbert Romerstein
Special Assistant to the Associate Director of Programs,
U.S. Information Agency

Mr. Richard Sandza
Newsweek

Mr. Gustave Schick
Office of Program Evaluation, Inspection Department,
Federal Bureau of Investigation

Mr. Daniel Schmidt
Program Officer,
Lynde & Harry Bradley Foundation

Dr. Gary Schmitt
Executive Director,
President's Foreign Intelligence Advisory Board

Dr. Paul Seabury
Professor of Political Science,
University of California—Berkeley

Mr. Theodore Shackley
President,
Research Associates International;
Former Senior Official,
Central Intelligence Agency

Mr. Donald Sheehan
Office Director,
Active Measures Analysis and Response Unit,
U.S. Department of State

Dr. Abram Shulsky
Senior Fellow,
National Strategy Information Center;
Former Minority Staff Director,
Senate Select Committee on Intelligence

Dr. Richard Shultz, Jr.
Associate Professor of International Politics,
Fletcher School of Law and Diplomacy

Mr. Ted Snediker
Chief,
Counterintelligence Operations,
Department of the Army

Mr. Jed Snyder
Deputy Director,
National Security Studies,
Hudson Institute

Dr. E. Miriam Steiner
Senior Analyst,
Defense Systems Incorporated

Mr. Lawrence Sternfield
Former Senior Official,
Central Intelligence Agency

Ms. Nina Stewart
Assistant Director,
President's Foreign Intelligence Advisory Board

Mr. David Sullivan
Professional Staff Member,
Senate Foreign Relations Committee

Mr. Charles Symes
Special Assistant to the Executive Director,
Defense Intelligence Agency

Mr. B. Hugh Tovar
Former Senior Official,
Central Intelligence Agency

Ms. Michelle Van Cleave
Assistant Director for National Security Affairs,
Office of Science and Technology Policy,
Executive Office of the President

Mr. John Walcott
The Wall Street Journal

Mr. Robert Walker
Vice President,
National Affairs,
Adolph Coors Company

Mr. W. Raymond Wannall
Former Assistant Director,
Intelligence Division,
Federal Bureau of Investigation

Mr. George Warner
Assistant Deputy Director for Collection Management,
Defense Intelligence Agency

Mr. Earl Anthony Wayne
The Christian Science Monitor

Dr. Dalton West
Editor,
Foreign Intelligence Literary Scene

Colonel Robert Wheeler
Assistant Deputy Director for Security and Counterintelligence,
Defense Intelligence Agency

Mr. Michael Wines
The Los Angeles Times

Mr. John Wobensmith
Senior Staff,
Department of Defense

Mrs. Roberta Wohlstetter
Author;
Pan Heuristics

Mr. William Worochock
Director of Counterintelligence,
Naval Security and Investigative Command

Index

About the Contributors

Eberhard Blum was a West German professional intelligence officer for thirty years, working closely with allied intelligence services. From 1982 to 1985 he was the director of the Federal Republic's foreign intelligence service, the Bundesnachrichtendienst (BND).

Robert Butterworth is director of the Mobilization Concept Development Center at the National Defense University. From 1985 to 1988 he served as deputy director of the President's Foreign Intelligence Advisory Board. Previously he was an analyst at the Department of Defense and a professional staff member of the Senate Select Committee on Intelligence.

Eliot Cohen is a senior research fellow at the U.S. Naval War College. He participated in the 1987 Department of Defense–National Security Council Commission on an Integrated Long Term Strategy and is a consultant to the President's Foreign Intelligence Advisory Board.

Kenneth deGraffenreid is a senior fellow on intelligence at the National Strategy Information Center. From 1981 to 1987 he served as a special assistant to the president and senior director of intelligence programs at the National Security Council. Previously he was a professional staff member of the Senate Select Committee on Intelligence.

Stephen Engelberg is a Washington correspondent with *The New York Times* specializing in intelligence and national security.

Robert Gates is the deputy director of central intelligence. From December 1986 to May 1987 he served as the acting director of central intelligence. He joined the CIA in 1966, working in the Directorate of Intelligence. In 1974 he was assigned to the National Security Council staff. After returning to the CIA in 1979, he became the national intelligence officer for the Soviet Union. In 1982 he was appointed deputy director of intelligence, and in 1983 he also became chairman of the National Intelligence Council.

James Geer has been the assistant director in charge of the FBI's intelligence division since 1985. He joined the FBI as a special agent in 1964 and has served in a variety of posts, including assistant director in charge of the laboratory division.

Fred Ikle served as the under secretary of defense for policy from 1981 to 1988. Previously, from 1973 to 1977, he was director of the U.S. Arms Control and Disarmament Agency. Prior to entering government service, he was a professor of political science at the Massachusetts Institute of Technology and was a senior official with The Rand Corporation.

George Kalaris served in a series of managerial and operational positions including a stint on the Counterintelligence Staff at the CIA, between 1952 and 1981.

R.N. Keeler has been a scientist, university professor, and government consultant. Currently he is with Kaman Diversified Technology Corporation and serves as a consultant to the Los Alamos National Laboratory. Previously he held management positions at the Lawrence Livermore Laboratory.

Merrill Kelly is a staff consultant to the Senate Select Committee on Intelligence. He is a lifelong military counterintelligence specialist. From 1982 to 1985 he served as the director of the Special Advisory Staff in the Department of Defense, handling matters relating to human intelligence and psychological warfare.

Andrew Marshall in 1973 founded the Department of Defense's Office of Net Assessment, which he still directs, to provide the secretary of defense and military commanders with assessments of the military balance in major geographical theaters. From 1972 to 1973 he was a professional staff member of the National Security Council.

Leonard McCoy served in both staff and operational assignments at home and abroad for the CIA between 1952 and 1985, specializing in Soviet affairs and counterintelligence.

Donald Nielsen has been involved for more than fifteen years with intelligence operations at the national and international level. From 1977 to 1982 he was director of the Special Advisory Staff in the Office of the Secretary of Defense. He also has served in senior intelligence positions in both the Atlantic and Pacific commands and as executive assistant to the director of the Defense Intelligence Agency.

Paul Seabury is a professor of political science at the University of California—Berkeley. From 1981 to 1985 he was a member of the President's Foreign Intelligence Advisory Board.

Richard Shultz is an associate professor of international politics at the Fletcher School of Law and Diplomacy and chairman of the Intelligence Studies Section of the International Studies Association. He is also a member of the secretary of defense's Special Operations Policy Advisory Group.

Miriam Steiner is director of studies in political military psychology at Defense Systems Inc. She also has taught at the University of Georgia.

B. Hugh Tovar has had extensive managerial and field experience with covert action. His intelligence career began in the Office of Strategic Services, and he later became a senior official at the CIA prior to retiring in 1978.

About the Editor

Roy Godson is an associate professor of government at Georgetown University, coordinator of the Consortium for the Study of Intelligence, and program coordinator of the Intelligence Studies Section of the International Studies Association.

Dr. Godson has taught at Georgetown University for eighteen years, specializing in international relations, national security and foreign policy, and U.S. and Soviet intelligence. In 1979 he helped establish the academic Consortium for the Study of Intelligence to promote teaching and analysis of intelligence policy under the auspices of the National Strategy Information Center. He has served as a consultant to the National Security Council and since 1982 has been a consultant to the President's Foreign Intelligence Advisory Board.

He is the editor of the seven-volume series *Intelligence Requirements for the 1980's.*

INTELLIGENCE REQUIREMENTS FOR THE 1980's

Roy Godson, *Series Editor*

Volumes one through five are published by the
National Strategy Information Center, Washington,
D.C., and New York, N.Y.

Volumes six and seven are published and distributed
by Lexington Books, Lexington, Massachusetts.